THE AUTHOR

Tom Gorman has been a professional ship modeller since his retirement from the marine engineering industry in 1983, and has had a lifelong interest in merchant ships and the sea. Beginning by producing model kits, he now concentrates on building models commissioned by specific customers, such as shipowners. He contributes frequently to the modelling press both in the UK and the USA, and articles by him have appeared in the journals *Model Shipwright* and *Model Boats*. He is an active member of his local model boat club and gives talks on aspects of ship modelling and also on techniques of model ship photography.

WORKING SCALE MODEL
MERCHANT SHIPS

WORKING SCALE MODEL MERCHANT SHIPS

Tom Gorman

NAVAL INSTITUTE PRESS
Annapolis, Maryland

Front illustration:
Steam tug *Knight of Saint Patrick* built by David Abbott to scale 1:48
COURTESY OF TERRY OSBORNE PHOTOGRAPHY, CHISLEHURST, KENT

Frontispiece:
Scale model of the Second World War Liberty ship *Francis J O'Gara*, built by
Peter Chappell, on the water at Sandal Park, Doncaster in May 1997.
DAVID MILTON

Back illustration:
Sternwheeler *Susie* built by John Fryant to scale ½in to 1ft.
JOHN FRYANT

First published in Great Britain in 1997 by
Chatham Publishing,
61 Frith Street
London W1V 5TA

This edition reprinted 2001

Published and distributed in the United States of America and Canada by the
Naval Institute Press, 291 Wood Road, Annapolis, Maryland 21402-5034

A library of Congress Catalog Card No. 00-105424

ISBN 1-55750-909-3

Manufactured in Great Britain

Contents

Introduction & Acknowledgements   6

1 Model Selection   9

2 Drawings, Scales & Interpretation   16

3 Researching the Chosen Model   21

4 Selection of Materials   26

5 Tools and Adhesives   29

6 Building the Hull   37

7 Detailing the Hull   51

8 The Moulded Hull   54

9 Running Gear   59

10 Electric Motors   68

11 Steam Engines   76

12 Decks & Hatches   87

13 Superstructures   98

14 Masts, Derricks & Rigging   108

15 Deck Fittings   115

16 Lifeboats & Davits   129

17 Winches, Windlasses & Capstans   135

18 Radio Control   142

19 Auxiliary Working Features   149

20 Unusual Drive Equipment   156

21 Painting & Finishing   160

22 Ballasting & Sailing Trials   165

23 Building & Sailing for Competitions   169

24 Hints & Tips   175

Appendices   181

Index   183

Introduction & Acknowledgements

The object of this book is to provide the best possible guidance into the building of working scale model ships which fall into the broad category of 'Merchant Ships'. This category includes tugs, tankers, tramps, liners, pilot cutters, oil rig support ships and fishing vessels, and, for the purposes of this book, all such vessels which are power-driven.

Working scale models are comparatively new to the model ship scene. Some twenty to thirty years ago, fully-detailed scale models were only found in glass cases in museums and exhibitions, and it was generally thought that fine scale model ships could not be made fully working. Most working models were fairly crude and bulky, and were looked down upon by the skilled museum model builders. The principal difficulty which faced most modellers in the years prior to and immediately after the Second World War was the lack of suitable materials from which to build model ships. Most were built from timber, one of the methods still used today and described later, but the timber available was of poor quality by today's standards. Some models were built using tinplate soldered to brass frames, and this method could result in a fine hull, but they suffered badly from rust unless very carefully painted and maintained.

Furthermore, there were no small motors or steam engines for driving models to be found in what few models shops there were. Some modellers with access to and experience of using a lathe could make small steam outfits, but the electric motors available were large and heavy. Radio con-trol equipments were equally large and very expensive, and the only batteries available were the heavy acid accumulator type. The early radio equipment used reed switches and relays to control current to the motor and therefore speed was regulated in steps, usually only on/off switching was available and the heavy equipment meant that hulls had to be built deeper than scale in order to hold it. Some miniature electric motors were available, but they had insufficient power to propel a ship model, and were only suitable for driving the tiller or similar controls.

There were few manufacturers of fit-tings for models and it was generally felt that small detailed fittings could not with-stand the rigours of sailing on the pond. Fittings for working models tended there-fore to be built overscale and were often quite crude. For example, ventilators were made solid so that water could not pene-trate through them. A few firms such as Bassett Lowke, Web and Billings did pro-duce fine scale fitting for model ships and there were some fine scale working models, but these were rare and certainly not the norm.

Few working models seem to have survived from the years prior to and just after the Second World War, probably for the reasons set out above. The model illus-trated opposite, *Duchess of Fife*, dates from 1956 and during overhaul was found to contain remains of a reed radio system and an old Taycol motor. The tinplate on brass frames hull was, however, in excellent con-dition and well-protected with paint. This is a fine model built to the large scale of

1:32, allowing a degree of detail which would not be found on a smaller-scale model of this period.

Modern materials and drive equipment have brought about a complete change in the model ship scene. Fine scale models can be seen operating regularly on ponds and lakes throughout this country and all over the world. Companies specialising in fine scale fittings have proliferated and kits for building scale working models can be purchased quite readily. Many ship plans and drawings are available from specialist suppliers, and the advent of glass-fibre techniques for modelling has given the modelmaker a virtually watertight hull to start from. The following chapters deal extensively with the use of these modern materials.

Based on tried and tested practices, the methods described in this book will guide the modeller through the various stages of building a working scale model merchant ship from building the hull to the finer points of detailing, for ships ranging in size from the small motor-driven cutter to large twin-screw vessels, and fitted with radio equipment ranging from simple two-channel systems to the large multi-channel controls for a variety of functions.

The layout of the book is designed to guide the modeller progressively through the stages of building in sequence and while the beginner will be able to follow this easily, it is hoped also that the experienced modeller may find useful hints and tips. It should be noted that the drawings and sketches which follow are not of a single model but are of different ones, in order to illustrate methods of building rather than the detailed building of a single ship. Furthermore, they are not drawn to scale, being provided for general information only.

Which model shall I build? This matter is essentially one of personal choice but guidance is required and this is given in Chapter 1 where the modeller is offered help in choosing the merchant ship type best suited to his or her skills. It should be noted that shipmodelling is not confined to the male of the species and there are some very fine women modellers working today.

Materials are discussed and advice given on how to combine varying materials to achieve the best results. Notes on suitable tools are included with the best methods to adopt when using such tools. With the huge range of adhesives available today, space is devoted to showing which adhesive(s) to use with which materials.

The selection and sizing of electric motors and propellers to suit the model selected is also covered, along with such other auxiliary equipment as batteries, speed controllers etc. The increasing popu-

Paddle-steamer *Duchess of Fife* built of tinplate and brass in 1956 and overhauled in 1990. Scale 1:32. Electric drive, with radio control and smoke generator in funnel.

larity of steam plant is not ignored and the fitting of such equipment is dealt with in some detail. No attempt is made to provide building details for steam plant, which is a highly specialised task beyond the scope of this book.

Details are given of painting techniques and the types of paints that can give good results, as well as the lining and lettering on ships and such details as lighting etc. The final chapters deal with the ballasting and sailing of the finished model and how a fine model may best be displayed at exhibition and in competitions.

It is hoped that the prospective ship-modeller will see the attraction that the merchant ship has to offer and that this book will be an aid to setting good models on the water. The merchantman is a ship apart and a fine sight on the pond. A new modeller will soon realise that while a full-size ship is built by people of more than twenty different trades, a model ship has but one builder who has to combine all the trades in one. This is a daunting prospect and one which, even after building over forty models, still raises doubts in the mind of the author when facing the challenge of a new model. It is hoped that the readers of this book will be enlightened and guided into building a working scale model merchant ship and that they will find inspiration and assistance herein.

Acknowledgements

The preparation of a book such as this is very dependant upon the assistance of others and I wish to thank all those who have so willingly rendered that assistance to me. Among those to whom my special thanks are directed are: John Orriss, my friend and colleague for more than twenty-five years, whose modelling skills have been and are invaluable to our association; John Bowen, who has over the years been a source of much information without which some of my models would not have been built; Dave Milton, David Holland and Peter Chappell of the Conisbrough & District Modelling Association for their encouragement, help and photographs, including their derisory remarks *re* my model sailing abilities, which are poor to say the least; Barry Shanks and his staff at Westbourne Model Centre; Peter Lewin and David Sambrook at Maritime Models, from whom much valuable help has been received over the years; and Scottie Dayton from the USA, who published my first articles over twelve years ago and who has been a guide to my writing and a firm friend ever since. I must also thank John Noble of the Onward Fishing Co for the information and help he has given relating to fishing vessels, and Neil and June Patterson of IMT Marine Consultants for their assistance and permission to use some of their design drawings in this book. All photographs are by the author unless othwise indicated. There are many others whose names are not mentioned here but to whom I say thank you for their help. Finally I would like to dedicate this work to my grandchildren and my godson James, all of whom are a joy forever.

1
Model Selection

The classification 'Merchant Ships' covers a wide range of very different ship types, which can best be described as vessels built for commercial operation. In this chapter the ship types covered appear under the headings of their designated service. When selecting a type of ship to model, this must be done in conjunction with the scale at which it will be built and this in turn is governed to a certain extent by the desired size of the model. It is much easier to build a small ship to a fairly large scale than to build a large ship to a very small scale. Today, for many modellers, one of the main factors which determines the scale, and hence the size, of a proposed model is that it must be readily transportable within the family car. The subject of scale will be dealt with in Chapter 2.

This book is concerned with working models of ships that are power-driven.

Steam was the first mechanical motive power used. Small tugs were among the first commercially successful ships, but the early steam passenger ships were initially less so. The paddle-wheel was the prime mover, but the development of the screw propeller eventually displaced it, although it continued to be used on certain craft until well into the 1970s and even after that. Similarly, sail was soon displaced by steam power in all manner of ships. Later, steam power, whether in the form of the reciprocating engine or the turbine, was itself overtaken by the marine diesel engine, and today even more advanced forms of propulsion have been and are being introduced.

Tugs

These range in size from small harbour tugs to ocean-going salvage tugs and all

Thames-type tug *Yvonne VI* built in Canada by Captain T C Pullen.
T C PULLEN

US Harbour tug *Akron* built to 1:32 scale by the author and fitted with electric motor, radio equipment and operating navigation lights.

Steam trawler *Kingston Peridot* built by the author and John Orriss to scale 1:48 and fitted with Proteus steam plant made by Cheddar Models and radio control. Construction of this model is featured in *Model Boats* magazine.

tugs differ in that the accommodation extends much further aft and they tow from cruciform-type bollards (called bitts) and not from hooks or winches.

Fishing vessels

Fishing vessels are another group in which there is a wide variety of types, their design and size being related to the purpose for which they were built and also to local conditions. Steam was first applied to the herring drifters of the UK east coast and hundreds of such vessels sailed from the ports of Scotland and England from about 1910 to the early 1950s. The herring drifters mainly plied the North Sea, spending about seven days at sea at one time, their catch being packed in ice in boxes or baskets. Between the wars the steam trawler was developed and sailed mainly to the middle distant waters, as did the drifters. After the last war they began to go to the distant waters of the Arctic and were soon being built to quite large sizes, up to 200ft (61m) long, and carrying crews of up to thirty men. Such ships sailed for a maximum of three weeks. Any

sizes could be found over the years. The steam tug served in many ports and rivers until fairly recent times and some, with tall funnels and bright paint schemes, make eye-catching models. Modern tugs are equally colourful and offer a diversity of propulsion methods, which will be covered in a later chapter. Plans and data for many different types of tugs can be found in the catalogues of the plans services available from many ship model magazine publishers or from commercial firms specialising in this field. Most tugs world-wide follow European practice and have a generally similar appearance. However, in the USA

Steam herring drifter *Formidable* built to 1:24 scale by the author and John Orriss and outfitted with a Maxwell Hemmens steam plant and radio control.

longer would have caused deterioration in the catch, since they lacked refrigeration. In later years some were so fitted. Today trawlers operate in the same sea areas. Although often smaller than their predecessors, they are better equipped, safer and carry smaller crews, most of whom can work well-protected from extreme weather. The fish are gutted and cleaned below decks and stowed in fully refrigerated holds.

The fishing boats which sail the middle distance and coastal waters are different again and catch fish in different ways. Some use purse seine nets and fish for herring etc, which swim near the surface and are known as pelagic fish. Some use special methods to fish for crabs, lobsters, scallops etc, each ship being designed or adapted to suit the method of fishing. Another attractive feature of fishing vessels is the way in which many owners paint their ships in bright and distinctive colours, making them highly visible. On the east coast of America the lobster fishers are noteworthy craft and they deserve to be modelled much more than they are. Illustrations and drawings of these fine craft are, unfortunately, very difficult to find.

Coastal craft

The coaster and short sea trader, the latter being so called because they were designed to sail over comparatively short distances coastwise or to the nearby continent, in early days were quite small ships and frequently plied on a regular port to port service. Some had accommodation for a small number of passengers. Coasters have always carried a wide range of cargoes between ports round a country's coastline. In many places they were the sole means of supplying essential goods to communities with no internal road connections. Slightly larger coasters now carry a limited number of standard cargo containers, usually on top of the hatch covers. Few coasters today are fitted with their own cargo-handling gear, relying instead on the equipment of the ports they serve. Coastal or estuary tankers, powered by triple-expansion steam engines or more lately by diesel engines, ply between the large oil refineries and the tank installations located on riverside sites. Bunkering ships in port is another activity calling for small, specialised craft, though in some ports these bunkering tankers are little more than large powered barges.

Pilot cutters and Customs vessels

A Pilotage Authority provides an essential service in all ports, rivers and estuaries. The pilots today are taken out to or from the larger ships by high-speed launches, some of which are quite large and make good subjects for models. In the past it was com-

Twin-screw coaster *Arran Mail* built to 1:32 scale by the author and John Orriss. Sold by Westbourne Model Centre to unknown owner.

mon for large pilot cutters to embark a number of pilots and take up station off the port or river they served. The pilots transferred from the cutter to their respective charges and, having brought another vessel out of port, they returned to the cutter. Early pilot cutters were quite often converted from vessels such as large steam yachts or fishing boats, but others were specially built. Almost all pilot cutters make attractive models and drawings for several

are included among those available from plans services. The ships of Trinity House have always been attractive and some of them are very specialised, for example, the buoy handling vessels whose large cranes mark them out from other ships. The ships servicing lighthouses are always very smart and often have a profile not unlike a small liner. The Customs cutter is a vessel used by HM Customs & Excise to put their staff on board ships entering or leaving port.

Customs and Excise cutter *Badger*, scale 1:32, built by the author and photographed by Ray Brigden at Blackheath, London. Model fitted with Decaperm motor and radio equipment. This model was researched and is soon to be released in kit form by Maritime Models, London.
RAY BRIGDEN

Most Customs cutters are fast ships, the earlier ships being steam driven and frequently very similar in appearance to a tug. Later ships were larger until, today, they are large high-speed launches akin to police boats. A number are illustrated in plans service catalogues and some are delightful ships to model.

Cargo ships and passenger liners

All the ships described thus far fall into the category of small ships. Most are not much longer than 200-300ft (60-90m) and thus lend themselves to being built to a fairly large scale and enable the modeller to include a great deal of detail. The ships which follow, though larger, may need to be built to smaller scales, in which case the detail becomes tiny and sometimes difficult to produce.

Cargo ships were to be seen in large numbers between and just after the wars. They varied in size from 200 to 500ft (60-

150m) or more in length. Some operated regular voyages between specific ports, while others went where there were cargoes available. Some carried up to twelve passengers. The three-island type ship between the wars, the Liberty ship of the war years and the later motor ships all make good models. Most tramp ship services have now disappeared being replaced by larger and ever larger container ships, oil tankers and ore carriers travelling between the larger ports and container and oil terminals. These vessels can be modelled but their great size does not make for an easy task.

The passenger liners that sailed so regularly right up to the late 1960s and early 1970s and their successors, the modern cruise liners and the giant ferries, also vary in size. The smaller passenger ships make wonderfully bright models and plans are available for some of them. The larger liners, such as those of the P & O, Union Castle, Cunard and British India companies, fall into the category of those having

Oil tanker *Shell Technician* built to 1:96 scale by Roger Thayne and fitted with electric motor and radio controls. This model took first place in a number of competitions.
ROGER THAYNE

North Seas Ferries
Norland model built by
David Holland to 1:96
scale shown sailing at
Doncaster. Model is
fitted with twin
electric motors and
multi-channel RC
equipment.

to be built to a small scale. However, roll-on/roll-off ferries fall into the size category where some can be built to a reasonable scale. Smaller ferries that run between places on opposite sides of a river or between mainland and nearby islands make good subjects for modelling, a large scale permitting the inclusion of plenty of detail.

Paddle vessels

Apart from the large vessels which made ocean voyages, paddle-steamers have provided regular passenger and excursion services on rivers, estuaries and along some coasts even as late as the early 1970s. Some of the most attractive vessels ever seen were to be found on these services. Their motive power was not confined to steam engines, one Clyde paddle-steamer being fitted with diesel generators to power the electric motors which turned the paddle-wheels, whilst in others the power was provided by diesel engines. Paddle-steamers carrying passengers in the UK were required by the Board of Trade to have their paddles linked together, only paddle tugs having independent paddle drive. In the USA, even today, there are paddle-steamers on the Mississippi and other large rivers. Most of the American paddle-steamers were of the stern-wheel type with long stroke, slow-running engines, with some others being side-paddlers. All were most beautifully decorated and painted and had a wealth of fine carving and ironwork. They make very

(Below)
Mississippi river packet
Idlewild, built in 1:48
scale by John I Fryant
and completed in 1972.
Originally electrically
driven with radio control,
the model is currently on
display at the Museum
of American History,
Washington DC.
JOHN L FRYANT

fine models indeed for the modeller who has patience to give to the wonderful detail. To have the stern-wheeler as a working model does require care since they were mostly shallow-draught vessels and that means that, with few exceptions, stability may present some problems. Radio-controlled models of stern wheel paddle-steamers suffer more from manoeuvrability problems than from stability ones. Stability problems arise when the hull is made from a lightweight material and the superstructure of heavier timber such as marine plywood. This gives a top-heavy structure. The prospective builder of American stern wheelers should consult *The Western Rivers Steamboat Cyclopaedium* by Alan L Bates which is available from Taubman Plans Service or other reputable book dealers.

Miscellaneous

Finally there are specialist vessels such as oil rig support, standby and rescue ships. They are very similar to large tugs and many are finished in bright colours, with company logos on funnels and occasionally with large white letters along each side. Some are fitted with unusual means of propulsion such as azimuth thrusters, Schottel drives or Voith Schneider propellers and these are dealt with in a later chapter. Then there are the heavy-lift ships, fitted with powerful equipment capable of lifting and transporting very large, heavy indivisible loads.

Although whale factory ships were rarely seen, their attendant steam-powered catchers were very similar to fishing trawlers and make a good subject for a model and one leading kit manufacturer (Graupner) has produced a kit. Dredgers, too, make interesting models, varying from large barges fitted with grab cranes to sophisticated vessels with a continuous chain and bucket system or, in some cases, a powerful suction-pipe system which can be lowered to remove mud and silt from river or harbour and discharges it into self-propelled barges for disposal at sea. Some dredgers not only bring up the spoil but transport it to sea themselves for disposal. Plans for a number of vessels of these types are available from plans services or other sources.

The newcomer to the hobby of ship modelling is strongly advised to begin with a simple type of ship and one with not too many fittings. This can be built in a comparatively short time, will not involve too much in the way of detail work and allows the model to be completed and sailing before the first flush of interest has waned. It can be followed by more ambitious and larger models as the experiences of the first model are absorbed.

Sand dredger *Sand Heron* built by Roger Thayne to a very high standard with minute detail and seen on the water during a regatta. The model won a number of high placings in competition.
ROGER THAYNE

2
Drawings, Scales & Interpretation

To build a fine scale model ship successfully requires a set of accurate drawings from which to work. These are available from many sources and probably the easiest to access are those of the many plans services run by magazine publishers or commercial firms and other sources (see Appendix 3). The plans offered by the plans services are generally drawn specifically for the model shipbuilder and are based on those produced by the builders of the full-size vessel. Quite often they include detail drawn to suit the modelmaker and give information on how a model may be built. Following the closure of most of the shipbuilding companies in the UK the plans collections of some of these yards are held in the archives of maritime museums and other organisations. It is possible to obtain copies on payment of a suitable fee. Those shipbuilders who are still in business are usually helpful to the modeller who respectfully requests assistance when wishing to build a particular model. A polite letter asking for help will usually get a sensible and helpful reply. If the shipbuilder is no more but the ship is still in service, a request for assistance from the ship's owners will often bear fruit. It may even be possible to visit the vessel in question and to take photographs, as the author has been invited to do on a number of occasions.

Having decided upon which ship is to be modelled and located a source of suitable drawings, it is necessary to be able to interpret them and decide on a scale and thus the size of the model. Shipbuilders' drawings can be huge, measuring as much as 14ft (4.27m) or more in length for a General Arrangement drawing produced to a scale of $1/_4$in to 1ft. Plans service drawings are generally to smaller scales and up to 60in (152cm) long. As a minimum the modelmaker needs drawings called 'Lines' and 'General Arrangement'.

There are occasions when the modeller will find that the plans bought are to a scale that gives a model smaller or larger than shown and thus the plans need to be rescaled. This is not such a serious matter as it was some years ago. There was a time when the only answer to making a model different in size to that shown was to redraw the whole set. Today it is possible to go to a specialist copy shop or drawing office supply company and have the plans enlarged or reduced very accurately either on plain paper or transparent film for a reasonable charge.

Lines plan

This is the key plan for the shape of a ship's hull, which it shows from three viewpoints. At the top is a side elevation, or sheer plan, comprising a horizontal base line, as often as not corresponding to the bottom of the keel, a line showing the shape of the stem, another showing the shape of the stern and one showing the line of the deck. Superimposed on this are three sets of lines. First, at intervals along the base line, there are a series of vertical lines, equally spaced, known as ordinates or station lines. Second are a number of horizontal lines, parallel to the base line and equally spaced and carried up as far as the deck line, called waterlines. Finally, running from bow to stern are two or three oddly shaped, curved lines, known as bowlines (from bow to midships) and buttock lines (from midships to stern).

Below the sheer plan is the half-breadth plan. This shows one half of the hull from the longitudinal centreline outwards and by convention is always the port side of the hull as seen from above. Along the centreline and at right angles to it are vertical lines corresponding to the ordinates or station lines on the sheer plan. The several curved lines on this plan show the outline of the hull as if sliced through from end to end at each of the waterlines shown on the sheer plan, together with one, usually the outermost one (unless the hull has

tumble home), showing the outline of the deck. Also on this drawing are two or three lines parallel to and at equal distances from the centreline. These indicate the positions of the bowlines and buttock lines and those oddly shaped curved lines on the sheer plan show the outline of the hull as if sliced vertically from end to end along each of these lines.

The third plan is the body plan, comprising the base line in the centre of which is a vertical line representing the longitudinal centreline of the ship. On the right hand side of this are a number of curved lines which show the shape of the hull as if sliced through transversely at each of the ordinate/station lines from bow to midships. On the left hand side is shown the shape of the hull if similarly treated at each of the ordinate/station lines from midships to stern. Convention has it that ship plans are always drawn with the bow to the right, with the port side shown on the half-breadth plan and the sections on the body

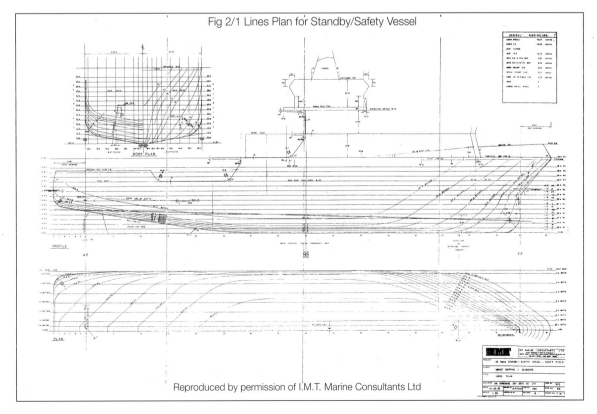

Fig 2/1 Lines Plan for Standby/Safety Vessel

Reproduced by permission of I.M.T. Marine Consultants Ltd

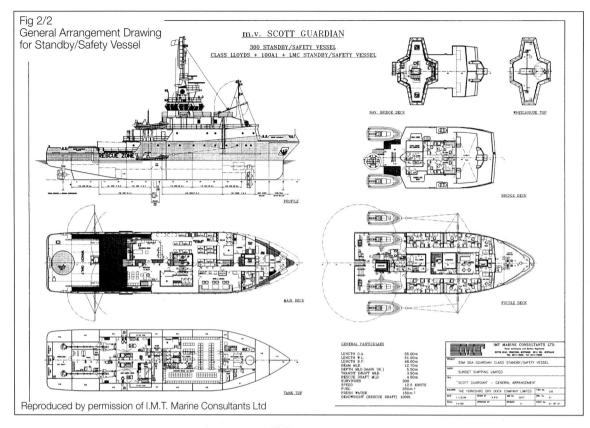

Fig 2/2
General Arrangement Drawing
for Standby/Safety Vessel

m.v. SCOTT GUARDIAN

300 STANDBY/SAFETY VESSEL
CLASS LLOYDS + 100A1 + LMC STANDBY/SAFETY VESSEL

Reproduced by permission of I.M.T. Marine Consultants Ltd

plan as described above. Also on the body plan are horizontal lines parallel to the base line and corresponding to the waterlines shown on the sheer plan and the two or three vertical lines equally spaced out from the centreline showing the position of the bowlines/buttock lines. The top of each ordinate/station line stops at the deck line and a line drawn through tops of these lines shows the line of the deck.

It will be as well to differentiate between the various vertical lines which appear on sheer and other plans, to avoid confusion later. On a sheer plan, at either end of the base line, are two key lines. At the fore end is a line perpendicular to the base line passing through the point where the stem cuts the designed load waterline. This is known as the Fore Perpendicular (FP). At the after end is a line perpendicular to the base, passing through the point where the designed load waterline cuts the after face of the sternpost (where a ship

does not have a stern frame it passes through the centre of the rudder stock). This is known as the Aft Perpendicular (AP). The distance between these two lines is the key dimension known as the 'length between perpendiculars'. As this length is frequently used in the displacement calculation, it is divided into a number of equally-spaced sections, usually ten, and these are the ordinate/station lines referred to above. Just to confuse matters they are also known as displacement sections. These lines are not structural lines and have no connection with those representing the frames or 'ribs' of the ship.

The frames are a structural part of the ship and, except in certain circumstances, are not equally spaced throughout its length. Basically they are more closely spaced towards the ends and more widely spaced in between. The exact spacing depends upon a number of factors and is laid down in the Classification Society's rules. The position of the frames and their spacing is shown on the general arrangement, profile and sectional profile plans. When understood it is very useful for determining accurately the fore and aft position of deck structures and fittings etc.

Sometimes, on plans prepared specifically for modelmakers, the person who drew the plan may have selected purely arbitrary positions for his cross-sections. Lines plans are illustrated in Fig 2/1.

General arrangement plan

The General Arrangement (GA) drawing(s) show the layout of a ship in some detail but can vary in quality and also the amount of information included, depending upon which shipbuilder drew up the plans or who drew the plans for the plans services. Usually a shipbuilders' GA drawings, as well as showing the layout of fittings and other items on the open or weather decks, also include the internal layout of the accommodation areas and machinery

spaces. Very few of these latter details are needed by the modelmaker and they can cause confusion. Much of this data is omitted from plans services drawings. Unfortunately the re-drawing of builder's plans to simplify them sometimes leads to errors and therefore as much research of the proposed ship as possible should be carried out before starting, so that the model will be accurate when completed.

The following recent experience shows the differences that can occur between shipbuilders' plans and the ship itself. The author had obtained a plan for a trawler from a museum source which had been prepared by the builder of the ship. When compared with a very good and obviously professionally-taken photograph of the ship, he found very considerable differences in the whole superstructure. The line of the boat deck was different, as was the shape of the wheelhouse and other parts of the deckhouses. Further research was undertaken and proved the photographs to be correct. When the ship and its sister had

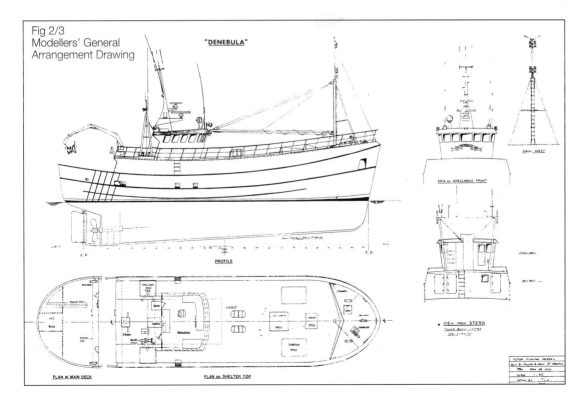

Fig 2/3
Modellers' General
Arrangement Drawing

been altered is not known. It may have been during construction, but, as the GA drawing covered four ships, two may have been altered with only detail drawings being issued for the alterations, or they may have been altered by their owners very early in service.

The differences between shipbuilders' and prepared (*ie* plans service) GA drawings are illustrated in Figs 2/2 and 2/3. Note how the second drawing shows less detail but is still perfectly suitable for producing a fine scale model. A GA drawing is vital but does not always provide all the data needed. Information on how the deckhouses appear when seen from front or back is needed so that they can be built correctly, as are the positions of portholes, doors etc. Also needed are details of rails, stanchions, davits, lifeboats, rafts, skylights, bollards and other deck fittings. On many plans these are shown in outline only and more detailed information, diagrams etc, will be needed. Many fittings used on the merchant ship are built to standard sizes and patterns, many laid down or approved by the Classification Societies. It is possible to supplement the data given on the general arrangement drawings by searching through technical magazines and books written to assist the modeller. One such is *A Ship Model Maker's Manual* by John Bowen which lists alphabetically many of the fittings, boats, winches, mast fittings, blocks etc, to be found on the merchant ship and which is an excellent reference book. Regretfully this book is now out of print but a copy may be found through the library services.

Scales

Scale is the ratio by which the model/plan compares with the full-size original. It is expressed in two ways, either as a ratio such

as 1:96, 1:50 or, when using Imperial units, as a fraction of an inch equalling one foot on the original. For example, many models/plans are built/drawn to a scale where $^1/_8$in, $^1/_4$in or $^3/_{16}$in on the plan/model equals one foot on the original. Such scales are also expressed as a ratio. As there are, for example, 96 eighths of an inch in a foot, a scale of $^1/_8$in to 1ft can be expressed as a ratio of 1:96. Similarly $^1/_2$in to 1ft is 1:24. The same applies when metric units are being used, though these are more usually shown as ratios, *eg* 1:25, 1:50, 1:100 and so on. Scale should always be expressed in one of these two ways. To say that a model is to, say, $^1/_8$ scale is meaningless. Does it indicate that the model is to $^1/_8$in to 1ft or is it to 1:8 (ratio) scale?

The Metric scale is in wide use today, all ships built in the UK, Europe and most of the rest world using Metric measurements. In the USA, however, Imperial measurements are still used. Drawings prepared in UK shipyards before the early 1970s will certainly be in Imperial measurements. From then to the present day UK shipyard drawings are in Metric units. To convert from Imperial to Metric measurement for the purposes of building a model is hardly worthwhile and it is easier to use the scales in which the drawings were prepared. It is not necessary for the ship modeller to have drawing office experience or to be able to produce very accurate drawings, as most of the draughting work is already done when the plans are purchased. Photographing details on board can provide vital information and, if a rod or stick marked clearly in set bands of measurements (such as 100mm if metric dimensions are being used or in 3in for Imperial) is placed against the object to be photographed, it will be possible to gauge the size of the piece from the photographic print.

3
Researching the Chosen Model

The first step to take after obtaining plans for the chosen ship is to ascertain for what date in its life they have been drawn and to check that they show the vessel correctly for that date. A model can be made of the ship as completed or as it appeared at a later point in its career. Many ships are altered in some way during the course of their life. Some of these changes may or may not alter the above-water appearance but others, such as the fitting of a different propeller or the addition of a Kort nozzle, will change the underwater configuration. In a scale model these changes, as well as any elsewhere, will have to be incorporated, if the model is to represent the ship at that stage of its life. It sometimes happens that a vessel can undergo a major reconstruction and emerge bearing little resemblance to its original appearance.

Another way in which ships are altered is by lengthening them. This is generally done by cutting them in half amidships and

Model of motor fishing vessel *Keila* shown on the water. This model shows the ship as lengthened by 16.5ft (5m) and with revised deck machinery on the shelter deck.

adding a new section. The model of the trawler *Keila*, illustrated here, is interesting in that it shows the ship as it would appear lengthened by 16ft 5in (5m). It was built at the owner's request so that he might see how the ship would look if so altered. However, at the time of writing the ship itself has yet to be altered.

Researching the history of a particular ship is far from easy but can be both interesting and rewarding. If the model is to be entered in one of the national competitions or exhibitions, it is necessary to provide the judges with research data to support the model and prove its accuracy. Such data gains valuable points in these competitions. Inevitably also, once the model is displayed on the local lake, there will be the onlooker who knows all about the hobby and who seeks to criticise the model that is the builder's pride and joy. It is easy to flout such comment by having the correct data at one's fingertips.

Research work can be helped by making out a schedule of the various points to be covered, thus for example:

1. Search Lloyd's Registers in your local library, collate entries and confirm information on the ship.
2. Seek drawings of the ship through plans service catalogues.
3. Use information gained from Lloyd's to enquire at a local museum or at the National Maritime Museum.
4. Contact owners, if possible, should drawings not exist elsewhere.
5. Contact shipbuilders, if they still exist, for help.
6. Contact all possible sources of information if the drawings came from a plans service. Try the service and through them the draughtsman who produced the drawings.
7. Seek information from local or central libraries.
8. Search local press files at or about the dates of the ship's launch, commissioning, breakup or other event in its career.

9. Talk to members of the local model boat club, where there may be a member who has knowledge of the ship, or may know of articles written about it in a specialist magazine, or be able to suggest other possible sources of information.
10. Contact the editorial staff of any of the magazines which deal with ships, shipping and or ship modelling. They are generally helpful and may be able to point the researcher in the right direction.
11. List and contact any other persons or bodies who may be able render assistance – it never pays to be a nuisance but persistence is often rewarded.

Lloyd's Register of Ships

An enquiry at the central library of the nearest fairly large town will indicate where a copy of *Lloyd's Register of Ships* can be consulted. Some libraries have copies of the Register going back for a number of years, so that it may be possible to trace ships which no longer exist. This Register, now in three volumes, is published annually and contains the names etc, of ships classed by Lloyd's Register of Shipping and particulars of all ocean-going merchant ships in the world of 100 tons gross and upwards. A supplementary volume contains the names etc, of all owners and managers and lists their vessels. The information shown for each ship now includes name, previous names (if any) and date of such change of name, official number, call sign, type of ship, tonnages, where, when and by whom built, yard number, name of owners, principal dimensions plus, in some cases, the lengths of poop, bridge and forecastle, type, make, manufacturer and power of engines and other data. Fig 3/4 shows a typical page from the Register.

This Register should not be confused with another Lloyd's Register of Shipping annual publication, namely *Rules and Regulations for the Construction and*

Fig 3/1   Reproduction of page from Lloyd's Register

Rdr Rt	Yiu Lian Dockyards Ltd. Hong Kong — Hong Kong (British)			RFD 4.0 1 dk rf 1245	2 Directional propellers
7615799 Esd RdrRTm	YLANG ex Osa Hawk-89 Societe Comorienne de Cabotage Navale et Commerciale Havraise Peninsulaire (N.C.H.P.) Moroni — Comoro Islands	458 203 664	BV GL	51,01 12,83 2,761 45,83 12,81 3,41 RQD 11,6 *1 dk	1976 Singapore Slpwy & Eng. Co. (Pte.) Ltd.—Singapore (96) TM RoRo Cargo/ Landing Supply Ship Water Oil Bow door/ramp L 10,20 W 5,00 Mchy.aft — Deutz 2 Oil 4SA each 6Cy. 220 × 280 reverse reduction geared to sc. shafts 1 740bhp (1 280kW) Kloeckner Humboldt Deutz Koeln 10,5kn
8904305 SBCJ Rt	YLVA A/B Goteborg-Styrso Skargardstrafik Goteborg — Sweden	315 137 50		34,15 31,50 7,55 3,43	1989 AB Nya Oskarshamns Varv—Oskarshamn (518) M Ferry 450dk P — Caterpillar 3508TA Vee Oil.4SA 8Cy. 170 × 190 with clutches, flexible couplings & sr geared to sc. shaft 638kW (867bhp) Caterpillar Inc. Peoria, Illinois Thw. thrust propeller fwd
5395797 SFVL	YLVA AF KARINGON ex Ylva-85 Bjorn Kenneth Tobin Karingon — Sweden	125 59 500		26,50 6,00 2,420 5,95 2 dks RW	1951 De Haan & Oerlemans—Heusden (261) M Ferry 243F — Mchy.aft Oil 2SA 5Cy. 250 × 340 325bhp (239kW) Nydqvist & Hoim A/B Trollhattan Gen 1 × 1,5kW 24V a.c. Fuel 5,0t (d.o.)-1,0pd 12kn
7505346 SDIA Df Esd Gc Pfd Rdr Rt AMVER	YMER Government of The Kingdom of Sweden (Svenska Staten Sjofartsverket) (The National Swedish Administration of Shipping & Navigation) Norrkoping — Sweden	6 908 195 2 600		104,70 23,86 7,081 96,02 22,52 12,12 2 dks	1977 Oy Wartsila Ab—Helsinki/Helsingtors (413) TD-E Icebreaker — Pielstick 12PC2-2V-400 5 Oil 4SA each 12Cy. 400 × 460 total 23 250bhp (17 102kW) driving 5 gen. connected to 4 elec. motors each of 5 500shp (4 046kW) & geared to sc. shafts Oy Wartsila Ab Turku/Abo 2 Controllable pitch propellers , 2 fwd 18,5kn
7920584 XYFZ BT-10102 Df Esd Gc Rdr RTm/h/v	YMIR KG Schiffahrtsgesellschaft Beutelrock G.m.b.H. & Co. Friedrich Beutelrock G.m.b.H & Co. K.G. Yangon — Union of Myanmar	1 599 1 193 4 210	GL	99,95 (BB) 15,75 5,090 95,31 15,71 5,29 F 6,8 2 dks	1980 Werft Nobiskrug G.m.b.H.—Rendsburg (700) M General Cargo Ice strengthened 3 Ho ER G.7 280 B.7 086 TEU 287 C.Ho 140/20' C.Dk :147/20' 3 Ha (stl) (12,3 × 10,1) (24,6 24,6 × 12,5) ER — Deutz SBV6M540 Oil 4SA 6Cy. 370 × 400 reduction geared to sc. shaft 2 000bhp (1 471kW) Kloeckner Humboldt Deutz Koeln Gen 1 × 208kW 2 × 176kW 440V 60Hz a.c. Controllable pitch propeller Thw. thrust propeller fwd 12,25kn
8709822 TFUG 1880 HF 343 Df Esd Gc Pfd Rdr Rt	YMIR Stalskip H/f Hafnarfjordur — Iceland	540 187 529	✠100A1 stern trawler Ice Class 1D ✠LMC EL 412,5/34,0U2 FN 993	53,00 (BB) 12,55 4,952 50,60 12,10 7,50 F 23,5 Upr.F 20,8 2 dks rf 1003 Box K 419	1988-5 Sigbjorn Iversen M/V. Skips.—Flekkefjord (72) M Fishing Stern Trawler Processing Ref Mchy.aft In.525 — Wartsila 6R32 Oil 4SA 4Cy. 350 × 350 with clutches, flexible couplings & sr geared to sc. shaft 2 005kW (2 726bhp) Oy Wartsila Ab Vaasa/Vasa Gen 1 × 1200kW 1 × 253kW 1 × 113kW 380V 50Hz a.c. Controllable pitch propeller Thw. thrust Contr. pitch propeller fwd Fuel 176,92t (hvf)
7042239 Df Esd Gc Pfd Rdr Rt	YMIR ex Ben Lui-78 Jluz — Uruguay	491 173 305	✠Classed LR until 20/11/89 DAMAGED BY FIRE 4/90	48,19 10,09 3,887 42,68 10,06 6,71 B 6,8 RFD 21,7 2 dks rf 686	1971-4 J. Lewis & Sons Ltd.—Aberdeen (364) M Fishing Stern Trawler Ref Mchy.aft — Polar Vee Oil 4SA 12Cy. 250 × 300 reverse geared to sc. shaft 1 214kW (1 650bhp) British Polar Engines Ltd. Glasgow Gen 2 × 125kW 1 × 44kW 415V 50Hz a.c. 13,5kn
7933086 JG3930 121714	YOBYO No. 53 Toa Kensetsu Kogyo K.K. Tokyo — Japan	173 — —		27,01 1,801 25,51 9,01 2,70 1 dk	1979 Toa Tekko K.K.—Yokohama (5) TM Anchor Hoy — Yanmar 2 Oil 4SA each 6Cy. 200 × 240 reduction geared to sc. shafts 480bhp (353kW) Yanmar Diesel Engine Co. Ltd. Amagasaki
8922113 JI3416 131671 Rdr Rt	YODO MARU Osaka City (Port & Harbour Bureau) Osaka, — Japan Osaka Pref.	153 — —		30,20 9,50 2,700 25,50 8,60 3,77 1 dk	1990 Kanagawa Zosen—Kobe (337) TM Tug — Niigata 6L25CXE 2 Oil 4SA each 6Cy. 250 × 320 with flexible couplings & sr geared to sc. shafts Niigata Eng. Co. Ltd. Ota Gen 2 × 64kW 225V 60Hz a.c. Fuel 27.52t (d.o.) 13.15kn

Reproduced by kind permission of Lloyd's

Classification of Steel Vessels. This lays down the scantlings for all parts of a vessel's structure in order to comply with Lloyd's rules and regulations.

Shipbuilders' plans

Unfortunately, over the years large numbers of shipyards in this country and throughout the world have closed down, in many cases with the destruction of all their plans and technical data. Even so, much has been saved and is to be found in the archives of some universities and city councils, in maritime museums and, in particular, in the massive collection of plans held by the National Maritime Museum at Greenwich, London. In most cases the source concerned is able to supply prints of plans upon payment of the requisite fee but, some may advise that, while they hold the collection of a particular shipyard, they do not have the facilities or finance to have them catalogued and thus are unable to assist with research.

If the modeller is really lucky and finds the shipbuilder still exists and is helpful, then he or she may well obtain some of the detail drawings prepared for different parts of the ship. For instance, plans of the ship's bridge and interior, plans of the various decks and deck houses and of the main superstructure with cabin detail, even drawings of the engine room and its machinery. All these will give detail that the usual plans available from the services do not, and all such information leads to the building of a good and accurate model. Quite often these plans will show how the various parts of the ship were built from

Oil rig rescue ship *Scott Guardian* pictured at her fitting-out berth in St Andrews Dock, Hull and nearing completion. Pictures of a model (under construction) of this ship can be seen later.

steel sections, plates etc, and it may be possible to enhance the model by simulating some of the constructional features. A shipyard produces hundreds of drawings, sketches and data sheets for a single ship and some of them can be of help to the modelmaker while others will only baffle and be of no value.

If the plans have come from a model shipbuilder's plans service the person who drew the plans may have additional information on the ship, or may even have built a model. Polite letters asking help, always enclosing a stamped self-addressed envelope and offering to defray any costs involved in providing assistance, will usually receive attention and gain some help for the researcher.

Photographs

If the selected ship is one of historical interest then research can be easier. Local press files can often provide information and photographs of a ship built at a local yard. Larger magazines such as the *Illustrated London News* can often supply photocopies of sections of their publications if details of the ship required can be given.

If the ship has been concerned with a newsworthy event, the national and local newspapers may have some photographs on file. In these times it may have appeared on one of the local television channels in which case the modeller might be able to obtain access to the pictures, particularly if the powers that be think the completed model would be worth a few moments of airtime. This was the author's experience recently, when local television spent a whole day with him making a three-minute documentary on only one model. Every avenue needs to be explored and often the outcome can be both surprising and rewarding.

Books

Library searches may reveal titles of books

relevant to the ship being modelled. Also of value are the catalogues put out by the publishers of maritime books and by the specialist second-hand maritime book-sellers. Selections of books by the former are often to be found in model shops which cater for the shipmodeller, while the latter are a useful source for obtaining maritime books which are no longer in print. Apart from those books which may deal with a particular vessel, others may cover ships of the same class while others again are devoted to ships of a specific period, in which some information relevant to the model may be found.

There are some excellent books written on steam tugs, coasters and ferries all of which can be of help to the modeller but it must be born in mind that these books deal with the full-size vessels and make no concessions to the model ship. Quite a lot of books cover individual ships or shipping companies, the latter listing all the ships that the company own or has owned and usually with a photograph or two of each ship. These can be helpful but, except when dealing with only one ship, give little to the researcher. The books devoted to a single ship are frequently concerned with the large passenger liners, or ships of particularly special interest. These vessels are generally well-documented although they may be too large to interest the shipmodeller.

Model clubs and societies

There are over one hundred such clubs operating in the UK alone, and many more in the USA, Europe and other countries. The members meet regularly to talk about their work and to sail their models, mainly at weekends, at a local lake or boating pool. Most are friendly and very willing to talk of their hobby, having a wealth of knowledge of ships and shipbuilding which they are willing to share. Membership of such a club costs little and the benefits are great. The measure of what one gets out of such a club is frequently governed by what one puts into it and the members do usually enjoy the hobby to the full.

Other sources

Research need not necessarily be confined to the UK, since the ship may have spent some time in other countries. It may have been modified in Europe or it may now be owned by an overseas company. All avenues need to be explored. In the USA, for example, there are many museums and archives holding large volumes of data about ships of all kinds. There seems to be one associated with almost every port large or small. Some technical societies, such as the Royal Institution of Naval Architects, and the Institute of Marine Engineers in this country and their counterparts in other countries hold specialist libraries, as do some universities. Research can occupy periods of time spread over months if the chosen ship has a long history, but in the case of a modern or fairly new ship then the time needed for research will be shorter.

It is possible to build a model ship entirely from the drawings and a few photographs without ever seeing the ship, if it still exists, and without any of the pleasures of research and of seeking out all the little items that make the model that much more personal and interesting. Though some people do not consider research to be important, it is essential if a truly accurate model is to be built.

4
Selection of Materials

The types of materials used to build a model ship are varied and wide-ranging, including tin plate, pasteboard, a wide variety of timbers, styrene sheet and glass-reinforced plastic, used variously for building the hull and for superstructures and detailing. There are many materials which are impervious to moisture but yet are not suitable for model building and frequently their suitability is only learned by trial and error. The working ship model is always painted, without exception, and this does give a great degree of protection from immersion in water. The paint finish on a model ship therefore needs to be very good and details of paint and paint working is given in a later chapter.

Tin plate

Some modellers have built working model ships from tin plate sheets fastened to brass frames and there have been a number of very fine models built with hulls constructed in this manner. A few even had tin plate superstructures. This material does not really lend itself to the easy construction of a working scale model ship, because metalworking requires considerable specialist skill and tin plate needs careful treatment and painting to prevent rusting.

Cardboard and pasteboard

Although not frequently used, scale model ships can and have been built from cardboard and pasteboard. This is a very flexible material which can be easily rendered waterproof by applying coats of cellulose dope to stiffen the card followed by a number of coats of paint. The hull of the working ship model needs to be fairly strong and a keel of plywood or similar strong timber is needed unless the hull is built up from sections in the same way that a full-size steel hull is constructed. Unless the modeller has a great deal of patience to spend the time forming hull sections from card, this material is best left alone. Mention must be made, however, of one scale ship model which is offered in kit form and made entirely of cardboard. It is of a standard merchant ship produced in the late 1970s/early 1980s known as an SD14 and is some 7ft (2.13m) long (see Appendix 2 for address of supplier).

Plywood

Model ship hulls are commonly made in quality marine plywood using the sizes readily available from the local model shop or a timber importer. Good quality plywood comes mainly from either Russia or Finland and it is obtainable in sizes of 0.4, 0.8, 1.5, 3.0 and 6.0mm thicknesses and in sheet sizes up to 1500mm square. The thicker plies are usually used for making keels and frames while the thinner sizes are used for decks, superstructures etc. A very useful type of plywood, which is soft and freely worked, is 'Liteply' (mainly used for model aircraft) and it is very suitable for deckhouses and superstructures. However, its light and open grain needs to be sealed well before painting.

Balsa wood

Many modellers use balsa wood in block form to build up the bow and stern of a hull where it is so not easy to run planking. Balsa is a very open-grained and almost knot-free hardwood, although the extremely soft nature of the timber belies its classification. It is easily worked but needs very sharp tools and cutting it across the grain can cause it to flake and leave gaps. Most model shops stock balsa in sheet and block form and many modellers find it ideal for basic hull making. It needs to be treated with a sanding sealer to give surface strength and to fill the open pores of the wood. Sanding is easy but the surface of the wood is very easily marked and therefore it requires care if it is to be part of the visible area of a model.

More suitable than balsa, but used in the same manner, is a knot-free wood called 'Jelutong'. This is harder than balsa and is extensively used by pattern makers because of its knot-free properties and the ease with which it can be worked, carved and cut. It is not so easily marked as balsa and is ideal for making bow and stern blocks and for carving detail that can be found on some ships round cabin windows and companions. It is stocked by most good timber importers and may be found at a few specialist shops dealing in exotic timbers.

Miscellaneous timbers

Other timbers that can be used in model building are mahogany, teak, walnut, obeche and birch. All of these have their uses: mahogany for cabin doors and insides of workboats, teak for decks and bulwark linings etc, and walnut for decorative work. Obeche in thin strips is suitable for planking decks and even the outside of the timber hull. Birch, found in good marine ply, can also be an excellent material for ships' planking. Lime is also a fine material for planking the timber hull. All these timbers can be bought in both sheet, strip and block form from specialist model suppliers. The more exotic the timber the higher the price.

Teak will be found to be oily and not easy to fix with the usual woodworkers' glues and resins, and it therefore needs care. It is also very open-grained, requiring to be well filled and sealed before it can be varnished. Although ships' decks are normally made from teak planks, the timber becomes bleached by constant washing and scrubbing until it is almost white. It is therefore much easier to simulate deck planks using a lighter wood such as birch or lime.

For models made in the 'bread and butter' (explained later) fashion, planks of English lime or basswood etc, are ideal, such planks need to be about 0.5 to 0.75in thick and truly flat. Thinner strips of the same timbers are suitable for the planking of the 'plank on frame' hull.

Mahogany and walnut should be used where the full-size ship was so fitted, but it is often only necessary to use veneers of such timber. Large areas can be made from plywood and covered with veneer to simulate the real timber. The scale shipmodeller really does not need much in the way of exotic timbers for working merchant ships, since most ships used cheaper materials unless they carried farepaying passengers who demanded a high standard of comfort and décor. More information on the uses of plywood and timber is given in the chapters relating to the building of the ship's hulls and superstructures.

Styrene sheet

The material that has come into greatest use in recent years is styrene in sheet form (sometimes erroneously called plastic card). This is available in a variety of thicknesses from 0.02 to 2.5mm and in sheets up to 1500 x 1000mm and even larger. It is a hard white material which gives a fine surface for paint and which is readily glued together using liquid polystyrene cement. It can be moulded when heated and is used quite often in a vacuum-moulding unit to give repeated copies of a given part. It is easily cut with a sharp knife and can be snapped along a line scored by the knife. The edges can be sanded smooth and trimmed to follow a curve or uneven shape. The material is impervious to water and ideal for making decks and deckhouses etc. Liquid polystyrene adhesive can be applied with a brush to a joint held together in the hand or with clamps and a very rapid bond results. The liquid is drawn into the joint by capillary action and takes only a few seconds to create a sound join. It is wise to leave it for a short while to allow the adhesive to dry out before sanding and preparing the material for further work.

Glass-reinforced plastics

Glass-reinforced plastics (GRP) are materials from which model boat hulls and sometimes superstructures and other parts are frequently made today. In its raw state the material comprises a liquid resin, a catalyst and a glass cloth formed of loosely-woven glass fibres. The commonest form of resin is polyester and it is generally purchased in activated form requiring the addition of a catalyst to set up a chemical reaction which results in the formation of a hard compound. This resin has a pungent smell and needs care in use in its liquid state. In the solid state it is easily worked. It can be drilled, tapped, sawn and sanded and can give a first-class surface for treating with paint. When solid it is impervious to water and resistant to oil. It can be treated, in the liquid state, to render it heat-resistant to a certain degree, making it suitable for hulls for use with steam plants. A later chapter is devoted to the use of GRP and particularly to polyester resin compounds. There are more expensive compounds of GRP using epoxy resins and woven Kevlar or carbon fibres, but these are used mainly for making model yachts and high-speed power boat models, where a very light but strong construction is required. The expense of the more exotic resins is not really justified for the model merchant ship hull or superstructures.

Other materials

The materials most used in building a model ship have been detailed above but there are many other materials which are necessary even if they are only used in small quantities. Brass and stainless steel are needed for propeller shafts, brass or bronze for propellers, brass strip and angle have their uses as does sheet brass which can be used as bought or etched to provide small parts, rail stanchions etc. Aluminium sheet, tube and rod is also useful in certain places on some models. Copper wire, tube and sheet is easily obtainable and many uses can be found for such material in the working ship model. Very useful too is white metal, which is generally bought as small slabs or pigs. It is easily melted and poured into silicon rubber moulds to produce castings of small parts such as bollards, fairleads etc. A modeller needs to make a single bollard to provide the master from which a number can be cast. The rubber used is also easily obtained and details of the method of casting small parts is also covered later.

The more ingenious modeller will find and make use of many other materials. However, it is necessary to make sure that the material will withstand the strain it may have to suffer and that it will accept paint and exposure to water. Most of the materials listed are those tried and tested by the author and many other modellers and have been found to be suitable for the uses to which they are put.

5
Tools & Adhesives

Some average household tools will be useful for modelmaking, but in general they tend to be too big. It is not necessary to have a huge range of different tools but start with a few basic necessities and expand these as one proceeds. One golden rule which should always be applied when buying tools is to buy the very best that one can afford. Cheap tools rarely do the work for which they are intended and often have to be replaced because they have failed. The more expensive tool will last longer and will prove cheaper in the long run. A second rule, which is often misunderstood, is that the very sharp chisel or knife rarely causes accidents; it is the blunt one needing to be used with a heavy hand which is more dangerous.

Tools must always be treated with care and respect. Do not force tools, particularly cutting tools, when working. If a tool will not cut easily it is either not sharp enough or the cut being taken is too big. With sharp tools take small cuts in preference to large cuts and the result will be a more accurate finish with less need for filing or sanding. Apply the rule 'measure twice and cut once', that is, double check all measurements before cutting. Think before selecting a particular tool and be sure it will do the job before it is used. Consider the sequence of cutting and assembling before doing any cutting. In this way both material and time can be saved and there will be less chance of errors creeping into the work. Study the drawings and read any instructions carefully before proceeding to do any work. Good models cannot be built without good tools and good workman-

ship. The latter comes with learning how to use the good tools.

Hand tools

The first consideration must be the material(s) which will be used when making the model. For plywood and timber, one needs at least a fretsaw frame and blades and a good-quality small tenon saw. If the model is to be constructed on a purchased GRP hull using mainly styrene sheet, then priority should be given to a good strong craft knife which will accept replacement blades. The craft knife is a valuable tool to have in the tool chest in any case. A knife that takes blades which have snap-off sections is particularly useful as the point of the blade frequently wears or breaks and the snap-off blade readily provides a new point. For measuring and for straight cutting with the knife there is no substitute for a good stainless steel rule preferably marked in both Imperial and Metric units.

For safe cutting of thin ply or styrene sheet a cutting mat is ideal. It is usually self-healing, does not blunt the blade when it cuts through the material and generally has a non-slip surface to assist in holding the material that is being cut. Cutting mats come in a number of sizes but the one most suitable for modelling purposes is probably the A3 size. Such mats can be purchased from hobby stores, artists' materials shops and some good stationers. The craft knife and cutting mat will probably be used more frequently than most other tools

An essential tool necessary for drawing and producing square corners is a good

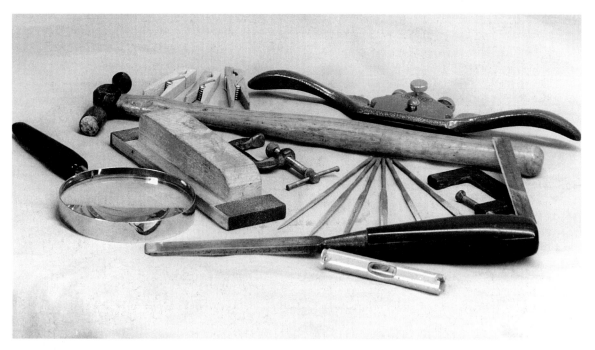

Useful tools for the modeller. Clockwise from top right: spoke shave 'G' clamp, abrasive slip, wood chisel, spirit level, magnifying glass, sanding block, pin hammer, small files and spring clothes pegs.

engineer's steel square. These are available in 3in, 4in and 6in (75mm, 100mm and 150mm) sizes and the 4in is ideal. The square can be used to ensure that the sides of a hatch are assembled vertically and that the corners are square, as well as being useful for marking off. A second, equally useful square is one which is adjustable and can be set to a given angle – one such is illustrated opposite. This type of square can be set for drawing accurate angles for cutting margin planks to fit round deck machinery etc, and it can be useful as a marking gauge for drawing the waterline round the hull.

Most large marine engineering works would have had a steel 'surface table', the top of which was carefully ground truly flat. It was used when marking off on castings and sections of work. A series of marking gauges with fine points were used to mark on the workpiece centres for drilling and planing or cutting lines. The workpiece was coated with blue marking compound so that the fine lines of the scriber would show clearly. Building a model needs the facility of a surface table but obviously a steel table is not feasible. A sheet of plate

glass, about 12 x 24in (300 x 600mm), will adequately serve the same purpose for far less cost. Sections of a model can be assembled on this with the knowledge that the base of the assembly will be truly flat and the sides set at the correct angles. The glass should be cleaned periodically with warm water and detergent and polished using methylated spirit to remove any grease.

A small hammer will be needed for driving small pins and nails into the timber beams and to secure planking when building a plank-on-frame hull. Most suitable will be a small ball pein type hammer, often called a pin hammer, of only a few ounces in weight. The hammer must be kept clean, especially the surface of the head used to drive the pins or nails. When making a plank-on-frame hull there is a tendency for the hammer head to become coated with glue and if it is not removed the head will slip as it contacts the nail and cause the nail to bend. The head is easily cleaned by rubbing it over with a damp rag or lightly with a slip of fine abrasive paper. To drive small pins and nails into the timber without marking the timber with the head of the hammer requires the use of a pin punch,

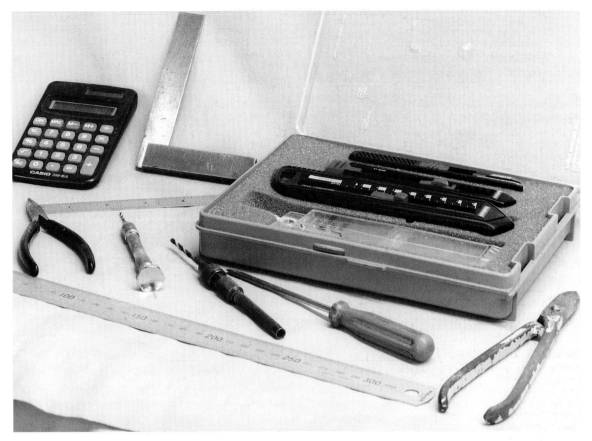

readily obtainable from good tool stores. A centre punch is also useful to ensure that holes are drilled in exactly the right spots. A light tap on the punch with a hammer when the point is on the centre of the location of the hole will indent the centre and guide the drill accurately.

A pair of small, long-nosed pliers will serve to hold the very small pins in place while tapping them with the hammer (fingers never seem small enough), and be useful for other tasks. There is little need for large pliers but those within the size 4in to 6in (100mm to 150mm) are sensible. They come in a number of forms – long nose, square jaw, snipe nose etc, as shown in the illustrations. The side-cutting type is useful when fitting the wiring and cabling of the model. To complement the pliers it is useful to have one or two pairs of fine tweezers. Most good chemists will have a range of surgical steel tweezers. A sharp-pointed

pair and possibly a pair with angled jaws will be of value. A very useful type of tweezer is that in which the jaws are normally closed and opened by squeezing the handle. Such tweezers hold small parts quite firmly and are ideal for positioning parts while glue is applied or holding them in place while small pins are driven through.

Wood chisels are necessary when building the model in timber and, providing they are kept sharp, will rapidly remove excess timber. Used with a mallet they are good for cutting square-cornered window openings in thin plywood or styrene. With care they can be used to cut away the corner of a timber or styrene box to form a small radius curve that can be finished with abrasive paper. Good chisels are expensive and need to be chosen carefully. A sharpening stone will be needed to keep the chisel in good condition. Among the range of

Necessary tools, left to right: calculator, small pliers, engineer's square, box of snap-off blade knives, two types of pin vice (chucks), screw driver, tin snips and 12in (30cm) stainless steel rule.

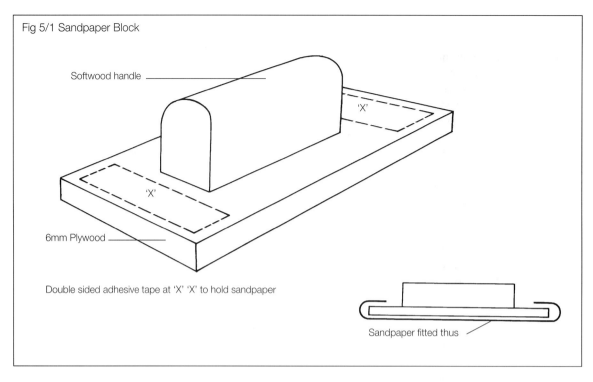

Fig 5/1 Sandpaper Block

Softwood handle

'X'

'X'

6mm Plywood

Double sided adhesive tape at 'X' 'X' to hold sandpaper

Sandpaper fitted thus

chisels found in most stores is the gouge with its convex, curved blade. This is useful for shaping timber where it is hollow and where other cutting tools cannot be used.

There are a number of boxed selections of tools produced by makers such as Exacto and these can be of excellent value. They offer a number of craft knives with interchangeable blades, a sanding block, a small saw and a small plane which also uses replacement blades. The plane can be bought separately from most model shops and is generally known as a 'David' plane, presumably after its designer. It is a very useful tool which can be held comfortably in the palm of the hand and used to smooth off the surfaces and edges of many parts of a model. As with chisels and knives, a plane is only as good as the sharpness of the blade and a blunt blade will only mar the workpiece. Larger planes will clean up the edges of plywood and other timbers and produce good, flat surfaces on the larger pieces of wood.

A very useful tool akin to the plane is the spokeshave, so called because it was

designed to be used to make the spokes of wagon wheels. This tool comes in two forms, one with a flat blade for use on outside curves and the other with a convex blade shape for use on inside curves. The flat-blade unit is the most useful and is suitable for very accurately shaping the outer edges of decks made in ply and for removing the excess material from corners of deck houses etc. The spokeshave has two handles and thus requires the workpiece to be clamped firmly, this being the only disadvantage.

Finally, a screwdriver or two is needed, such as a small 4in (100mm) long flat blade and a similar size having a cross point. Larger screw drivers will generally be found in the home. One with a spring clip arrangement for holding the screw when inserting it into an awkward spot is also useful.

Files and abrasives

Abrasives are needed to smooth corners and rough surfaces and under this heading there is a range of suitable tools. A second-cut half round file, 8in (200mm) long, complete with handle is ideal for removing excess timber or styrene quickly but will leave a coarse surface. This can be smoothed by using a finer file but much better results can be gained by using various grades of abrasive paper fixed to a block. For small areas a selection of needle files are best and these can be bought from almost all tool stores and by mail order from many outlets. It is always better to use a file fitted into a suitable handle and these, even for needle files, can be bought or fashioned from blocks of hardwood.

When it comes to abrasive paper, many modellers have their preferences but, in general, a sheet or two of aluminium oxide paper in grits of 80, 120, and 200 will suffice, complemented by some sheets of wet-and-dry paper in 180, 400, 600 and 1200 grit. Whenever possible abrasive paper should always be used fixed to a suitable sanding block and there are several shapes of such blocks available from the specialist DIY stores. It is easy however, to make sanding blocks from $^1/_4$in (6mm) thick plywood and to attach a block of scrap soft wood for a handle, the paper can be attached to the ply using double-sided adhesive tape (Fig 5/1 illustrates a homemade sanding block). The finer wet-and-dry papers can make useful files if cut and attached to strips of $^1/_8$in (3mm) plywood approximately 6in (15cm) long. Such small strips can be used in awkward places and can easily be replaced. Wet-and-dry paper will last much longer when it is used wet but the water will raise the grain on timber parts and require the part to be dried thoroughly before it can be sanded again. Therefore on timber, it is best used dry. For finishing paintwork the fine grades of wet-and-dry paper used wet are almost unbeatable.

Power tools

A workshop fully equipped with lathe, pedestal drill, powered saws, air compressor and large working surfaces is unfortunately only a dream for most modellers. However, a comprehensive range of tools and equipment can be built up over a period of time particularly if one buys carefully and takes care of the tools.

An essential tool is a drill, whether electrically driven or hand operated. A range of drill bits in various sizes will be needed and it is wise to buy only the sizes required at the time they are wanted as buying a package of drill bits can be expensive if only one or two are required. It is also useful to have a drill stand into which the drill can be fitted and so be able to drill holes squarely through a workpiece. A four- or five-speed pedestal drill is a wonderful item of workshop equipment but very expensive for the modeller unless he has a great deal of use for it. Much more useful, even essential, are two or three pin chucks with different size collets to accept very small drills. These can be held in the hand to drill tiny holes in most material. Small holes are needed through which to insert the blade of a fretsaw for hole cutting or to form the corners of windows and also for locating pins and to pilot small screws. The photographs illustrate some tools used by the author including some pin chucks. Miniature electric drills (12 or 24 volt) have many uses and are often sold complete with a range of drills, grinding stones and burrs, buffing wheel and arbors. There is also a range of attachments for such drills comprising drill stand, lathe, saw table etc. Though small they can perform many tasks, but bear in mind that their power is not that of mains machinery and make due allowances.

A soldering-iron of the copper bit type that had to be heated by a fire or blowlamp is a rarity these days as the range of electric irons is adequate for almost all tasks where soft soldering is needed. An iron of 15 to 20 watts is suitable for soldering parts to circuit boards and doing other jobs associated with the radio or electrical sections of a model ship. A larger iron, of perhaps 75 or 100 watts, will be needed for joining together larger pieces of copper, brass etc. Both will have only intermittent use, but will prove a worthwhile investment. Chapter 24 details methods of soldering.

In the range of power-driven saws can be found the bandsaw, which is very powerful and suitable for cutting timber up to 3in (100mm) thick in both straight and curved cuts. It is only really useful to the modeller who buys timber in large sizes. Much more useful is the power fretsaw which can be found in two or three forms, one which is of the magnetic, vibrating type and which is very safe to use as it does not usually cut soft material such as fingers, and two which are motor-driven with vertical reciprocating motion. Power fretsaws all accept the usual fretsaw blades as well as blades suitable for cutting sheet metal such as brass and aluminium. The powered pedestal drill has already been mentioned but for those modellers who wish to turn up their own fittings and, perhaps, make their own working gearboxes and even steam engines, a lathe is a necessity. Lathes come in all manner of sizes from the smallest, which can be bought from the average model shop, to the large expensive machines with comprehensive facilities. The small lathe is one driven by a 12-volt motor from a transformer and suitable for turning wood for masts and spars and making other small pieces in brass, aluminium, wood or plastic. This type of lathe can cost less than £100 ($150) and is useful for the modeller who works mainly in wood.

Power-driven sanding machines, powered files and similar tools can be found in the catalogues of many manufacturers such as Black & Decker and Bosch and offer labour savings at a reasonable price. Many of these tools will be very useful within the home and thus may be a good buy. A power sander will reduce the time required to sand a timber hull and make the work much easier. However, a powered jigsaw is less likely to be useful to the modeller unless it is an attachment for a drill. Not all modellers will have a need of a precision circular saw but if it is an attachment for an electric drill then it can be used for cutting timber into smaller sizes.

One very useful tool not yet mentioned is the airbrush. Like so many tools, air brushes come in a range of types and prices. It is a miniature paint spraygun designed to apply paint over small areas down to thin lines. The simpler brush is similar to a scent spray where an air current over a small pipe draws liquid up from a reservoir and sprays it out. The more expensive air brushes mix air and paint within the brush itself and control the spray very accurately. Cans of airbrush propellant can be bought from many model shops and artists' material stores and are adequate for intermittent use and short spray runs. Much more suitable is the oil-free air compressor specially made for use with an airbrush, which will give a constant supply of compressed air at a fixed pressure. The only very necessary extra to the compressor is the water trap and filter. Most compressors deliver air which contains a small amount of moisture and this moisture must be trapped to prevent it spoiling the paint finish. While an airbrush is very useful and will give the model a high-quality finish, it is not an essential for the beginner and it is necessary to become proficient in its use before it will justify the expense.

Adhesives

Many adhesives are available in shops and stores today and the variety can be daunting. Only a few are needed when building a working scale model merchant ship. Each adhesive is generally useful only for a particular task, as indicated here. In all cases it is essential to ensure that the surfaces to which an adhesive is to be applied are clean and free from grease or other contaminant. Once a surface has been prepared avoid touching it with the fingers as they will leave grease even if the hands are dry. This applies to all adhesives without exception.

Wood to wood or card

Two adhesives are recommended, Cascamite and Polyvinyl Acetate (PVA). Cascamite is a resin glue which comes in powder form for mixing with water to the required consistency. It is slow to cure but waterproof when dry. It gives an extremely strong bond which will not deteriorate when immersed in water, but its slow grab and curing times can be a disadvantage. PVA is a resin glue in general use throughout the woodworking industry. It comes in the form of a thick, almost white, cream and in two types. The first is a general adhesive for indoor use while the second, listed as aliphatic, is a water-resistant type. Both have fairly fast grab times – in other words they will hold parts firmly after only a short period of time – down to five minutes in a warm atmosphere and both are fully cured in about twelve hours or less. When using PVA it is essential to wipe excess glue from the joint immediately with a damp cloth or tissue as it is difficult to sand away later. When using any of these three glues it is wise to use spirit or water stain on the timber first and to allow the stain to dry before applying glue and joining the parts together. If the parts are glued first, the glue fills the grain and will prevent the stain from penetrating the timber close to the joint and the glue, showing up as white marks on otherwise well-coloured wood. PVA is the quickest way to go but it is also the more expensive. Both types of adhesive should be available in a local model shop and certainly in a DIY store.

Wood to GRP or styrene

For joining timber to GRP or styrene (and also as a stand-by wood glue), two-part epoxy is very useful. This adhesive comes in two forms; the five-minute, fast-grab type and the slow cure type. Be warned – the former is not suitable for use where the parts may be subject to immersion in water and thus must not be used to secure propeller shafts and rudder bearings to timber or GRP hulls. The slow-cure type epoxy can be used for this purpose and is safe underwater when cured. Both types need to be used in a warm atmosphere and will cure more rapidly in warmer places. Both epoxies and resins need warmth to allow the volatile gases produced by the reaction of the chemicals making the bond to evaporate. Epoxy cements are very useful for attaching small metal parts to a model. Epoxy adhesives can be used to attach timber to GRP hulls but it is necessary to roughen the area where the joint is to be made to provide a key for the epoxy.

Styrene sheet

The best adhesive to join styrene parts is liquid polystyrene cement. Tubes of polystyrene cement can be bought but it is prone to stringing and it is not easy to place the glue precisely where. Holding two styrene parts together while a brush loaded with liquid polystyrene cement is applied to the joint is, however, easy and quick. The resultant joint will be firm in only a minute or two but should be left for at least twelve hours before any attempt is made to sand or dress it. As with the epoxy and resin glues, liquid polystyrene cement works by chemical action and time is needed for the volatile gases to evaporate. Always use liquid polystyrene in a well-ventilated place, for the fumes can be unpleasant. There is no real substitute when working with styrene.

Metal to other materials

In recent years cyanoacrylate adhesive (Superglue) has become extremely popular and it is now available in a number of forms ranging from thin liquid to heavy jelly. There is also a release agent that will remove unwanted glue. This type of adhesive also needs to be used in a well-ventilated atmosphere. As its name indicates, it is a material using cyanide in its makeup and is therefore poisonous. It is very fast in effecting a bond and will join most materials used by the modelmaker. The most useful and certainly most widespread use for Superglue is for gluing of metal parts to timber, styrene, GRP and metal. Where white metal parts are used the only alternative to cyanoacrylate is low-melt solder which requires the use of special flux, special solder and a temperature-controlled iron. When using it with timber, the timber piece should be coated thinly with the Superglue and allowed to dry and a second application used to bond the timber to the other material. The open grain of timber will benefit from being sealed by the first coat of Superglue and the second will create the required strong bond.

Veneers to timber etc
A contact adhesive such as Evostik or Durofix is ideal. Within the last year or so Evostik has been modified to lose the smell so enjoyed by the glue-sniffer and it comes now with a small sponge applicator which can be washed in warm water after use and re-used. As before and with all contact adhesives, both surfaces to be joined should be thinly coated with the glue and set aside until they are touch-dry, whereupon they are brought together and a firm bond will be the immediate result. Accurate location of the parts is essential as the immediate bond does not allow time for movement or repositioning of the two pieces. A period of two or three hours should be allowed for the bond to gain full strength.

Paper to timber etc
The best adhesive for this purpose is that used by artists and photographers for fixing prints to cardboard mounts. This is known as 'spray-mount' and comes in a spray can. The advantage of this adhesive over others used on paper is that it does not wet the paper and cause it to stretch, so it can used safely to glue frame shapes to plywood without fear of distortion. Such spray cans are fairly expensive and three types are available; one which allows a degree of repositioning, one which gives an immediate bond and one which is considered to be safe for archival work. Obviously the first is best for model ship work.

Among the many adhesives sold in tubes is one which may be of value in the construction of display cases using clear acrylic sheet and timber mouldings. This is known as 'general purpose' or 'all-purpose' glue and it can bond acrylics to timber and timber to timber. The grab time is short and the bond good after about twenty-four hours but it is expensive compared to PVA for using purely with timber.

The range of adhesives today is wide ranging and bewildering, so that the beginner is advised to seek those listed above and to become proficient in their use before attempting to use one of the many others that advertise specific uses. Never forget that the surfaces to which the selected glue is to be applied must be clean and free from grease, dirt or paint to get the best results with any adhesive.

6
Building the Hull

Having chosen the ship and obtained the drawings and data, attention may now turn to the building of the working scale model merchant ship. As with the full-size ship, the model is built from the keel upwards and a flat working surface is an essential prerequisite. A piece of fairly thick block board or plywood coated on at least the working surface with Formica or similar hard plastic is ideal. It should measure about 6in (150mm) longer than the overall length of the model and about the same measurement wider than its beam. Ensure that the board is truly flat and that there are no bumps or hollows in it. A centreline should be drawn down the length of the board in such a way that it will be readily visible at all times.

Ships were built of wood for thousands of years and this is a very suitable material from which to build the hull of a scale model. There are a number of methods of producing a model ship hull. The first is to carve the hull from a solid block of timber but this is not feasible for a model of any size. The amount of work needed to shape the outside of the hull, followed by a similar amount of work to hollow out the inside, all adds to making this method unsuitable for all but the very smallest of craft. The second utilises planks of timber cut out to the shape of the outside of the hull at various waterlines and glued together, after which it is carved to shape. This is known as the 'bread-and-butter' method, where the timber is the bread and the glue is the butter. The third and most popular method is to build a framework of keel and

frames and cover it with thin planks in the same way as a ship was and is built of timber today, known commonly as the 'plank-on-frame' method. The fourth is a variation of the third but using bulkheads instead of frames. This is often used when the framing is to be removed later or if the hull is needed as a plug from which to make a GRP hull. One further method which is detailed in some magazines and which is a saving in timber is that propounded by Mr Steve Kirby for the bread-and-butter method. These methods will be described in some detail here and it must be understood that, as with all tried and tested methods there are variations on each theme, often too numerous to mention, although one or two will become obvious.

Bread-and-butter hulls

Referring to the lines plans, bread-and-butter hulls follow the shapes of the waterlines on the half-breadth plan, except of course that this drawing shows only half of the ship and the 'bread' must be cut to full width. Obviously to follow the plans as they are drawn means that timber planks of the same thickness as the depth between each of the waterlines are needed and this is the best route to go. If, however, the distance between the drawn waterlines is a great deal more than the thickness of timber available, then it will be necessary to use two or more planks per waterline. In this situation it is essential that the thickness of timber used conforms to the distance between the drawn waterlines to ensure accuracy. If the timber is thicker

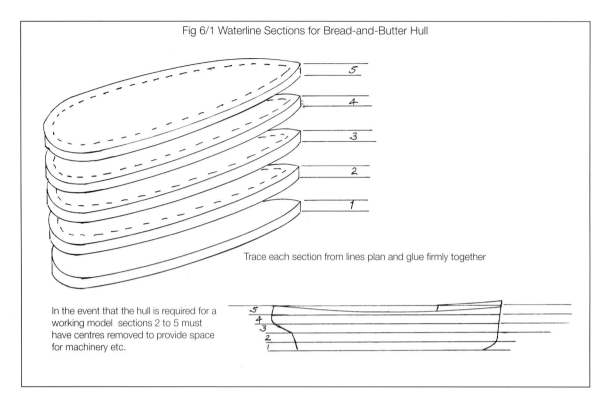

Fig 6/1 Waterline Sections for Bread-and-Butter Hull

Trace each section from lines plan and glue firmly together

In the event that the hull is required for a working model sections 2 to 5 must have centres removed to provide space for machinery etc.

Five templates used to shape the bow blocks of *Scott Guardian* correctly. Each was cut to a specific waterline.

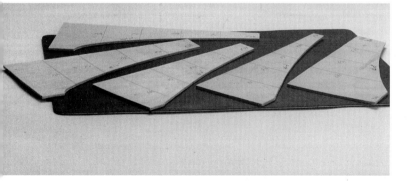

then it will have to be reduced (planed or sanded) to the required thickness. This is most easily done by your local timber merchant or joinery company. Their power-driven planers and/or sanders will reduce the planks to the required dimensions very quickly. Once the timber has been cut to the necessary thickness the 'bread' slices can be prepared.

Trace the outline of each waterline on to a separate timber plank (see Fig 6/1). The bottom plank will remain solid, while the remaining planks can have the centres cut away to leave a gluing margin round each edge. Each plank is then glued down to the preceding plank and weighted or clamped to hold it firm until the glue has set. It is wise to drill for and fit dowels between each layer of timber so that they do not move during the gluing and setting period. Some modellers use brass screws between layers but this needs care to ensure that the screws will not be revealed in the subsequent carving and sanding. The adhesive needs to be waterproof or at least water-resistant and the best, but, with the slowest grab time is Cascamite – this comes in powder form to be mixed with water before use. An alternative is woodworkers' glue of the polyvinyl acetate type (PVA) and the water-resistant type should be selected.

The oddly-shaped hull should be set aside, long enough to allow the selected glue to set thoroughly, before proceeding to plane and shape the outside of the hull. Shaping the outside of the hull needs to be done with care and the only way to ensuring that the work proceeds correctly is to use templates. These are cut to the shape of the ordinate/station lines on the plans so that they can be tried against the hull repeatedly at each appropriate station during the process. Templates can be made from thick card or, preferably, from thin plywood. They must be cut with care as the accuracy of the finished hull will depend upon their accuracy. Sample templates for a hull can be seen in the photograph. Great care must be taken when planing and sanding the hull. It is easy to remove too much material and much harder to replace it. Frequent testing using the templates is essential and final finishing of the outer surface of the hull needs to be done progressively with successively finer grades of abrasive paper. The best way to control the sanding operation is to use the sandpaper on a rubber or timber block. Sanding by holding the paper in the hand will often lead to hollows being left and hills being exaggerated. A very fine surface is needed on which to apply the paint.

The inside of the hull also needs to be smoothed out and the thickness of the sides and base is determined largely by the space required for the equipment to be fitted inside. A bread-and-butter hull will usually terminate at main deck level, any bulwarks being added later as normally they are too thin to be carved out from the hull timbers. It must also be realised that the thickness of the timber will affect the weight of the model and its behaviour on the water. It is wise to remove as much timber from the sides as possible while still leaving an adequate thickness for strength. At the bottom the thickness will similarly depend upon the machinery to be installed. The bottom of most merchant ships is not flat, when seen in section, but rises slightly from the centre line outwards. This is known as the 'rise of floor'. The propeller shaft or shafts need to be accurately located and any bossing or brackets must be marked and prepared. Some ships have a prominent bar keel and this must be made and fitted to the hull accurately. Thin ply-

wood keels can be fitted by cutting a groove in the timber of the hull just wide enough to accept the ply keel and then gluing it in place. With some vessels the keel may be fabricated and attached to the hull only at the stern between twin propellers. Such a keel will need to be built up or carved from solid timber before being glued in place.

Many merchant ships have bilge keels running low down on either side of the hull and over a third of the length of the hull, to reduce the rolling moment of the ship. They must be made and fitted before the hull is finally painted and details of these are given later. However easy it is to describe the making of a bread-and-butter hull, the work is time-consuming and does need regular sighting by eye in addition to using the templates to ensure that the final shape is true.

A modified method of making a bread-and-butter hull using less timber was devised some years ago by Steve Kirby and his system is fully described in a number of publications which are still available (see Appendix 3 for further information). The timber plug for the model of *Rovuma*, shown in the photographs, was built using the Kirby method and was completed in about two-thirds of the time needed for building a plank-on-frame hull of similar size. In brief the Stephen Kirby method of building a bread-and-butter hull allows the laminations to be cut from a single plank. The system suggests an overlap of individual laminations of $1/2$in (12.7mm). The thickness of the timber needs to be selected as for the bread-and-butter hull described above, ie to coincide with the depths of the waterlines of the plans. To calculate the minimum width of timber from which to cut the hull the formula below is used, the length of the timber will remain the length of the hull overall.

Width of plank = 2 [(number of laminations - 1) x overlap] + beam.

For a model with 10 laminations, a beam of 8in and an overlap of $1/2$in the calculation is:

$$Width = 2\,[\,(\,10 - 1\,)\,x\,1/2\,] + 8$$
$$= 2\,(9\,x\,1/2\,) + 8$$
$$= 9 + 8 = 17in$$

To obtain wood of this width (balsa), several planks will have to be glued edge to edge. Marine plywood is, however, very suitable and obtainable in various thicknesses. A centreline is drawn on the selected timber and stations are marked at right angles, as many stations as there are on the plans. The bottom lamination is traced from the plans at waterline No.1 above the keel. Datum lines No. 2 (false centre lines) are drawn $1/2$in away and on either side of the drawn centreline, waterline No. 2 is next traced but on either side of the No.2 Datum lines. This is repeated with datum lines for all the remaining waterlines on either side of the previous lines and the waterlines marked from the appropriate datum lines until the deck level is reached. Finally the plank is cut to all the drawn lines producing laminations, except for No. 1, of half hulls. These are glued together to give the full hull and the whole assembly is carved and sanded to the finished hull shape. As for the other timber joints described, Cascamite or PVA adhesives are suitable for assembling the hull parts.

Plank-on-frame hulls

This system of building the timber hull is more widely used than the bread-and-butter method as it leaves a clear internal space in which to fit drive gear and radio equipment. The lines drawings need to be enlarged or reduced to the desired scale for the model if they are not to scale when obtained. The sheer plan will give the bottom outline for the keel and this should be traced on to a suitable piece of 6mm ply or similar-sized hardwood. It is sometimes preferable to cut the keel in two pieces and join the pieces in the middle with a scarphed joint (see sketch Fig 6/2 and photographs pp41-43). This method helps to eliminate any slight twists in the timber as of course the keel must be absolutely true and straight. Once the keel has been cut to the outline traced from the sheer plan the inner part can be marked off and cut. The depth at which the keel should be cut depends upon the model that is being built. For example, if the vessel has an obvious bar-type keel then it will be necessary to cut the keel to a depth of at least 1in or even $1^1/_4$in (25 to 30mm). If the keel is cut in two parts they must be assembled with a good-quality woodworker's adhesive and clamped to a flat surface until the glue has cured. Two or three hardwood trenails through the scarphed joint (as illustrated) will assist the alignment and the strength of the joint. In some cases the sternpost can form part of the keel and in others it will need to be made and added once the keel is ready. The drawings will assist here.

Frames dictate the shape of the hull and cutting and assembling these must be done with care. First count the number of frames that will be needed to provide sufficient support for the hull planks. They should be not more than 3in (76mm) apart and spaced more closely towards the ends where there is more curvature. Photocopies should be made of each of the frame drawings (ordinate/station lines) to the correct scale, or if the drawings are to model size each frame can be traced through carbon paper on to good-quality paper. Extend all the frames at the outer edges to a datum line at least 1in (25mm) higher than the tallest frame, This will allow the hull framework and keel, when assembled, to be inverted and attached firmly to a work board for planking of the hull (Fig 6/3). Fold the paper pattern of each frame down the centre and carefully cut at the required line to obtain a full frame. Glue the paper patterns to a sheet of good-quality marine ply and cut them out. At this point they

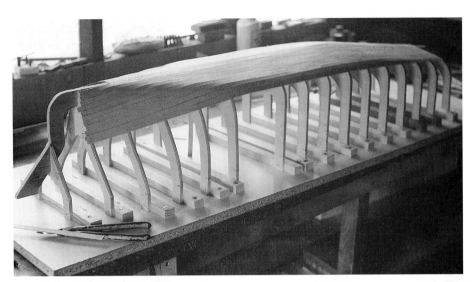

Keel and frames for model of *Scott Guardian* mounted on building board with some of the bottom planking fitted.

View of keel and frames from the stern. Note that the planks terminate at the last frame to allow the later fitting of timber blocks.

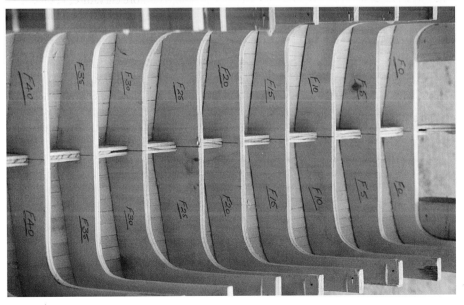

Stern of fully planked hull for model of *Scott Guardian* from the inside showing stern quarter timber blocks. Note frame numbers running forwards from stern.

Bow view of planked
hull showing space for
timber bow blocks
forward of front frame.

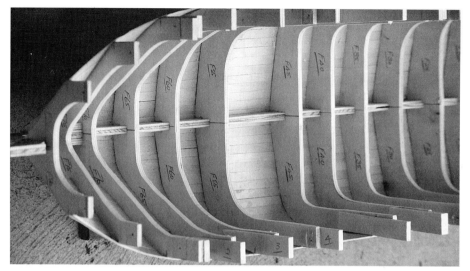

Side view of planked
hull illustrating how
planks have been fitted
at the bow leaving
space for timber blocks
needed where the
curvature of the planks
would be too severe for
easy fitting.

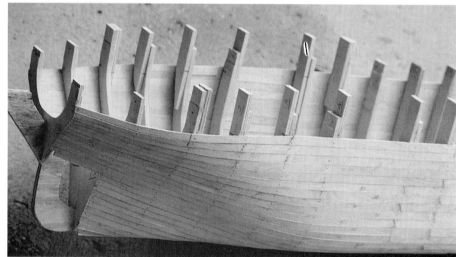

Stern quarter of planked
hull showing lines
marked for guiding cut-
ting to correct deck
height. Note how some
of the planks have been
numbered to aid correct
fitting after cutting.

Side view of model hull amidships to illustrate how the diagonal plank ends are butted and fitted to alternate frames to give strength to the construction.

Midships view showing deck lines marked for cutting. The frames will be cut back to deck level once the hull has been sanded and rendered smooth.

View of stern quarter of hull for *Scott Guardian* showing planked detail befor the planks have been sanded and dressed. The spaces between the stern quarter blocks will be fitted with strips of planking running athwartships.

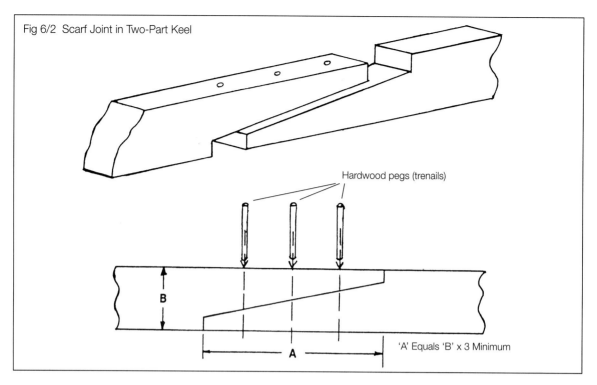

Fig 6/2 Scarf Joint in Two-Part Keel

Hardwood pegs (trenails)

B

A

'A' Equals 'B' x 3 Minimum

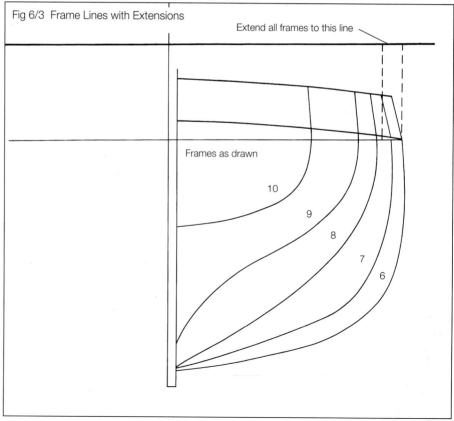

Fig 6/3 Frame Lines with Extensions

Extend all frames to this line

Frames as drawn

10

9

8

7

6

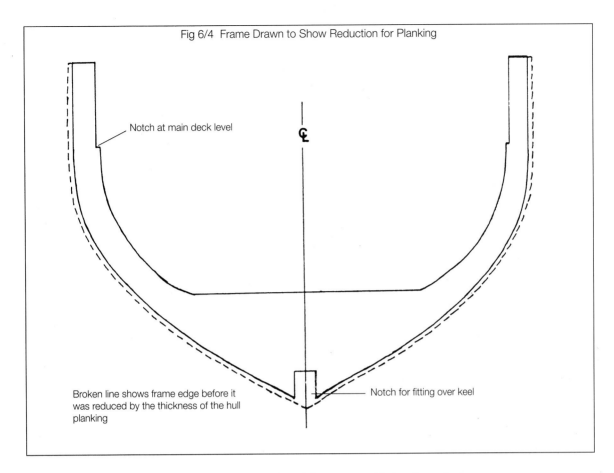

Fig 6/4 Frame Drawn to Show Reduction for Planking

Notch at main deck level

Broken line shows frame edge before it was reduced by the thickness of the hull planking

Notch for fitting over keel

will be bulkheads so the insides will have to be cut away. But before doing so, trim back the outsides of the frames to match the thickness of the planking that is to be used to clad the frames. It is important to remember that the frames and indeed all the lines of the lines drawings are drawn to the outsides of the plating. Therefore they need to be reduced by the thickness of any planks to avoid making the model too wide in the beam and therefore out of scale (Fig 6/4). It is a simple matter to use a marking gauge or a pencil fixed to a timber block to mark round each frame to the thickness of the planks and then to saw away the excess. The inside of each frame can then be removed to leave a frame depth of $3/8$in to $1/2$in (10mm to 15mm) or less if there is a need for the maximum possible room in the hull.

Some of the photographs illustrate keels and frames assembled and attached to a working board. Each frame should be notched to fit over the keel at the appropriate station and to leave a part of the keel showing at least equal to the thickness of the planks or more if a keel is to be visible (Fig 6/5). Each frame must be vertical to the keel and equidistant on either side of the keel. Therefore each frame must be trial fitted and adjusted for accuracy before it is glued in place. When gluing these timber parts together a fast grab will be obtained if a PVA adhesive is used, but a joint using Cascamite will be more suitable for use in water. Before gluing any of the frames to the keel mark the centres of all frames on both sides of the keel and number them so that no errors may occur during construction. The sketches show frames cut to give a flat floor inside the model and notched at the position of the main deck. They were

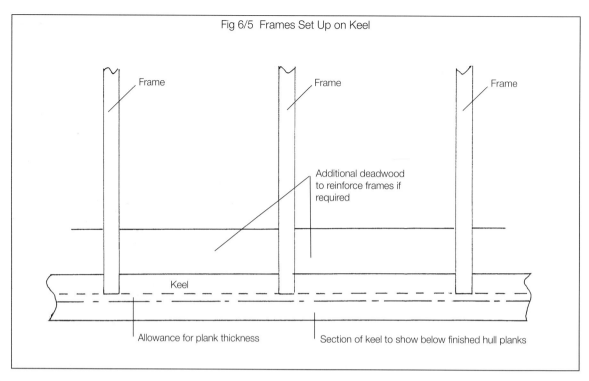

Fig 6/5 Frames Set Up on Keel

for a model herring drifter, but the principle can be adapted to suit other models. Once all the frames have been set to the keel the assembly should be set aside for at least forty-eight hours to allow all the adhesives to dry out, it is wise to clamp a straight edge (a length of angle iron such as Dexion or similar) to the keel to hold it perfectly straight while the glue dries.

When the keel assembly is dry it should be inverted on to the work board and the tips of the frames should all touch the surface. Fit small packing pieces of timber under those frames which do not touch the work surface. Strips of square or similar scrap timber can be attached to each frame and to the board by five-minute epoxy and pins, or a similar fast-curing adhesive, and allowed to set. The result will be a solid assembly to which the hull planks can be fastened and glued. Before any planks can be fitted, however, it is necessary to bevel the edges of the frames towards the bow and stern so that the hull planks will lie flat. This work should be carried out using a plank as a guide. With coarse sandpaper on

a block, or with a coarse file, bevel the edges of the frames fore and aft until the guide plank lies flat to each frame edge over a number of frames. The guide plank should lie over the maximum frame width so that it can truly follow the curve of the hull. To avoid severe bends in the hull planking it is acceptable to use blocks of balsa, Jelutong or similar timber at bow and stern; such blocks can be added after the hull planks are fitted and sanded. More about the block works follows later.

Whatever timber is used for the hull planking it needs to be free from knots, straight-grained and of good quality. Lime is ideal, as is spruce, but so is good-quality plywood. The planks should be about $^3/_8$in (10mm) wide and not more than $^1/_8$in (3mm) thick, since anything thicker is difficult to bend. When planking the hull always work on alternate sides of the keel and *never* lay more than two planks on one side before going to the other. Failure to follow this rule can cause stress which will warp and twist the hull when it is removed from the work board and the only cure is

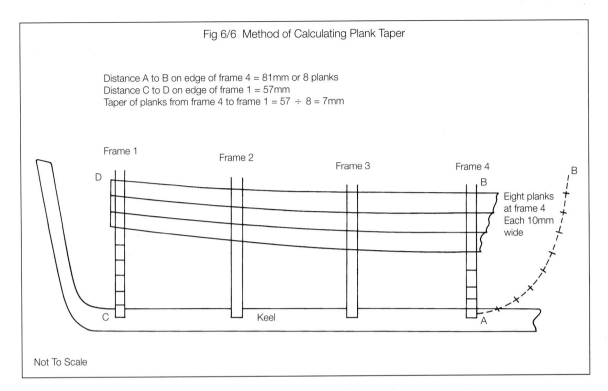

Fig 6/6 Method of Calculating Plank Taper

Distance A to B on edge of frame 4 = 81mm or 8 planks
Distance C to D on edge of frame 1 = 57mm
Taper of planks from frame 4 to frame 1 = 57 ÷ 8 = 7mm

Frame 1   Frame 2   Frame 3   Frame 4   B

Eight planks
at frame 4
Each 10mm
wide

Keel

Not To Scale

to scrap the work and start a new hull all over again.

Start by laying one plank along each side of the keel. If the planks are short, fit two so that they join on a frame amidships, diagonally cutting the ends that butt together. For adequate strength further planks should have their midships joints staggered over two or three frames. Glue each plank to each frame and the edge to the keel using the recommended adhesives previously mentioned. Small pins should be used to fasten each plank to each frame. Brass pins $^3/_8$in (10mm) long are ideal as they are easily sanded along with the timber. If steel pins are used they will need to be removed and the holes filled before the hull is sanded. It is wise to number each plank as it is fitted to keep a record of the work, ie S1 and P1 for starboard and port sides. This avoids mistakes and ensures that each side of the hull is kept as near identical to the other as possible. The first planks must be fitted accurately at the stern but they may overlap the forward frame for trimming back later. From here on the work becomes a little more exacting, each plank needs to be tapered towards bow and stern to maintain the correct shape of the hull. This is effected as follows (see Fig 6/6):

1. Measure the deck position from the plans and mark each frame with this position, making a deep score in the frame.

2. Find the widest frame of the model and, with a pair of dividers set to the plank width, determine the number of planks that will fit from the keel line to the deck position.

3. Measure the remaining frames from the keel plank to the deck position. Note the measurements at each frame and divide by the number of planks needed. This will give the required taper. For example, if twenty planks are needed on each side at the widest frame and the frame at the bow measures 5in (125mm), then the planks at the bow will need to be $^1/_4$in wide (6mm), 5in (25mm) divided by 20 .

4. Checking the distances at each frame will determine the points at which tapers commence, mark the hull accordingly.

Proceed by measuring each successive plank for length against the framing, not forgetting to stagger any joints amidships, then mark and cut the plank to the appropriate taper. Apply adhesive to the bottom edge and to each frame and pin each plank in place. If necessary use small clamps to hold the plank in place but, where the curve of the hull prevents the plank from fitting easily, the plank may need to be pre-bent. This can be done in a number of ways. A plank bender may be purchased and each plank curved with it. Planks may be soaked in very hot water for a few minutes when they will be found to be more flexible or they may be steamed to render them flexible. Soaking planks in household ammonia solution is also very effective although the fumes can be troublesome. All these methods will work quite well but not if the planks are of plywood. Plywood planks are best bent by stroking them gently over the shank of a hot 75- or 100-watt electric soldering-iron clamped in a vice. The heat from the iron will soften the glue between the layers of ply and allow the strip to be bent easily. When removed from the heat the glue will harden and the plank will remain permanently bent.

As the work proceeds it may be found that a plank will not easily run fair with its neighbour because of the curvature of the hull and the need to twist the plank. This usually occurs at the stern. In this case it is necessary to fit a 'stealer'. A stealer is a short wedge-shaped length of plank cut to fit between the last strake and the one now being applied (Fig 6/7). Fitting stealers will upset the plank taper measurements which will need to re-assessed each time a stealer is used. In fact it is often best to leave the fitting of stealers until the hull is completely planked, when each one can be tailored to fit its location. Stealers are, of course, glued and pinned in place in the same way as the main planks. Fitting stealers is not out of scale or bad practice, as they were often fitted to full-size wooden vessels. However, restrict their application to those places where they cannot be avoided.

Work slowly when planking the hull until the planking reaches a point just above the deck level. Fit only a few planks at each session and allow ample time for glue to dry before proceeding further. Ensure that each plank is butted tightly to its neighbour for a gap-free run. Where the turn of the bilge is a tight curve, planks which are not bevelled on their edge will leave a gap which must be filled. This is not a problem with the hull that is to be painted. However, it is not acceptable to use a filler compound if the hull is to be stained and varnished. In this case it will be necessary to bevel the edges of all planks to ensure one lies true to the next. Bevelling planks also affects the taper measurements which, again, will need to be checked constantly as the work proceeds.

Where the ends of planks have been left free beyond the bow and stern frames they must be cut back and the ends sanded flush with the face of the end frame. The whole surface of the planking must be examined and any gaps filled. The hull will generally be found to be fairly even and true and a thorough sanding, using progressively finer grades of paper from about 100 grit down, will produce a fine surface finish. At this point the hull can be cut from the work board and the board cleaned up for future use. A suitable stand to hold the hull while work proceeds should now be made and, later, a stand made to display the model when it is completed.

The next step will be to make and fit the bow and stern blocks. Balsa is the first timber to spring to mind as it is easily cut and sanded but it is also easily marked and crushed even after it has been sealed and surface-hardened. If the model is to be

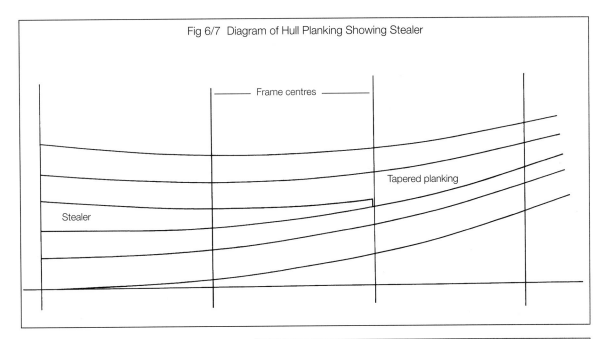

Fig 6/7 Diagram of Hull Planking Showing Stealer

Frame centres

Tapered planking

Stealer

sailed then these blocks should be of a harder material. Jelutong is recommended. This is almost as easy to cut and sand as balsa but is much harder and less prone to damage if accidentally bumped. The bow blocks are easily marked out by holding them in turn against the hull (Fig 6/8) after which each can be roughly cut before being glued to the keel and hull at the bow. The stern blocks are not quite so easy (Fig 6/9) but again can be marked off using the gaps in the hull at the stern. They can also be roughly cut before being glued in place. An important point to remember when fitting stern blocks to the hull of a working model is to cut away the inside to allow clearance for the rudder stock or propeller shafts.

The final dressing of the hull is a time-consuming task requiring care and attention to surface finish. The bow and stern blocks must be sanded until they are very close to their final finish. Next the whole hull must be examined carefully and all those places which may be high or where filler needs to be used marked with a soft pencil. All pin positions must be checked and, using a high-quality filler compound, any holes and gaps made good,

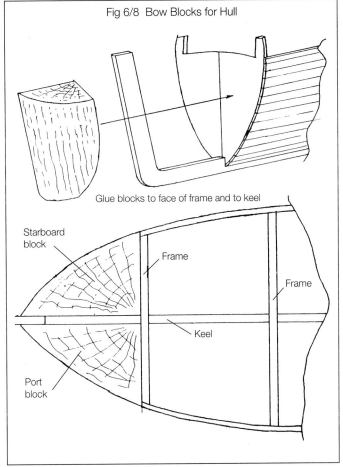

Fig 6/8 Bow Blocks for Hull

Glue blocks to face of frame and to keel

Starboard block

Frame

Frame

Keel

Port block

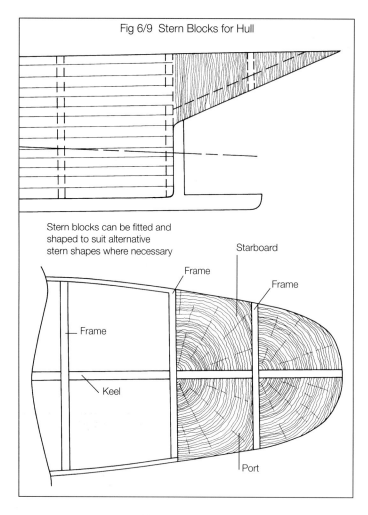

Fig 6/9 Stern Blocks for Hull

Stern blocks can be fitted and shaped to suit alternative stern shapes where necessary

which can be rectified. Cut away the tops of the frames that protrude above the planks. To assist with waterproofing it is wise to treat the inside of the hull with a number of coats of varnish but, better still, coat the inside with a skin of polyester resin to which the necessary catalyst has been added. The use of polyester resin for model ships is described in Chapter 8. The resin when fully cured will stiffen the planks and assist in providing a good surface on the outside of the hull. Once the hull is complete to this stage the outside can be treated with two or three coats of suitable primer and set aside for a few days to dry. It will also be an advantage to paint the outside of the hull with polyester resin and catalyst but this will require careful rubbing down once it has cured. Painting the hull is described in a later chapter. To complete the hull at this stage mount the model vertically on a smooth work surface and carefully mark the heights of the deck at each frame station. With a thin spline of timber join the marks to gain a fair curve and trim the top edge of the hull to the curve.

A hull built in one of the methods described above is quite suitable for completing and outfitting to make a fully working, radio-controlled scale model merchant ship. However, such a hull is also suitable for using as a master from which to produce a hull in glass reinforced plastic (GRP). Should a GRP hull be the ultimate objective the only differences from those described above that would be of value are:

(a) the bread and butter hull need not be hollow but can be left solid.
(b) the plank-on-frame hull can be built with solid bulkheads instead of open frames.

One further point when making a plug (master) for a GRP hull is that the timber need not be of high quality. Almost any flat and true timber can be used, even that recovered from old furniture. A bread-and-butter hull could be assembled from well-seasoned old floor boarding.

allowing adequate time for filler to cure. Using a medium grit sandpaper on a block commence to rub down the entire hull, removing any high spots and then carrying on until the whole hull has an even finish. Continue to examine for and rectify any blemishes and, with successively finer grades of sandpaper, bring the hull surface to a superfine finish. There is no shortcut to this work although electric sanders of the orbital type will bring the surface down more quickly.

Finally, clean up the interior of the hull by removing any excess glue which may have penetrated between the planks. Careful scraping with a sharp instrument such as a chisel will effectively remove this. Examine the inside for any obvious faults

7
Detailing the Hull

Whether the hull is to be fitted out and used for the finished model or used as a plug for a GRP hull, details need to be applied. The location of the propeller shaft(s) at the exit point or points of the hull need to be added. The anchor hawse hole trims must be fitted or the anchor recesses cut into the sides of the hull near the bows. The positions of bow and stern thrusters, if fitted, need to be marked into the hull as do the positions of any bilge keels or stabilisers.

Plating

Ships in earlier years and up to the last War were invariably built of steel plates riveted together and to the frames. During the War welded ships became more and more common as they could be built faster.

There is a measure of controversy about fitting shell plating to a model. The question of scale comes into this matter quite decidedly. For example, a steel plate which is 1in (25mm) thick at a scale of $^1/_2$in to 1ft would be represented by material of 0.042in (1mm) thickness and this is quite visible on a model and card and styrene sheet of this thickness is readily obtainable. At a scale of $^1/_8$in to 1ft then the thickness becomes 0.010in (0.25mm) which is very much less, although still visible to the naked eye at a short distance. Ships' plates were and still are a matter of Classification Society Rules and how a ship is plated is governed by such rules. With reference to Fig 7/1 it can be seen that some strakes of plates are 'in', some are 'out' and yet others are 'in and out'. This refers to whether the plate overlaps or is overlapped by another on both edges or whether it is only overlapped on one edge. Obviously the 'ins' and 'outs' are dictated by the curves of the bilge etc. A plate expansion drawing will be a great help to the modeller wishing to plate a model and one such is illustrated in Fig 7/2. They are not easily obtained so the modeller must rely upon photographs if they are available. In general, plate lines on a ship run parallel to the keel and then the deck edge and it is possible to plate a hull provided some data on plate sizes and runs can be found.

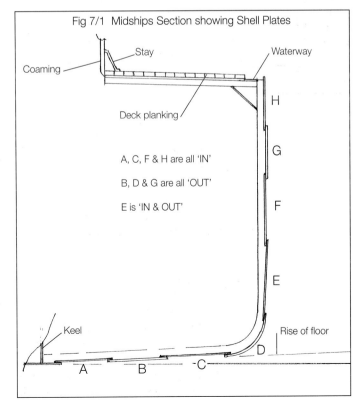

Fig 7/1 Midships Section showing Shell Plates

A, C, F & H are all 'IN'

B, D & G are all 'OUT'

E is 'IN & OUT'

Fig 7/2 Plate Expansion Drawing

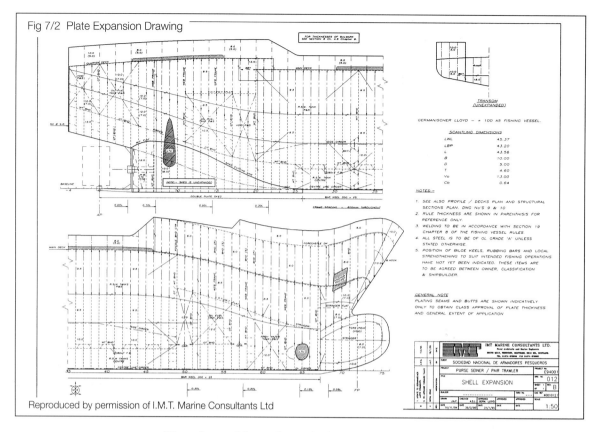

Reproduced by permission of I.M.T. Marine Consultants Ltd

Plates for models can be made from thin sheets of pasteboard or cartridge paper found in most good stationers or artists' materials supply shops. Thin styrene sheets are suitable but need care in fixing and thin sheets of aluminium such as used litho sheets from print shops will also suffice, as will sheet cut from used aluminium cans. Select the material that is nearest in thickness to that dictated by the scale of the model. The plate expansion drawing cannot be used to obtain the shape of the shell plate as this has been expanded only vertically, not horizontally. It is best to mark the strakes of plating on the model and lift the shapes of the plates from that. A contact adhesive such as Evostik is the best to use with styrene or litho plate, whereas a PVA glue will work quite well with card. Start working from the keel and from the stern moving towards the bow and upwards. Plates overlap towards the stern in all cases. It will be necessary to lay those plate runs which are 'in' first, followed by any which are 'in and out' and finally those that are 'out'. It is necessary to take great care with this work as even small mistakes will show clearly on the finished hull.

Rivets

A much more serious matter, and one which has provoked great debate, is the question of showing rivets. Here again clear rules are laid down by the Classification Societies regarding the spacing of rivets, the number of rows of rivets and the size of such rivets. On most merchant ships the rivets on the outside of the hull were countersunk with a small dome head which renders the rivet almost invisible, particularly when the hull of the full-size ship has had a number of coats of paint. In these circumstances it is very debatable whether rivets should be shown on the scale model. Certainly they would not show in scales much less than $\frac{3}{8}$in to 1ft (1:32). More important is the need to show rivets correctly if they are to be added to the model. A row of blobs of glue is not sufficient and will be seen as poor workmanship. Consult the Classification Societies' rules and apply rivet heads carefully and accurately. There are places where there are three and four rows of rivets and others where there are only two or even one row. Think carefully before 'riveting' and be very certain that the runs that are fitted are correct. Fig 7/3 gives some rivet detail.

There are a number of inlets and outlets, of different sizes and for various purposes, above and below the waterline of a ship's hull. These just above the waterline need to be clearly shown on models to the larger scales. A ring of the correct size glued to the hull is usually sufficient unless the builder intends to feature a working discharge on the model. How to do this is shown in a later section.

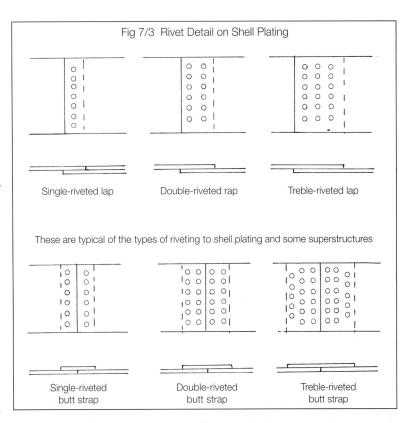

Fig 7/3 Rivet Detail on Shell Plating

Single-riveted lap

Double-riveted rap

Treble-riveted lap

These are typical of the types of riveting to shell plating and some superstructures

Single-riveted
butt strap

Double-riveted
butt strap

Treble-riveted
butt strap

Detailing a plug

When the hull is required as a plug from which to make a GRP hull any mark, blemish or scratch on it will be repeated in a GRP mould, so care must be taken when handling the hull needed for this purpose. Furthermore, nothing should be put on a hull that is to be used as a master which will prevent the moulded hull being released from the production mould. In this case it is wise just to make a suitable location mark upon the hull and to fit the part after it has been moulded. For example, a rudder post fitted to a keel extension and leaving space for a propeller will not allow the mould to be released and would thus need to be fitted later.

A further advantage of moulding a hull in GRP is that the ship's bulwarks can be moulded along with the hull and rubbing strips can form part of the master plug. Other small fittings found on the hull of the prototype vessel can be added provided they will not impede the release of the hull from the mould, so that each hull taken from the master mould will carry the same detail. Regretfully it is rarely possible to have a ship's bulwarks form part of the hull planking of a plank-on-frame hull or form part of the bread-and-butter hull, as in both cases the hull will be too thick. Bulwarks must be added separately later and will be described in a later chapter. In some cases the bulwarks will not form part of a GRP hull and thus they, too, will need to be added later. If bulwarks are to form part of the plug for moulding then ensure that any openings for wash ports, in way of fairleads, mooring pipes etc, are marked clearly on the master. Details of wash ports, Panama ports and similar items will be dealt with in later chapters.

8
The Moulded Hull

A hull constructed from timber as described in the previous chapter can, with sensible sealing and painting, be perfectly suitable for building up into a scale working model. It can easily be outfitted with decks, superstructure etc, all of timber or styrene sheet construction. However, a hull moulded in polyester resin and glass fibre will be proof against water damage and leaks, except through propeller shaft tubes or other skin fittings. Once a production mould is made, more than one hull can made identical to the first. It is possible for a number of modellers all wishing to build, say, a tug, to share the costs of the materials and each to have a hull to finish in the form he/she pleases.

Materials

The materials needed for making hulls of GRP are readily obtainable from a number of specialist suppliers. Polyester resin is a thick, clear liquid with a pungent smell, usually bought in activated form. The resin can be purchased without the activator but using it is complicated and unnecessary when ready-activated material is available. When a suitable catalyst is mixed with polyester resin in correct proportions a chemical reaction takes place which results in the resin solidifying. The chemical reaction generates a certain amount of heat and care is needed when handling the mixture. The catalyst is usually liquid although some car accessory dealers stock a resin which requires the addition of a catalytic paste. For the purposes of moulding a hull, such resin is expensive when compared to that of the specialist suppliers. To give a fine smooth finish to a moulded hull, resin in the form of a thixotropic jelly, known as 'gelcoat', is applied before any other work is done. This gelcoat has the property of drying (curing) in contact with another surface and free from air. If allowed to air-dry, the surface of the gelcoat remains tacky. Other resin, known as lay-up resin, has air-drying properties. To reinforce the resin and allow it to hold the shape of the hull or other type of master, chopped strands of glass in a loosely-woven state are used. The 'glass mat' comes in various thicknesses designated by weight – 1.0, 1.5 and 2.0 ounces per square foot or 300, 450 or 600 grams per square metre, the best for a model ship hull being 1.5oz/sq ft (450g/sq m). Glass cloth is also available in a woven ribbon form for reinforcing corners and seams of large areas – rarely used in model ships – and also in the form of a fine tissue which can give the inside of a model hull a fine finish although it is not so easy to handle.

All the materials such as resins, catalysts, wax, release agent and colouring, together with brushes, rollers and brush cleaners, can be obtained from the manufacturers listed in Appendix 2. Glass cloth, mat and surfacing tissue can also be bought in small quantities together with mixing cups and disposable gloves and even coveralls from these suppliers. Note particularly that polyester resins and fibreglass products are materials that should be handled with care and in accordance with the makers' recommendations. The smell is strong and unpleasant and some of the liquids are hazardous. Under these circumstances it is sensible to work in a well-ventilated area away from the home and where the odours will not cause distress. It is also sensible to ensure that small children are kept well away from the workplace and the materials. Some users will find that the resins and brush cleaners do have a deleterious affect on their skin while others can handle the liquids easily. In all cases it is wise to use a barrier cream before starting to work and to wear disposable gloves while handling the resins. It is also necessary in cold and damp weather conditions to have the work place heated, because most resins do not set hard in temperatures below 60° Fahrenheit. Best conditions are around 70 to 75°.

Preparing the plug

A timber hull which is to be used as the master ('the plug') must be completed to a very high standard. Ensure that all the detail required is fixed on the plug and that all blemishes, scratches etc, have received attention. Then spray the plug with two or three coats of good-quality gloss paint. The best gloss paints available at the time of writing are the acrylic finishes found in most car accessory shops. These have a very fine nozzle and give a superb finish. Each coat of paint should be lightly rubbed down before the next is applied. The whole plug should then be left in a warm dust-free place for some days to allow the paint to harden – seven to ten days is sensible. Full hardness is necessary before proceeding to the next stage.

Invert the plug and fix it firmly to a work board (plastic-coated chipboard or similar cheap material), so that it is raised an inch or so above the board. The sketches clearly show the method of fixing the plug to the work surface. Make a spine to fit round the hull at the centre of the keel and extending up the bow and stern. This spine should be of 6mm-thick plywood or similar timber and should be fitted with banana-shaped supports over one half of the hull as shown in the sketch Fig 8/1. Ensure that the spine is firmly in place and that it is at least 2in (50mm) wide. Fill any gaps between spine and plug with Plasticine or similar modelling clay, trimmed to give a clean surface to the spine with the joint at 90°.

Clean the plug and spine with a soft, lint-free cloth soaked in thinners or methylated spirit and allow to dry. Apply three to six coats of 'Mirror Glaze' or similar mould release wax to the open plug and spine. Each coating of wax must be applied with soft terry-towelling cloths and each must be buffed to a hard, brilliant finish before the next is applied. Six coats will normally take up to twelve hours, allowing hardening time between coatings. Cover the whole assembly between working sessions to avoid any possibility of contamination by dust. Finally, coat the whole exposed and waxed surface with a liquid release agent applied by brush.

Making the mould

Place sufficient resin gelcoat to cover the exposed area of hull and spine in a mixing

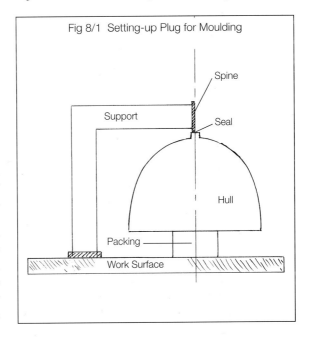

Fig 8/1 Setting-up Plug for Moulding

Spine

Support

Seal

Hull

Packing

Work Surface

pot. The maker's literature will usually give the quantities needed to cover a given area. Add the required quantity of catalyst specified and mix thoroughly. Note that the setting time for gelcoat is usually only about twelve to fifteen minutes and thus only the quantity that can be handled in that time should be mixed. Brush the mixture over the surface of plug and spine to a thickness of about $1/16$ in (1.5mm) and leave to set. Squeeze excess resin out of the brush and wash it in brush cleaner (Acetone).

While waiting for the gelcoat to cure, prepare some pieces of glass mat (2oz per sq ft), large enough to extend from the top of the spine to just overhang the edge of the plug and enough to cover from bow to stern with about an inch overlap at each joint. Test the gelcoat by just touching the surface with a fingertip. The surface is ready if the gelcoat is tacky but does not adhere to the finger as it is lifted off. Mix sufficient laminating resin with catalyst to allow working within fifteen minutes and brush coat the gelcoat with the mix. Progressively cover the plug with the glass mat, stippling it into place with the resin mix. Do not brush the glass mat with resin but use the brush to push the resin through the mat. Ensure that the mat is

taken well up the spine and that it hangs over the lower edge of the inverted hull. Continue with resin and mat until the whole plug half has been covered then allow the mat to cure for an hour or more. Repeat this process with mat and resin until the surface is about 4mm to 6mm thick and then set the unit aside for at least seven days to permit the resin to cure fully. While working with this glass mat and resin take care to ensure that there are no air bubbles left in the mat and for added security it is wise to use a roller over the whole surface while it is still wet and thus to eliminate any possibility of the surface delaminating due to air being trapped.

After seven days, remove the spine and banana supports and start the process again on the remaining half of the plug. Coat the hull and upstand of glass fibre with wax as before, treating this half exactly as the first. Apply gelcoat followed by resin and glass mat exactly as before and once again set the project aside for seven days. On the eighth day drill a series of holes round the upstand of the spine right through from side to side close to the point where the hull curves outward. These holes should be of a suitable size to allow the fitting of bolts with washers and wing nuts

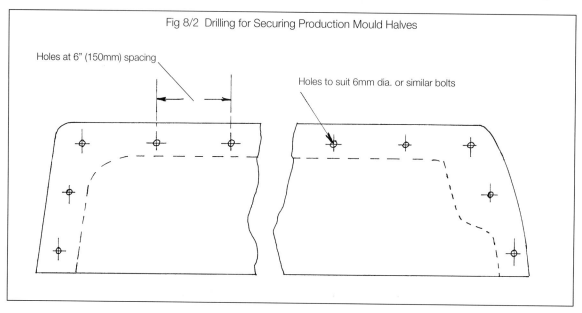

Fig 8/2 Drilling for Securing Production Mould Halves

Holes at 6" (150mm) spacing

Holes to suit 6mm dia. or similar bolts

necessary to hold the two halves of the mould together when making a hull. A suitable size for the securing bolts is $^5/_{16}$in (7.5mm) (see Fig 8/2).

The next job is to remove the plug from the mould and to separate the two halves. Carefully pour some boiling water between the plug and the mould, easing one apart from the other with a screwdriver or stiff flat blade. Progressively move round the plug easing and pouring in water. After a while, usually with the most frightening cracking and groaning sounds, the mould will split apart and the plug can be removed. It is quite possible that small pieces of timber from rubbing strips or other detail will remain embedded in the hard gelcoat of the mould and this should be gently removed by soaking with hot water and easing them out with slivers of wood. Do not under any circumstances attempt to use steel tools to remove embedded pieces as these will damage the mould, sometimes without any possibility of repair. Once the mould is free of unwanted debris it should be washed in warm water with detergent, rinsed and allowed to dry.

Moulding the hull

Before a hull can be moulded, the master mould needs to be treated. Join both halves together and apply three to six coats of mould release wax in the same manner as for the plug, polishing each to a brilliant finish and allowing time for each coat to set up. Coat the whole of the inside of the mould with release agent liquid – this is usually coloured to make it easily visible – and allow it to dry. Prepare pieces of glass mat of desired weight to completely cover the inside of the mould in one run with overlaps of no more than 1in (25mm) and put on one side. It is easier to try these pieces of mat before coating the mould with gelcoat than to guess requirements as the work proceeds. Mix sufficient gelcoat and catalyst to cover the mould. Note that

before adding the catalyst, the gelcoat can be coloured using a colour medium available from the makers and mixing it into the gelcoat before adding the catalyst. Colouring the gelcoat will make the hull opaque and the colour can be selected to match the required finish of the model. Only the quantity of colour medium specified by the makers should be used as it can affect the cure of the gelcoat if too much colour is added. Coat the whole mould with gelcoat brushing it in to a thickness not more than $^1/_{16}$in (1.5mm) and allow it to cure to tackiness as before.

Mix the laminating resin and catalyst as before and incorporate colour if desired. Paint the mould with the resin followed by the glass mat and stipple the mat into the mould in the same manner as for the master mould. Take particular care to avoid air bubbles and roll out the mat in preference to just stippling the surface. Apply a second layer of mat if necessary after the first layer has cured to a tacky surface. In the case of some hulls the upper edges of the mould will, in fact, incorporate the bulwarks of the hull. To give a good surface for paint on these top areas a layer of glass tissue can be put in place with resin. Tissue is very fine and the surface can only be stippled or rolled, as it will lift and run into ripples if brushed while still wet. Set the mould aside for approximately twenty-four hours to allow the hull to cure, ensuring that it is kept in a warm, dry environment. The first hull is easily removed by removing the bolts holding the two halves of the mould together and pouring hot water into the joint while prising it open.

The mould should then be thoroughly cleaned and given another coating of mould release wax. If a second hull is to be laid up then the same method applies as for the first except that only the one wax coat is needed. Subsequent hulls, up to a total of six, can be laid up at twenty-four-hour intervals before applying the next wax coating. After laying up each hull and before waxing the mould or applying release agent, the mould should be examined for any damage and such damage made good using the mould repair paste that the resin maker can usually supply.

Before the moulded hull is used it needs to be cleaned of all traces of wax and release agent. Such contaminants will prevent paint from adhering to the surface of the hull and/or show up as blemishes which will be hard to remove later. Cleaning is best effected by scrubbing the whole hull with hot water and a good detergent followed by a thorough rinsing with clean water. It should be left to dry naturally and then rubbed all over with 400 or 600 grit wet-and-dry abrasive paper to key the surface for the paint. It is important that the hulls be cleaned well and this cannot be overemphasised. All too many painting faults can be laid at the door of a poor and soiled surface. It is a good idea to apply a coat of etching primer to the hull before attempting any work at all. Even if this priming coat is damaged during further handling of the hull, it will still serve to keep the paint surface good for future applications. Etching primer can be obtained from specialist paint supply companies both for use by brush or in spray cans. Ordinary primer coatings such as are available from car accessory shops may adhere to the GRP hull, so the etching primer is by far the safest route to follow.

In the following chapters the subject of laying decks and building up the superstructures etc, of the model are dealt with in some detail. However, with the GRP hull it is almost invariably necessary to fit strips of square timber round the hull at deck level to support the edges of the decks. It is possible to secure such strips using epoxy cements, although those of the slow-cure type do take some time to cure and effect a grab. It is much easier to attach timber strips to the inside of the hull if they are coated on one edge with catalysed gelcoat, clamped in place and a fillet of gelcoat applied to the underside of the timber. This will bond within thirty minutes and as the adhesive is of the same chemical nature as the hull it provides a very strong bond. Gelcoat can also be used effectively to seal propeller tubes to the hull and to bond other pieces of timber or plastic when necessary. Obviously this applies more to the modeller who makes his own GRP hulls and thus has gelcoat to hand. Small quantities for use as adhesives can prove expensive particularly as all the resins do have a limited shelf life, sometimes of only a few months.

There are those readers who will have read or have experience of the more exotic resin products such as the epoxy resins often used to produce model racing yachts, the Kevlar and carbon fibres used to give added strength etc. These are not really needed for the model merchant ship. The extra strength provided by Kevlar or carbon fibre is not justified by the high costs, nor is it necessary to use the high-cost epoxies. As with all such products, there are sensible uses and costs for each of them, and polyester resins, glass fibre mat and tissue will adequately serve the merchant ship model builder and at reasonable cost. Most of the GRP hulls produced commercially for the ship modeller are built from polyester resins and there are often very informative articles on the use of these products printed in the model press from time to time.

The manufacturers of the resins, catalysts, colours, glass mat etc, generally provide a first-class information service in the form of informative leaflets and literature. All welcome the small quantity sales and will give help and advice. It is absolutely essential to observe and abide by the precautions laid down by the makers. They are for your own good. The materials are hazardous until cured and the dust from cutting the finished product is also hazardous. Wear face masks and gloves where advised to do so and treat the products with real respect. Do not ignore these warnings but act sensibly and enjoy the results of such labours in a safe manner.

9
Running Gear

The running gear of a ship comprises propellers, propeller shafts and shaft supports or alternatively paddle-wheels and associated gearing and shafting, and rudders. Before proceeding to fit the decks and to build up the superstructure of the model it is wise to fit out the hull with the propulsion gear, drive equipment and rudder(s) while access is easy. Careful measurement is required when locating such equipment so that suitable access arrangements can be built into the decks and superstructure to permit the equipment to be serviced or removed.

Propellers

Reference to the drawings will give the line for the propeller shaft(s) and the position of the rudder stock. With a single-screw ship, the shaft for the propeller exits through an opening in the stern frame and the rudder stock is exactly astern of the propeller, whilst with a twin-screw vessel the shafts exit on either side of the keel near the stern and there may be a single

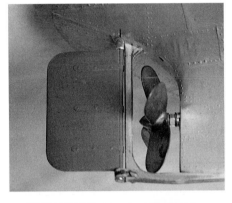

(Left)
Single propeller and rudder on model of fishing trawler built by the author to a scale of 1:48. Note propeller is of brass while the rudder is made from timber with a brass stock.

(Below)
Twin screws and single rudder fitted to a model of a French ship built to a scale of 1:30.

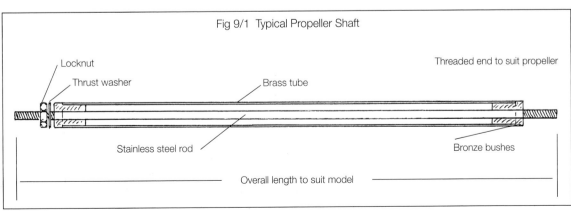

Fig 9/1 Typical Propeller Shaft

Locknut

Thrust washer

Brass tube

Threaded end to suit propeller

Stainless steel rod

Bronze bushes

Overall length to suit model

A selection of propellers
by the Prop Shop
(for address
see Appendix 2).

A selection of propellers
by E Radestock
(for address
see Appendix 2).

STANDARD

TYPE 42

LEANDER

WWII 3 BLADE

WWII 4 BLADE

units are positioned where suitable access can be sited. In the case of a steam plant the engine(s) are normally beneath engine room skylights. Suitable propeller shafts can be purchased from specialist makers or from those model shops that specialise in model ships. They are available in a range of lengths and diameters and can be threaded to suit the selected propeller(s). Commercial propeller shafts are sized by the length of the outer tube, the inner shaft being generally about 1in (25mm) longer. Shafts for twin-screw ships leave the ship's hull further forward than the single-screw shaft. On some vessels there is a bracket carrying a bearing to support the outer end of the shaft close to the propeller. This is called an 'A' bracket or shaft bracket. The section of the shaft which runs between the hull exit point (bossing) and the propeller is not carried in a tube but is bare and the 'A' bracket bearing relies upon the water for lubrication. Shafts with short tube lengths to suit this type of application are also available to order. It is possible to produce one's own shafts if there is access to a small lathe or if a friend can produce suitable bushes in brass or phosphor bronze to fit the brass tubing that is available from most model shops. Shafts should preferably be made from stainless steel. Mild steel will

rudder centrally as for a single-screw craft but there are examples of ships with two rudders, one aft of each propeller.

The propeller shaft or shafts need to be measured for length so that the drive suffice but will corrode and cause problems over time. It is not wise to make the shaft of brass or other material. Fig 9/1 shows a propeller shaft in section.

Most merchant ship propellers are of the three- or four-blade type. Propellers, like shafts, can be purchased from specialist suppliers. They are usually made from brass with the blades soldered into a tapped boss. The thread size of the tapping is dictated by the size of the propeller and can be 2 or 4 BA, or M4 or M5 in the metric scale. Obviously the propeller shaft needs to be tapped with the same thread. Note that the BA thread system is slowly being superseded by the metric and some suppliers can no longer provide propellers or shafts with these threads. Most commercial brass propellers have the same or closely similar pitches to the blades and this may not match the propeller of the full-scale ship. The pitch of the blades can be tweaked to match the real thing more closely but care is necessary to ensure that all the blades are turned the same amount and that the balance of the propeller is not altered. It is preferable to have the propeller altered by an expert.

Some ship modellers do make their own propellers and it is a fairly simple task for those with experience with a soldering-iron. Four pieces of thin brass sheet should be lightly tacked together with solder. The shape of a blade is then scribed on one face, cut out with good tin snips and the blade shape filed and dressed. Heat will release the four blades. A suitable boss needs to be made and, after drilling and tapping, a piece of brass rod can be filed into the required shape. Four slots equally spaced round the propeller boss are cut with a fine hacksaw

into which the blades are soldered. Silver solder is preferable but soft solder will suffice for doing this work. The blades need to be carefully curved to the required pitch and the unit needs to be balanced. The propeller is balanced by fitting it on to a length of straight steel rod and placing the rod across two flat knife-edged blades. The propeller will turn until the heaviest blade hangs down. Light filing of the blade and constant checking will lead to a propeller that will revolve but not stop at any particular point, indicating that it is truly balanced. There is a range of propellers on the market made from nylon or similar material. They are available in both three- and

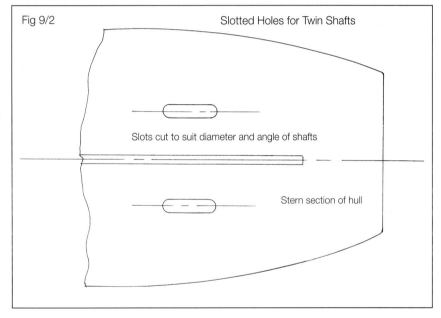

Fig 9/2

Slotted Holes for Twin Shafts

Slots cut to suit diameter and angle of shafts

Stern section of hull

four-blade forms and are comparatively cheap in price. However, they are restricted in diameter to about 2in (50mm) maximum and need to be painted before use.

All propellers are handed, that is they will move the model forward when turning one way or another. With a single-screw ship it does not really matter whether the propeller is left- or right-handed – ie turns clockwise or anticlockwise – to drive it forwards. The only effect is that the model will tend to turn slightly towards the hand-

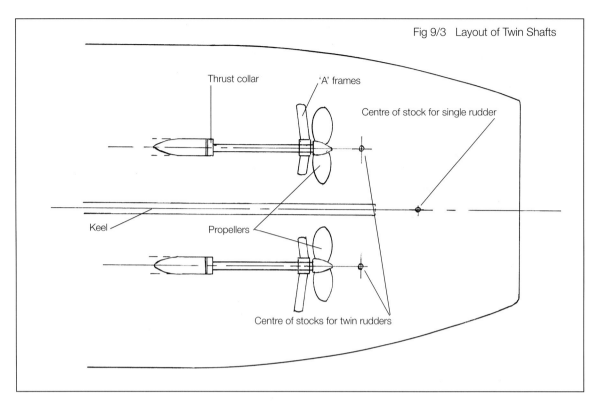

Fig 9/3   Layout of Twin Shafts

Thrust collar

'A' frames

Centre of stock for single rudder

Keel

Propellers

Centre of stocks for twin rudders

ing of the propeller. With a twin-screw ship the propellers must be of opposite hands. The screw which turns left when viewed from the stern should be fitted to the port shaft and the right-hand screw fitted to the starboard shaft. In other words the propellers of the twin-screw ship should turn outwards to drive the model forward.

It will be noted that no mention is made of ships having three or four propellers, since triple and quadruple propellers are only found principally on large passenger liners and warships, neither of which are covered here. The large cruise ships of recent years all have twin screws.

Whether one or two propeller shafts are fitted, their outer tubes need to be firmly fixed to the hull and well supported inside. Careful measurement will show the position of the hole or holes required in the hull to accept the propeller shaft. Such holes should be drilled carefully, starting with a small drill and progressively enlarging the hole until the outer tube of the shaft will just fit. Where twin screws are

concerned the holes in the hull will need to be slotted lengthwise so that the propeller tube can lie closely to the hull (Fig 9/2). To secure the shaft tube to the hull, it should be scored with the edge of a file where it fits to the hull and to provide a key for the adhesive. In the case of a timber hull the shaft tube can be secured with two part epoxy cement of the twenty-four hour curing type; the five-minute cure epoxy is not suitable for use in water. In the case of a GRP hull, while epoxy is suitable, the best adhesive is catalysed polyester resin gelcoat.

The degree to which the shaft rises from the stern forward is shown on the drawings, but it may be found that the angle shown places the inboard end of the shaft too low in the hull to allow the fitting of the drive unit without employing a severely out-of-line double coupling. While flexible couplings are designed to take up some degree of mis-alignment, they function best if they can be set as nearly true as possible. To avoid poor alignment of shaft, coupling and drive unit, it may be necessary to increase the angle of the shaft from that shown on the drawings or even to employ two shafts with a coupling between them (Fig 9/3). In either case the shaft tubes need support and should be fixed firmly to the hull. Under no circumstances should any shaft be stressed by slight bending as this will place undue strain upon the drive equipment with disastrous and costly consequences. The fitting of drive equipment and shaft couplings is covered in later chapters. Once the shaft tube has been sealed into the hull it should be packed with a light waterproof grease to lubricate the shaft and to prevent water from passing through the tube into the hull of the model. Some modellers fit a lubricating tube to the propeller shaft tube as shown in the sketches, but unless a very heavy oil is used grease is the most effective lubricant. The lubricating tube is easily fitted with a small grease nipple to allow the shaft to be greased from inside the model and obviate the need to remove the propeller for access to the shaft.

One important variation of propeller and shaft assembly and one which is seeing increasing use on the merchant ship scene is the variable pitch propeller. This propeller is fitted with blades which can be swivelled on the boss by a system of internal levers. This allows the propeller to move from neutral (with no movement of the ship in the water) to full ahead or astern by a shift of the angle of the blades and with the engine running at its most economical constant speed. Control of such a propeller, in full-size practice, is effected by a small lever on the bridge of the ship which changes the pitch through an hydraulic and electronic system, the lever being generally marked to indicate the percentage of pitch and thus the thrust. The use of such a system gives the master or officer of the watch on the bridge full control of speed and direction without any delays such as were experienced in the days of the telegraph and response from the engineers. Two or three manufacturers currently offer variable pitch propellers in model form but of only two sizes, 50mm (2in) diameter and 75mm (3in), and with the necessary shafts. Each is easily coupled to a servo to vary the pitch and the shaft diameter is very little larger than that of a standard shaft. Such units are expensive but, when compared to a standard fixed blade propeller with an electronic speed controller, there is little to chose between them, although the servo may be cheaper to replace than the speed controller should either unit fail.

Paddle-wheels

Paddle-steamers of the side-wheel type, such as those that carried out the Clyde and Islands services in Scotland and which were to be found in many places worldwide, were remarkably fast vessels reaching speeds of up to 17kts or more. In all but very basic paddlers in Europe and the UK, the paddle-wheels were of the feathering type. Feathering paddles allowed the floats to enter the water at an angle whereas fixed floats slap the water on entry (Fig 9/4 overleaf). Floats on US paddle-wheelers are called buckets. The German manufacturer Graupner is at present the only producer of model paddle-wheels with feathering floats. These are made in ABS plastic to one size only at a scale of 1:40. There are a number of detailed drawings available from the plans services to assist the modeller to make suitable paddle-wheels. Side paddles on passenger ships in the UK were, by law, locked together and a shaft to connect these wheels will span the model. Suitable bearings at either side and fitted into the hull are needed to support the shaft. If the model is of wide beam it may be necessary to install bearings on pedestals inside the hull to give extra support. Paddle-wheels run at slow speeds, 100rpm or less, and thus gears will be needed to reduce the speeds of either electric motors or steam engines, unless the steam engine is of the

Feathering paddles on model of Clyde steamer *Duchess of Fife*. Scale 1:32. This fully working paddle set was made from brass sheet, rod and tube with timber floats. Builder unknown.

The stern-wheeler *Bailey Gatzert* built at 1:48 scale by Glenn S Hensley of Kirkwood, MO. The model is electrically driven with radio control.
GLENN S HENSLEY

long-stroke, slow-running pattern made specially for the paddler. Suitable drives are discussed in the following two chapters. Stern wheel paddle-steamers, mostly found in the USA, have fixed floats. The wheels are particularly large and run very slowly. Drawings for these craft detail quite plainly where and what type of paddle shaft is needed and frequently how the wheel is driven. Successful models almost invariably utilise a belt drive from the motor within the hull to layshafts and thence to the stern shaft. With a steam plant the drive is similar. Most modern commercially-made steam outfits, which are rapidly becoming popular, are fast-running and therefore for paddle-steamers will benefit from having a gearbox fitted between the engine and the final drive shaft. The modeller who builds his own steam plants will know that long-stroke, slow-running engines are generally extravagant on steam and need large boilers whereas the smaller, fast-running outfits are economical on steam but will need to be geared to the drive shaft of the model.

In the case of the paddle tug, the paddles can be independently driven using

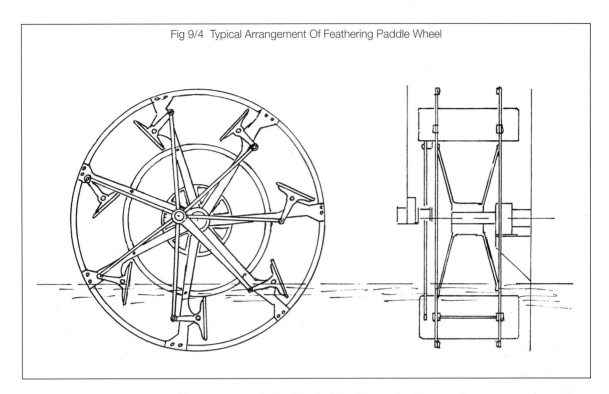

Fig 9/4 Typical Arrangement Of Feathering Paddle Wheel

two motors or steam plants. This means that each paddle shaft must have an inboard and pedestal-mounted bearing to support it. It means also two sets of reduction gears between the drive unit and the shaft. While this is a perfectly feasible method of driving the tug, most models with independent paddle drive tend to waddle like ducks in the water since it is virtually impossible to synchronise the two separate drive units accurately. One single shaft driving both paddles from one unit is by far the best arrangement.

Rudders

The merchant ship rudder has evolved over the years and the drawings of the chosen ship will indicate the type of rudder that was fitted. Some of the various types are shown in Fig 9/5. Movement of the rudder is normally limited to about 35° on either side of the fore and aft centreline of the ship. For the model ship, a rudder bearing tube must be fitted through the hull at the appropriate place. Should the

shell of the hull be thin, as in the case of a GRP hull, a block of hardwood should be secured inside the hull and drilled to accept and support the rudder tube. The rudder stock must be extended in the hull to suit the radio equipment. It will be fitted a tiller arm to be driven by a servo controlled by the radio and the position of the servo will dictate the length of the rudder stock with-

Keel extension shown for securing the lower end of the rudder stock on a model of a steam trawler. The brass propeller and propeller shaft was supplied by Westbourne Model Centre, the rudder was of timber with a stock of brass rod.

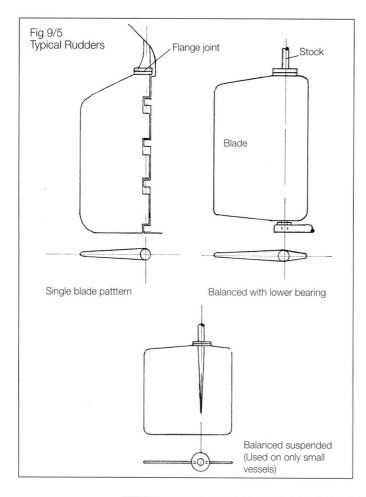

Fig 9/5
Typical Rudders

Flange joint

Stock

Blade

Single blade patttern

Balanced with lower bearing

Balanced suspended
(Used on only small
vessels)

in the hull (details of the radio gear are given later). This tiller is one of the points where some form of access is wanted in the deck of the model.

The model rudder blade can be made from solid timber, styrene sheet, plywood or brass and all have their uses. The most important thing is that, however they are made, they must be fixed very firmly to the rudder stock. The sketches show the construction of a number of rudders and indicate how the stock can be secured to the blade. Timber rudders need to be well sealed and painted to avoid water damage. The other types are, in general, impervious to water. In the case of a GRP hull it may be necessary to make and fit a keel extension to carry the lower bearing of the rudder and this is shown in detail in Fig 9/6. It is important that the rudder tube (upper bearing) is well sealed to the hull to prevent water entering the hull.

There are refinements to the rudder and steering systems, such as the steerable Kort nozzle, on certain types of ship and these are discussed in a later chapter. When the completed model is given its trials it may be found that the turning circle is much larger than is wanted. This would

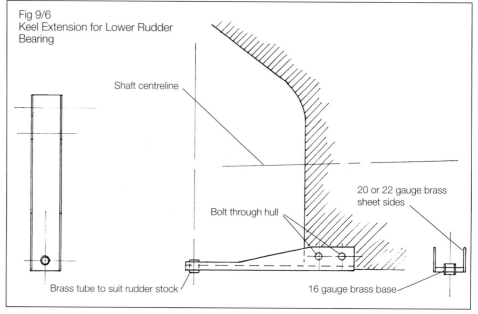

Fig 9/6
Keel Extension for Lower Rudder
Bearing

Shaft centreline

20 or 22 gauge brass
sheet sides

Bolt through hull

Brass tube to suit rudder stock

16 gauge brass base

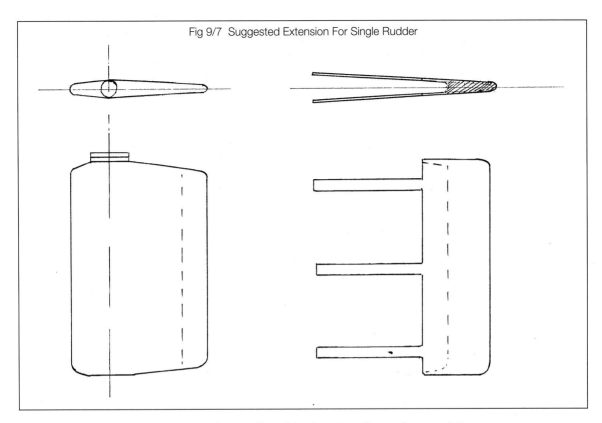

Fig 9/7 Suggested Extension For Single Rudder

apply particularly to a model required to perform on a steering circuit at a regatta. The usual cause is that the rudder blade is too short, fore and aft, in correct scale size. To avoid altering the rudder to an 'out of scale' unit it is possible to make an extension piece for the rudder which can be clipped in place for sailing and removed for display purposes (see Fig 9/7).

Final adjustments to drive shafts and to rudders are discussed in the individual chapters that follow and which detail the methods of driving the working scale model.

10
Electric Motors

The most usual drive for a working scale model ship is by electric motor with rechargeable batteries, the current being either 6 volts or 12 volts DC. There is a large range of suitable motors available, and they create the problem 'which motor do I fit in my model?'. This is not the easiest of questions to answer but a suitable motor size can be calculated from the formula given below.

The motor

In the case of a scale model, and particularly one which is a model of a full-size ship, it is very wise to calculate all the necessary data for propulsion using the data from the full-size ship, as follows:

SHIP'S NAME:- SCALE: 1 : 24
Required Information from full size ship.
Installed power per screw A

Top Speed (Metres/sec)	B
Screw Dia. (Metres)	C
Number of Blades	x
Number of screws	v
Screw pitch (not essential)	h
Screw revs	y

CALCULATION METHOD
1. Model Scale D
2. Prop shaft dia. l
2a. Scale speed vo

$$vo = \frac{B}{\sqrt{D}}$$

3. Scale power per screw (P):

$$P = \frac{1000 \times A \ (HP)}{\sqrt{A} \ 7} = watts$$

Merchant ships are not noted for high speeds, the majority running within the 9 to 16kts range. Reciprocating steam

Single Decaperm 6-volt motor fitted in hull of model pilot cutter *Chimera*.
Scale $^3/_8$ins = 1ft.
Note single resistance speed control board (Bob's board) and sealed lead acid battery fitted into frame for security.

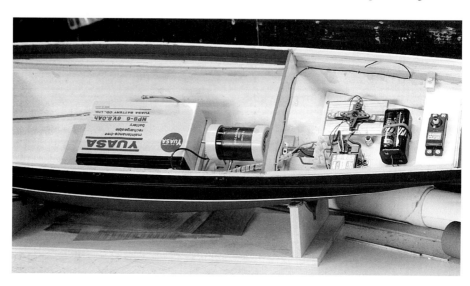

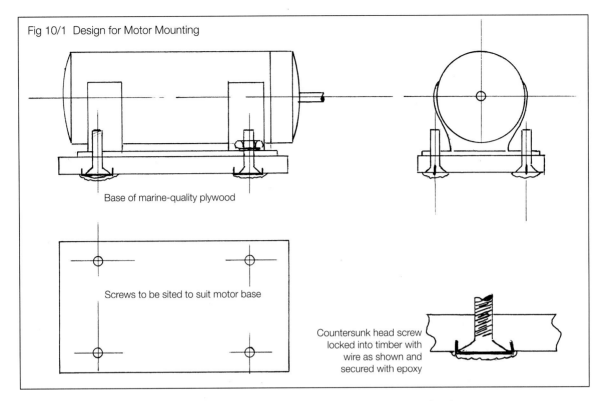

Fig 10/1 Design for Motor Mounting

Base of marine-quality plywood

Screws to be sited to suit motor base

Countersunk head screw
locked into timber with
wire as shown and
secured with epoxy

engines, which first powered merchant ship, ran at speeds of between 60 to 150rpm and drove the ship economically within this range. When the steam turbine was brought into service the final drive was geared down and propeller speed only rose to around 250rpm. The modern oil engine (diesel) is a comparatively slow-running machine and it, too, is geared down to give a maximum propeller speed of about 250rpm. A specification prepared recently for a 100ft (30.5m) long shrimp trawler lists the main engine as a 6-cylinder diesel engine of 850bhp at 750rpm driving a controllable-pitch propeller through a 4.25:1 reduction gearbox, giving a propeller speed of only 176rpm. A second specification for a 30.1m long trawler lists a 12-cylinder diesel engine of 750bhp at 1225rpm, driving a fixed 4-blade bronze propeller at a speed of 350rpm.

Modern 6- and 12-volt motors suitable for the model ship are generally high-speed units having free running speeds of up to 12,000rpm and this, even when

reduced under load, is much too fast for a model propeller. This means that it is preferable to drive the model through a reduction gear box but, if necessary, it may be direct-driven without using gears. A model driven through a gearbox always uses less power than when driven directly. For example if a motor driving a 2in (50mm) diameter, 4-blade propeller draws 10 amps when the model is in the water, the same motor, when fitted with a 2:1 ratio reduction gearbox, will drive the same propeller under load and draw only 4 amps, therefore producing a huge 60 per cent saving in power and a longer duration from the same size battery. As a matter of interest the speed of the model under the second and geared condition is very little different to the first. The explanation for this is that when a propeller is driven too fast it creates a condition known as cavitation where bubbles of steam, caused by the reduction of water pressure round the propeller blades, are formed and the propeller slips in the water without providing its full driving force. The cavitation also causes the propeller blades to corrode away quite seriously in the case of full-size ships, although the conditions prevailing in the model ship rarely damage the propeller simply because the model prop does not run for equivalent lengthy periods of time. It follows, therefore, that consideration should always be given to fitting suitable gears between drive motors and propellers (see below).

The drive motor or motors should be mounted securely within the hull and in a manner which will allow easy removal for attention. It is possible to fit the motor on a rubber bed to reduce noise and vibration but normally a firm mounting is all that is required. The motor shaft, coupling and propeller shaft should be carefully aligned before the motor is fixed in place. A simple but effective method of making a motor mounting is shown in Fig 10/1 (p69), where the removal of four nuts and separation of the coupling releases the motor from its base. The motor should be fitted in the hull so that it lies under a hatch or detachable portion of superstructure, the length of shaft being adjusted to suit the motor location.

Batteries

Batteries for powering the motor come in two forms, primary cells and secondary cells. The common dry cells used in many torches are examples of primary cells which produce electricity from a chemical reaction when connected to a circuit. These disposable batteries are not suitable for providing main drive power to a model ship. Secondary cells are those which can be charged using some form of battery charger. There are two main types of secondary cell batteries for modelling use, the sealed lead acid type and the Ni-cad type. The former are similar to, but much smaller than, the battery fitted in the average car except that they are sealed and do not require topping up of the liquid inside. They can be mounted in almost any way, even upside-down if necessary. Charging

sealed batteries requires an appropriate charger. The type used to charge a car battery is not suitable as it can cause overcharging which will damage the sealed battery and seriously shorten its life. Ni-cad batteries can be used but they come in fairly small sizes and need to be assembled into packs to give the current and duration required. Such packs must have the connections soldered or welded for safety. The type of charger used for the Ni-cad packs used in the radio equipment will charge this pattern of drive battery. However, the Ni-cad battery pack is really only suitable for the very small, single-screw ship fitted with a low-current motor. Larger packs for bigger motors and models will prove more expensive than the lead acid units. For the working scale model merchant ship Ni-cad batteries should be confined to use with the radio equipment.

The battery or battery pack must be fitted securely inside the hull. This unit or pack will form part of the ballast of the model and sometimes cover all the weight needed to bring the model to its waterline. Secure fitting is vital for, should this weight shift when the model is afloat, this could easily cause it to overturn and sink. A box fixed firmly to the hull and in which the battery is a snug fit is all that is needed, as illustrated in some of the photographs.

Control equipment

To control the motor or motors a speed controller is necessary and these units come in various forms. The simplest is a servo-operated on/off switch which will do no more than switch the current on or off and have no speed control. Such switches can be found in the lists of most radio control makers. By keeping the voltage fixed and altering the resistance and current flow the speed of the DC motor can be varied, and by altering the direction of the current flow the motor can be reversed. This is the principle of the resistance board controller which is the simplest type of speed con-

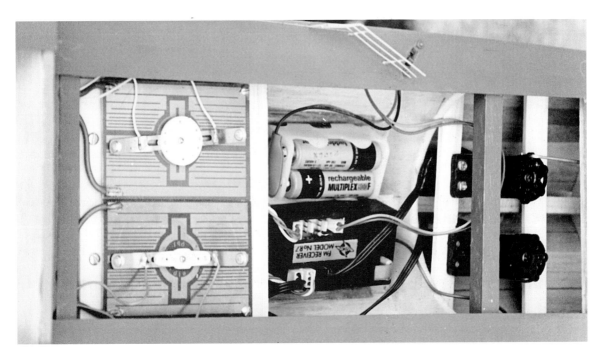

troller and which provides control of speed and direction. The board has a length of resistance material embedded in it and a servo rotating a wiper arm over the board changes the length of the resistance material through which the current has to flow. Greater length means greater resistance and a smaller current therefore less speed. Incorporated into the resistance board is a changeover arrangement allowing the driving servo in its midway position to have the current switched off and, in either direction of turn, to apply current to run the motor in one direction or another. Such boards come in a range of sizes to suit the motors to which they are applied, *ie* 1 to 2 amps, 2 to 4 amps and 5 to 8 amps. It is essential to fit the correctly-rated board to the motor otherwise there can be problems of board failure through overloading etc. Most motors give the loadings that can be expected. Some motors have their ratings given in watts and the following equation can be used to convert to amps: Amps x Volts = Watts.

The electronic speed controller is the third type of motor control available, which is becoming increasingly popular. This is the most expensive type but does give very precise control of speed and direction with very little current loss. In addition it usually includes an overload protection not fitted to other controllers. This is a desirable attribute particularly when a more expensive motor is fitted. This caters for the initial very high current that is momentarily needed to start any electric motor and which can cause damage to some controllers. When wiring up between any battery, controller and motor a suitable fuse should always be fitted into the positive lead. This should be of a size to blow should an overload occur due to the propeller stopping through weed or similar fouling, and thus preventing the motor from being damaged. This is mentioned at this stage as some controllers come complete with line fuses and others do not. Wiring up the motor, batteries etc, is dealt with in the chapter covering radio controls. Electronic speed controllers provide very good slow-running characteristics with almost all motors but, as for the resistance boards, they are available in sizes to suit certain motor size ranges. The controller must be matched to the motor, although

Twin resistance speed control boards controlling twin motors in model of French ship. Motors are Marx Luder Monoperm fitted with Richard gearboxes.

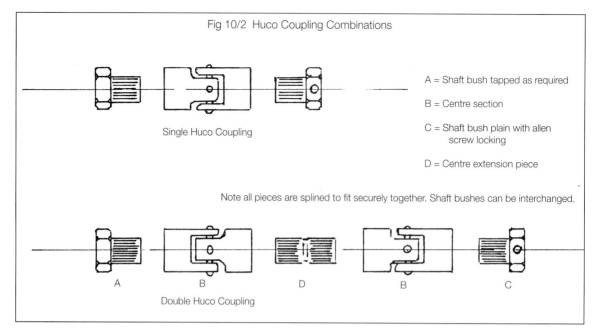

Fig 10/2 Huco Coupling Combinations

Single Huco Coupling

A = Shaft bush tapped as required

B = Centre section

C = Shaft bush plain with allen
      screw locking

D = Centre extension piece

Note all pieces are splined to fit securely together. Shaft bushes can be interchanged.

A   B   D   B   C

Double Huco Coupling

the electronic controller need not be so precisely matched as the resistance board. For example, an electronic controller rated at 15 amps will happily control a small motor of say 1.5 amps. A motor drawing 10 amps will need a controller of 30 amps, the high rating being geared to the stall current of the motor. A simple method of determining the stall current of a motor is to fit a sensitive amp meter in the leads to it. Grasp the motor in a vice or similar clamping system. Turn the power full on and then quickly and firmly grasp the motor shaft with a strong pair of pliers, having soft jaws to prevent damaging the motor shaft. At the moment the motor stops, the current can be read from the meter. Do not, of course, hold the motor shaft in the stalled position for more than a second or so or the motor will burn out and be irreparably damaged.

The majority of problems experienced with electric motors are due to poor installation. Correct alignment of motor, coupling and shaft is very important and can seriously load the motor if incorrect by imposing a high resistance to turning. A single coupling of the Huco or similar type (Fig 10/2) is only suitable for absorbing the very smallest of mis-alignments and needs to be lined up with shaft and motor very carefully. Where there is a more serious and unavoidable mis-alignment then double couplings (Fig 10/2) must be fitted. Sometimes it may be necessary to split the drive into two shafts, using an intermediate coupling. The current required by the motor to drive the model is proportional to the load imposed by the resistance of the shaft and the coupling to turning, and of the propeller to the water, all of which combine to prevent motion which the motor must overcome. It follows that the resistance of shaft and coupling must be kept to the absolute minimum to allow the motor to receive the maximum current needed.

Scale speed

The speed of the scale model is often a bone of contention when judged even by experts. There are very few models sailing on the ponds today that actually run at true scale speed. Most run at well over scale speed, and many at remarkable speeds which equate to full-size speeds in excess of 50kts - and this from a steam-driven tug! It

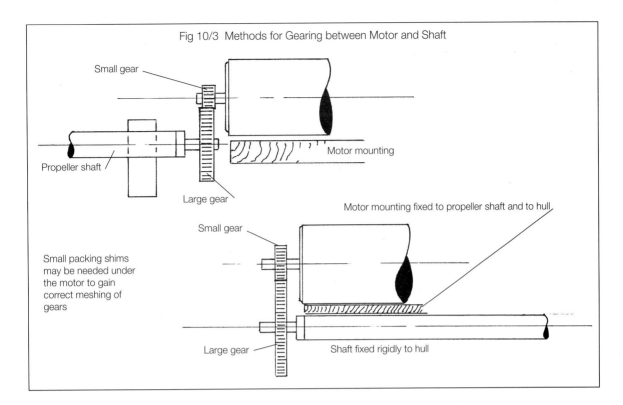

Fig 10/3 Methods for Gearing between Motor and Shaft

Small gear

Propeller shaft

Large gear

Motor mounting

Small packing shims
may be needed under
the motor to gain
correct meshing of
gears

Small gear

Motor mounting fixed to propeller shaft and to hull

Large gear

Shaft fixed rigidly to hull

is a simple matter to calculate the scale speed of a model ship from the formula:

$$\frac{V}{v} = \frac{L}{l}$$

Where V = speed of prototype

v = speed of model

L = length of prototype

l = equivalent length of model.

Alternatively L/l can be expressed as the scale of the model.

Scale speed equals prototype speed divided by the square root of the scale. For example, 12kts full speed full-size ship divided by the root of 48 (1:48 being the scale of the model) = 12/6.93 = 1.73 kts. 1 knot = 0.5 metres per second, therefore 1.73 x 0.5 = 0.865 metres per second or 2.84ft per second. It is an easy matter to test sail the model over a set distance on the water and to time the run. A few practice runs will soon provide the correct speed setting of the controls. A much more satisfactory method of controlling

the model at scale speed is by gearing the drive to suit.

To assess the requirement for a suitable reduction gear between motor and propeller the following simple formula will suffice. Note here that the scale propeller will need to revolve faster than the prototype unit to maintain correct scale. If the prototype speed of the propeller is 200rpm then the scale speed will be as follows: scale speed = prototype speed times the square root of the scale. Therefore scale speed =

Detail of twin motors with Richard gear boxes which allow selection of six speed ratios from 3 : 1 to 12 : 1 by turning the cover of the box to the required reduction point and locking it in place.

200 x √48 = 200 x 6.93 = 1386rpm. If the motor selected has a top speed of 12,000rpm free running then a gear set to give a reduction of 6:1 will give a free-running shaft speed of 2000rpm and this, under load, will be very near the required speed. More acceptable is the fact that the slower-running propeller will produce a model speed almost equivalent to the scale speed required with the throttle stick of the radio transmitter at the full-speed position. This last condition will not only give scale speed but impose a lower load on the drive battery leading to extended running time which is often important at sailing regattas.

Although fitting a propeller much smaller than correct scale size may allow the model to be direct driven at nearer scale speed, such practice is to be deplored. Modern nylon gears are very cheap, easily obtained and simply fitted. They require no lubrication and, as they allow the motor to be fitted higher in the hull, they overcome

the problem of not being able to sit a motor low down in the narrow stern section of a hull. As most nylon or plastic gears are a force fit on a shaft and 4mm diameter is a standard size both for the gear centres, motor shafts and for propeller shafts, it is easy to combine the set to give the necessary reduction. For example, a 20-tooth gear on the motor shaft coupled to a 60-tooth gear on the propeller shaft will give a 3:1 reduction. One UK supplier lists gears having 10 to 70 teeth (in multiples of 10) all in one pack of ten items with all but the smallest having a shaft bore of 4mm. Two such gears can be simply mounted as shown in Fig 10/3, but both propeller shaft and motor must be mounted firmly in the hull so that the gears mesh neatly with very little backlash. It is possible to mount the motor above and in line with the propeller shaft provided both are rigidly fixed together. This arrangement of gearing eliminates the need for a flexible coupling between motor

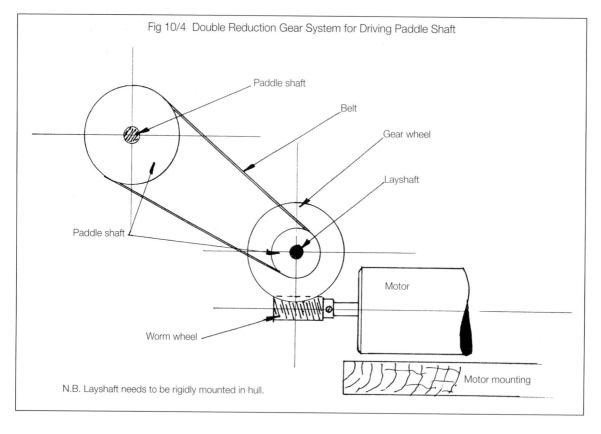

Fig 10/4 Double Reduction Gear System for Driving Paddle Shaft

Paddle shaft

Belt

Gear wheel

Layshaft

Paddle shaft

Motor

Worm wheel

Motor mounting

N.B. Layshaft needs to be rigidly mounted in hull.

and propeller shaft. Therefore the cost of a coupling can be transferred, with some savings, to the cost of the gears.

Paddle vessels

Driving paddle-wheels by electric motor demands a reduction gear of one kind or another. Paddles on full-size vessels rarely revolved at more than 120rpm and those on a model should not be driven much faster than 240rpm. 'Pile' gearboxes are available for a number of electric motors, most notably the Marx Luder range. They can be set to a number of different reduction ratios depending upon the segments of the gearbox which are used and these ratios vary from 3:1 to 360:1. Four segments are supplied providing 3, 4, 5 and 6:1 reductions. Together these provide a reduction of 360:1 (3 x 4 x 5 x 6), but each segment is easily detached and the combination of parts will generally give the ratio that is needed. With a pile gearbox it is necessary only to arrange a simple belt drive between the motor/gearbox unit and the main drive shaft for the paddles. For example, a motor running at 15,000rpm would require a pile gearbox using the No. 3, 4 and 5 segments together to produce a 60:1 reduction and a paddle speed of 250rpm.

A simpler method would be to purchase a worm and gear drive set from a model railway shop. These can be bought having ratios of 20, 30 and 40:1 and are used with most O and OO gauge model locomotives. The gear wheel is mounted on the paddle shaft and the worm on the motor shaft. It is necessary to mount the motor carefully to ensure that the worm and gear wheel mesh neatly without any appreciable backlash. A motor running at 15,000rpm will need a reduction gear set of 60:1 to give 250 rpm at the paddle shaft. Therefore it will be necessary to fit not only a 30:1 worm gear set but also a secondary 2:1 reduction to give the required shaft speed. The fitting of a simple 2:1 reduction can be achieved by a belt

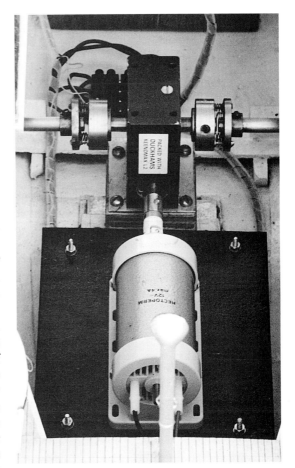

drive from a shaft driven by the worm gear to the main shaft of the paddle-wheels. Fig 10/4 illustrates these two methods of paddle drive which are suitable for a fixed pair of paddles. If a paddle tug is being built that needs independent paddle drive, it is necessary to fit two motors and two sets of reduction gears.

Obviously it is necessary to know the top speed at which the drive motor will run at before gears are fitted in order to calculate the reduction ratio required from the gear set, and this applies equally to a propeller-driven or a paddle-driven model. It follows that the speed of the paddles or propeller of the full-size ship must be known to use for reference in the calculations. If this information is not available data on similar ships may help to give a near approximation.

Paddle shaft drive in *Duchess of Fife* showing reduction gearbox giving 20:1 reduction and Marx Luder Hectaperm motor with 2:1 gearbox – total reduction 40:1 producing a speed at the paddles of 110rpm.

11
Steam Engines

In recent years the steam plant has become much more popular due to the efforts of a number of manufacturers in producing designs which have allowed compact and easily-installed outfits to be built. It is no longer necessary to own a lathe to build the steam plant in the workshop as suitable engines and boilers are available at prices not much higher than the cost of electric motors and controls. Such small steam engines can be easily con-

trolled by the radio equipment available in model shops.

Engines

There are, as for electric motors, a range of steam engines and boilers of varying sizes available and it is necessary for the ship modeller to select the size of steam plant that best suits the vessel. Almost all steam engines of small size run at quite high speeds but, like the full-size steam engine, they are easily controlled down to very slow speeds and they produce high torque at all speeds. The very smallest engines, usually of the oscillating type, will benefit from the fitting of a reduction gear system between engine and propeller shaft, but the larger engines will perform satisfactorily without gears. The oscillating steam engine is basically very simple with fewer moving parts than the slide valve unit. When fitted with properly-designed bearings and with satisfactory attention to lubrication, this type of engine will give long life and trouble-free running. In addition the oscillating engine has springs holding the cylinders and operating valve in position and all these act as additional safety valves making an inherently safer steam outfit.

The principle of the steam engine is quite simple. Water is heated in a boiler and produces steam which is passed through pipework to the steam engine where the steam, as it expands, drives a piston in a cylinder. The wasted steam exhausts to the atmosphere and the piston is driven back and forth by admitting steam to either side of it, and this reciprocating

Vertical boiler steam plant (Maxwell Hemmens Max II).
COURTESY OF MAXWELL HEMMENS PRECISION STEAM MODELS

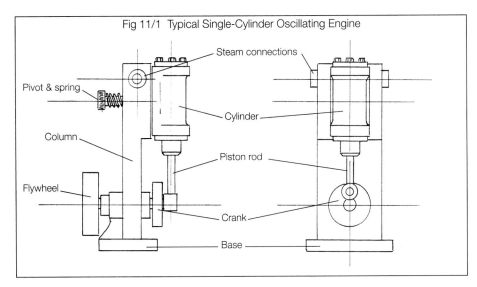

Fig 11/1 Typical Single-Cylinder Oscillating Engine

motion is used to turn a crankshaft and fly-wheel. The flywheel aids the turning motion and the drive is coupled to the ship's propeller shaft by a suitable coupling in the same way as an electric motor is connected.

The simplest steam engine available is the single-cylinder oscillating unit. In this engine steam is admitted only to one end of the piston and it is not able to start by itself but needs to be turned over by hand. Once it is running it can be controlled for speed to a certain degree, but it cannot be reversed unless it is first stopped and turned over by hand. In this respect it is suitable only for the very simplest of model ships. Oscillating engines with two or more cylinders and often with steam fed to either end of the piston in turn, are usually self-starting and can be reversed quite easily. They are obviously slightly larger than the single cylinder engine, mainly in overall length. Fig 11/1 gives basic details of an oscillating engine and some are shown in the photographs.

Single-cylinder slide valve engines can be self-starting and can be arranged with valve gear to provide reverse motion. They are rarely used for marine duty as they are usually long stroke, slow-running engines which, in full size, were commonly used to drive land-based machinery. Such

engines are not made for the marine modeller by the listed manufacturers since a single-cylinder engine can be stalled in one position and fail to re-start, thus allowing a model to fail on the water. However, twin-

Horizontal boiler and twin cylinder steam plant (Cheddar Models Puffin).
COURTSEY OF
CHEDDAR MODELS LTD

cylinder slide valve engines are very suitable for marine models. They are easily controlled both ahead and astern, often from a single lever, so that a two-channel radio system controlling rudder and engine is quite feasible. The more sophisticated twin-cylinder engines incorporate a feed water pump which can be used to keep the water level in the boiler constant and thus extend the duration that the model can

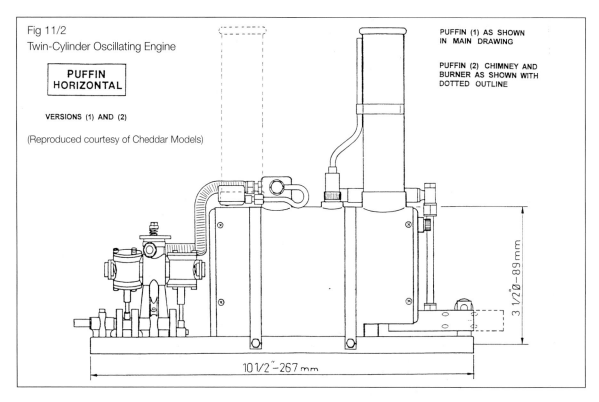

Fig 11/2
Twin-Cylinder Oscillating Engine

PUFFIN HORIZONTAL

VERSIONS (1) AND (2)

(Reproduced courtesy of Cheddar Models)

PUFFIN (1) AS SHOWN
IN MAIN DRAWING

PUFFIN (2) CHIMNEY AND
BURNER AS SHOWN WITH
DOTTED OUTLINE

3 1/2"−89 mm

10 1/2"−267 mm

spend on the water between boiler fillings. Brief details of a typical twin-cylinder engine are given in Fig 11/2.

One Japanese company produces a three-cylinder steam engine. This engine, like its two-cylinder equivalent, incorporates Stephenson valve gear to reverse direction of running, which requires two servos to operate it, one to control the valve gear and the other to control the throttle. The system of controlling throttle and direction of rotation separately is often also applied to twin-cylinder engines, depending upon the method used to effect directional running.

With all steam engines lubrication is important. Whilst the electric motor often has sealed and lubricated bearings, the steam engine does not. The instructions which accompany the commercial steam plant advise where the special steam oil needs to be applied and there is always a displacement lubricator located in the steam supply line feeding the engine. The displacement lubricator is a simple piece of

equipment having no moving parts. It comprises a small cylinder with a detachable top through which it can be filled with steam oil, a drain plug on the bottom and inlet and outlet connections for the steam supply. Fig 11/3 shows a typical displacement lubricator in section. Steam passing across the nozzle at the top of the cylinder picks up a small quantity of oil and in turn leaves behind a drop of water condensed out of the steam. The oil in the steam is carried into the engine where it is deposited on the cylinder walls and lubricates the moving pistons and slide valves. The water condensed from the steam collects in the bottom of the displacement lubricator cylinder and lifts the oil, progressively maintaining a supply at the top for collection by the steam. The size of the lubricator and the oil supply is geared to the running time of the engine and boiler and usually allows the engine to have a sufficient quantity of oil for this time with a small safety margin. At the end of each running period it is necessary to drain the water

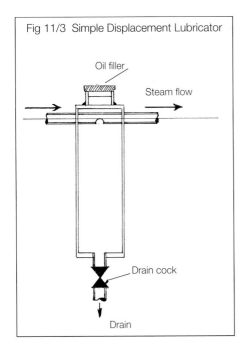

Fig 11/3 Simple Displacement Lubricator

Oil filler

Steam flow

Drain cock

Drain

from the lubricator and to refill it with steam oil. All steam engines need to have 'steam oil' for lubrication purposes. This is a specially-blended oil prepared to withstand the heat of the engine and the high steam temperatures. Steam oil is very thick but must not be confused with the oil that is used for car engines or gearboxes. Motor vehicle oils are not suitable for steam engines.

There is one unpleasant aspect of the model marine steam plant caused by the displacement lubrication system. The steam which carries oil into the engine also carries oil when it is exhausted and, unless it is cleaned first, it deposits oily water over the decks of the model. This is obviously not acceptable but is easily rectified. The exhaust steam from the engine needs to be led into a steam and condense trap or tank where the oil can be condensed out of the exhaust which can then be safely released to atmosphere. Furthermore, at some lakes the local authority or owners of the water will not permit oil or similar contamination so that the oily steam may not be exhausted through a hull skin fitting directly into the water. A suitable steam-trapping tank is easy to make from a short length of copper tube, capped at each end and fitted with intake and outlet pipes and possibly a drain plug as shown in Fig 11/12.

The steam engines available to the modeller today are finely engineered pieces of equipment and the quality of workmanship is reflected in the prices asked. The smaller oscillating engines are wasteful of steam as they cannot be sealed against leakage to the same degree as the other types. The rigid cylinder and slide valve engines are much more economical of steam and, when coupled to even a fairly small boiler, can give runs of up to thirty minutes

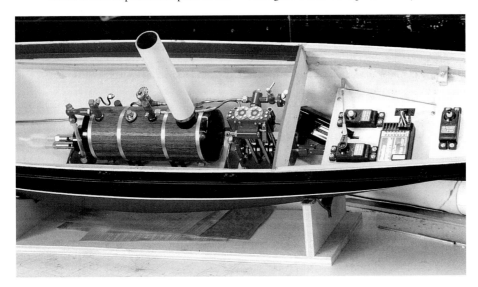

Hemmens Max II steam plant installed in hull of pilot cutter *Chimera*. A feed water tank is formed in the bow of the hull and the return water pipe is visible above the burner.

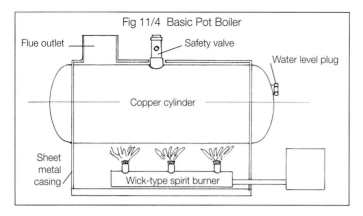

Fig 11/4 Basic Pot Boiler

ly allowed the steam to be used more than once before feeding it to the condenser system. In the small steam plants for the model ship the steam pressure rarely exceeds 50psi and the small size of engine does not lend itself to the use of the steam more than once. In addition the lubrication system of the small engine is vastly different from that of the full-size unit. Some small triple-expansion marine engines have been built for model ships but these have been specially made by modellers skilled in the use of lathes and milling machines etc, and this type of work does not fall within the scope of this book.

Boilers

The boiler is the source of steam for the model and these come in differing sizes and forms to suit the steam engine to which they are married. The huge cylindrical and water tube boilers of the full-size ship do not lend themselves to sensible miniaturisation and the model boiler is much less complicated. The simple pot boiler comprises a cylinder beneath which solid fuel pellets or a methylated spirit burner are located and with a detachable safety valve through which the cylinder may be filled and the steam led to the engine. This is shown in Fig 11/4 in diagrammatic form. Sensibly, this boiler

between boiler fills. The purist and more knowledgeable modeller will ask 'What about the compound and triple-expansion engines?' In full-size practice two-cylinder compound engines, and triple- and quadruple-expansion engines were the norm. In these the steam exhausting from the first cylinder was passed into the next to do further work until it was finally exhausted to the ship's condenser system where it was turned back to water to be fed again into the boiler. This system is very economical of steam and uses its expansive and working qualities to the full, but the small size of the engine needed for model work does not really lend itself to the multi-expansion system. In the full-size ship the steam left the boiler at pressures often over 250psi and the steam was super-heated to high temperatures. This effective-

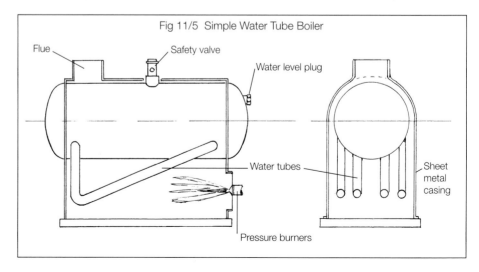

Fig 11/5 Simple Water Tube Boiler

should have a sight glass to show the water level or a level plug which, when removed, indicates the level in the cylinder. A vital addition is a suitable safety valve which will lift and release steam should the pressure rise above a set level. This valve prevents the pressure rising in the boiler to the point where it can fail and explode. All safety valves need to be accurately set and regularly checked as a matter of sensible precaution.

The pot boiler can be modified to be a more efficient steam generator by the addition of water tubes fitted so that they are below the water level and in the direct line of heat from the burner system as shown in Fig 11/5. With a well-made insulating jacket round the boiler and burner space, such a boiler would benefit from the addition of a gas burner which would give more heat than the fuel tablets or methylated spirit. Such gas burners are discussed below.

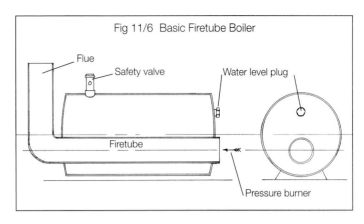

Fig 11/6 Basic Firetube Boiler

More efficient than the pot boiler is the firetube boiler, where a cylinder is fitted inside the larger boiler cylinder and in which the heat is generated by a gas or methylated spirit burner. Fig 11/6 illustrates this basic unit which is similar to the full-size cylindrical Scotch boilers. This boiler arrangement can also be improved by the insertion of water tubes across the furnace tube as shown in Fig 11/7 and by

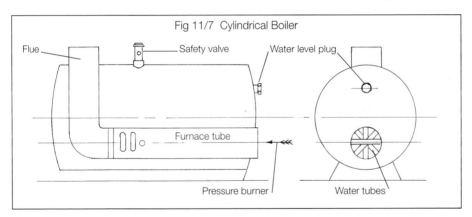

Fig 11/7 Cylindrical Boiler

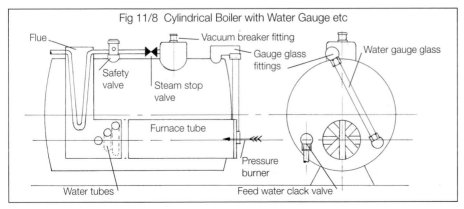

Fig 11/8 Cylindrical Boiler with Water Gauge etc

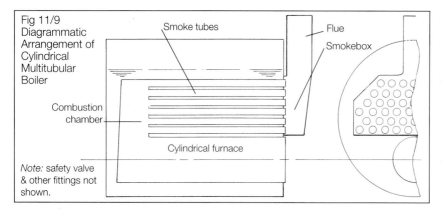

Fig 11/9 Diagrammatic Arrangement of Cylindrical Multitubular Boiler

Smoke tubes

Flue

Smokebox

Combustion chamber

Cylindrical furnace

Note: safety valve & other fittings not shown.

turning the flue vertically at one end to exhaust out of the boiler top and thus having the hot gases totally within the boiler casing. The addition of a water gauge, feed water clack valve and vacuum breaker and carrying the steam pipe through the flue gases results in the arrangement shown in Fig 11/8. Finally, the most efficient of all the boilers is that where return tubes carry the hot gases back through the water space of the boiler to exhaust through a smoke box above the burner as shown in Fig 11/9.

All the boilers used by today's makers with only one exception are made from copper, brazed or silver-soldered during construction and supplied complete with suitable certificates indicating the tests carried out before despatch. The one exception is that of the Japanese maker Saito whose boilers are made of brass and fired

with methylated spirit but only to pressures not exceeding 25psi. At this pressure the Saito engines with generous clearances run well. Brass, however, is not really a satisfactory material from which to build pressure vessels as it varies widely in its make-up. Copper is the accepted material for the model boilermaker and it will, when sensibly used and silver-soldered or brazed, stand up to pressures of 150psi or more depending upon the thickness of the sheet. The modern commercially-made steam plants generally run at pressures of 50 to 70psi and the boilers have safety valves which lift at 80psi. In this case the boilers are tested to twice the pressure at which the safety valve lifts, *ie* 160psi.

In addition to the horizontal form of boiler some can be bought in vertical form and, as illustrated in Fig 11/10, these are usually to be found fitted in open steam launches or models where space is restricted. Regardless of the pattern of boiler that is used, all need to be fitted with a means of filling and with a suitable chimney or funnel through which the exhaust gases can be vented. The funnel of the boiler, when it is fitted into a model with closed superstructure, should not be used as the funnel of the model but should be enclosed in a scale funnel attached to the superstructure and providing an air space between it and the boiler funnel.

Some of the steam engines available today incorporate feed water pumps driven from the engine crankshaft and with the boiler pipework and valve system arranged to allow the pump to feed the boiler with fresh water to maintain the water level and extend the duration that the system will run before refilling is required. A diagrammatic arrangement of such a pipework installation is shown in Fig 11/13. It is not usual to use the water of the pond or lake

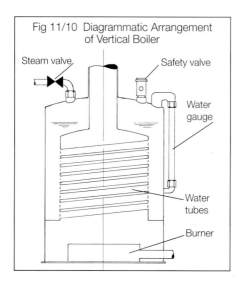

Fig 11/10 Diagrammatic Arrangement of Vertical Boiler

Steam valve

Safety valve

Water gauge

Water tubes

Burner

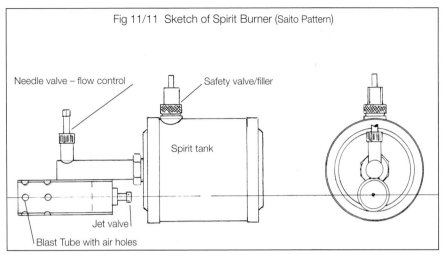

Fig 11/11 Sketch of Spirit Burner (Saito Pattern)

Needle valve – flow control
Safety valve/filler
Spirit tank
Jet valve
Blast Tube with air holes

to feed the boiler as it could be hard and contain contaminants which will coat the inside surfaces of the boiler and reduce the efficient production of steam. In fact it is wise to use only distilled or de-ionised water in model boilers or, at the very least, water which has been boiled once before being used. Where a feed water pump is fitted then it is necessary to arrange a feed water tank within the model and, while a suitable tank can be made of, say, styrene sheet and fitted into the hull in a suitable spot, it is often possible to utilise the unused space in the bows of the hull as a feed tank. To do this it is only necessary to fit a watertight bulkhead across the hull in a suitable position and to fit feed and return pipe connections to this bulkhead. The foredeck above the bulkhead will form the tank top and a suitable filler hatch could be arranged in the deck. If necessary, the bulkhead could be fitted with a water gauge glass to show the level of water in the tank or the bulkhead could be made of transparent perspex or similar hard material which would serve the same purpose. In any event the pipework needs to be sealed into the bulkhead and the bulkhead must be sealed to the sides of the hull to ensure that no water can leak into the hull. The only restriction on the duration of the running of the plant will be the quantity of water and the quantity of fuel available. It is vital to ensure that the boiler does not run short of water under any circumstances as a gas burner running in an empty boiler will rapidly cause the seams to fail and the boiler to become a total write-off with expensive results. Where a water tank is formed in the bows of a timber hull obviously the whole inside surface of the hull must be rendered waterproof either with a number of coat of paint or varnish or by

sealing the area with polyester resin which has been suitably catalysed.

Fuel

Model boilers can be fired by either solid fuel tablets called 'Meta Tablets', methylated spirits or by gas which can be bought

Cheddar Models 'Proteus' steam plant installed in model of trawler Kingston Peridot. This fine and powerful outfit was really a little too powerful for the model and the large boiler and engine was a tight fit in the slender hull. It performed excellently on the water under test.

for camping stoves and the like and is usually butane or a combination of butane and propane. Each method has its merits, although the modern tendency is to use gas as it is readily available and clean to use.

Solid fuel tablets need to be placed in a small tray and lit before being placed beneath the boiler to heat the water and provide the steam. Such tablets last only a short time and are not suitable for sophisticated boilers. They are used by one maker to power a simple boiler (SVS & R M Marine, see Appendix 2) and can be effective for short runs of small models.

Methylated spirits can be bought from most chemists and camping shops. In order to burn meths for the modern model boiler there are two types of burner in use. The first is the simple wick pattern where a tank of methylated spirit feeds a tube from which project a number of wicks which can be lit to give a hot and clean flame in a ladder format (see Fig 11/4). The second is the self-blowing pressure burner such as is supplied with the Japanese Saito equipment. This is a first-class type of burner and very efficient, with a distinctive roar similar to a paraffin blowlamp. This type of burner is ideal for the horizontal furnace tube boiler. The Saito burner is fitted with a safety valve to relieve any pressure build up in the feed tank and the valve can be fitted with a pipe to exhaust methylated spirit gas outside the model should the valve lift.

Methylated spirit burns with an almost invisible and very hot flame which is very clean and deposits virtually no soot on the boiler passages. As it is invisible in reasonably bright daylight, care must be taken when lighting up this fuel before locating the burner in the boiler (Fig 11/11).

Liquefied petroleum gas (LPG), as used in camping stoves, cigarette lighters etc, is an ideal fuel for model boilers and most manufacturers of such plants provide gas burners as standard equipment. Canisters of lighter gas are normally charged with butane and this is also the usual fuel for camping stoves and the like. Propane burns with a much hotter flame and comes in containers at higher pressures. It is commonly used to cut metals in burners also using oxygen and is frequently used on building sites to heat premises temporarily and to heat tar boilers etc. Butane can be used by itself as a means of firing the model boiler but a mixture of butane and propane is much more suitable. The mix should not exceed 70 per cent butane and 30 per cent propane or a flame that is too hot will result. The advantage of the mix is that it does not supercool as easily as butane alone does. Cooling the gas cylinder reduces the pressure of the gas inside it. Butane, by itself, as it is used tends to cool the cylinder in which it is stored and thus progressively reduces the available pressure until the burner fails.

LPG is stored, as its name suggests, in liquid form and is held as liquid purely by pressure and high pressure at that. When the liquid is released it instantly turns to gas and can be ignited and burned using specially-designed burners which are not unlike the gas burners of modern domestic central heating boilers. Alternatively the burner can resemble a blowlamp and in this form

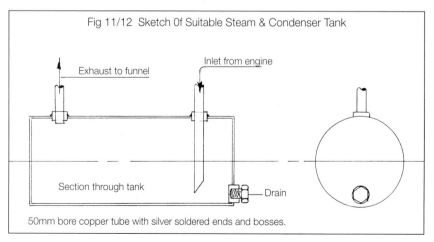

Fig 11/12 Sketch Of Suitable Steam & Condenser Tank

Exhaust to funnel

Inlet from engine

Section through tank

Drain

50mm bore copper tube with silver soldered ends and bosses.

is often used for soldering, paint stripping etc. In the model boiler either pattern may be used, the most important consideration being the rechargeable gas tank that is installed and the pipework that leads the gas from tank to burner. As the gas supply tank is a pressure vessel it must be constructed to the same strict standards as a boiler and tested to at least twice its normal working pressure. Some makers fit safety valves to gas supply tanks for use in model ships and, if such a safety valve is fitted, it must be arranged to exhaust outside the model. It is also important to remember that all LPGs are heavier than air and escaping gas will collect at low level in the hull of the ship. Such gas is explosive and will instantly ignite if not removed. If a gas leak is suspected, the gas burner should not be lit until one is certain the hull has been purged of gas and the leak rectified. The gas can usually be detected by its distinctive smell. The burner supply tank should only be recharged out of doors and well clear of surrounding buildings and, of course, well away from the curious eyes and fingers of children. When lighting the gas burner, a spark-type igniter is usually employed and, again, this should be done out of doors. Should the burner fail to ignite upon the second attempt make absolutely certain that no gas has collected in the model before making further attempts. A small fan to blow air through the ship is a good way of evacuating gas that has been left in the bottom.

It is possible to use the small containers in which the gas comes as supply tanks inside the model and they are perfectly adequate if the space in the hull is well ventilated. However, a well-made and specially designed rechargeable gas tank will usually be found to be much easier to locate inside the hull. The whole installa-

Detail of 'Proteus' engine.
DAVID MILTON

tion of gas tank, boiler and engine will generally occupy more space than the electric motor and batteries but spread along the length of the hull. It is also essential to provide adequate ventilation when a steam plant is installed. An electric motor and batteries needs little or no air but a boiler and burner system needs air for combustion. If there is inadequate ventilation the burner, regardless of the type of fuel used, will fail and the supply of steam will cease. Some years ago the author found that it was necessary to remove the glazing fitted to a steam yacht, as the burner slowly died and went out between the time of lighting up and the time it took to raise steam, replace the hatches and place the model on the water. Removing the glazing of the forward cabin gave some 6sq in more of clear intake for air and allowed the burner to remain lit when the hatches were closed up. Obviously the location of intakes for combustion air need to be sited well above the waterline of the model and high

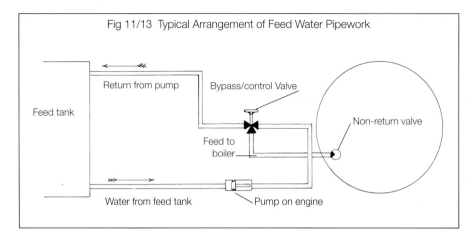

Fig 11/13 Typical Arrangement of Feed Water Pipework

Feed tank

Return from pump

Bypass/control Valve

Non-return valve

Feed to boiler

Water from feed tank

Pump on engine

intervals of two years. Test certificates provided by the testing station are valid for this period of time. Within the jurisdiction of the Model Power Boat Association in the UK and Naviga in most of the rest of the world, such certificates of testing are required before model steam ships may be sailed at regattas attended by the public. Failure to have pressure vessels tested invalidates any insurance cover and renders the equipment unfit for use. Many of the model boat clubs in the UK have facilities for boiler and tank testing with a suitably qualified person available to carry out tests and issue certificates.

enough up to avoid water from getting into the model.

Operating steam models

There are, these days, a number of regattas and meets for the model steam ship enthusiast and there is a great deal of friendly rivalry at such events. Both in the UK and France steam is rapidly becoming popular and there are a number of events each year attended by enthusiasts from both countries. One enterprising manufacturer in the UK has had a boating lake built at which clients can sail their models and where regattas may be held on a regular basis, where too, the steam plants made can be fully tested in working models.

All steam boilers and rechargeable gas supply tanks require to be tested at

When making the decision to drive the model ship by steam it is necessary to be fully aware that, of all the possible methods of propulsion, steam is the most potentially dangerous, particularly if elementary precautions are ignored. The danger arises from the boiler in which the steam is generated. Unlike fluid under pressure, which will disperse, steam has an expansive force which can cause an explosion if given half a chance. Escaping steam can seriously scald and due precautions should always be taken for one's own protection but more so for that of the innocent bystander. Most model boat clubs have facilities for boiler testing and carry insurance for members' and the public's safety. Modern steam outfits are, however, quite safe if handled with care and a model sailing over the lake with a plume of steam issuing from the funnel is a fine sight. In the same way that steam locomotives appeal, so do steam ships and there is a certain special something about the romance of steam with the smell of hot oil and the gleaming parts in motion to the gentle hiss of the exhaust.

Maxwell Hemmens steam outfit fitted into open framework of hull to allow easy alignment of shaft, coupling and engine before hull was planked.

12
Decks & Hatches

The methods of fixing decks to a model hull vary only slightly, what differences there are being mainly due to the material being used both for the deck and the hull. Whether the hull is made of timber, GRP or another material, the line of the main deck must be clearly defined. In the case of a plank-on-frame timber hull this is usually the top edge of the hull. This edge needs to be measured carefully, at the very least, at each frame station and vertically from the keel, and the line of the deck sanded true to these measurements. If the deck is to lie on top of the hull sides then the deck line must be drawn to make allowance for the thickness of the deck material. If the deck is to lie inside the hull planking then small supporting blocks of timber must be glued between the frames to support the sides of the deck.

In the case of a GRP hull, supports for the deck edges need to be fitted to the inside of the hull. Where the bulwarks of the ship have been included in a GRP moulding the deck supports must be fitted to allow not only for the depth of the bulwarks, but also for the thickness of the deck material. In the case of this type of hull the deck edge supports should be made from $1/4$in or $3/8$in. (6mm or 10mm) square timber stock, best secured to the hull with gelcoat resin suitably catalysed. Slow-cure epoxy resin adhesive will also serve. To permit the square timber to conform to the curves of the hull sides it should be saw cut half through at intervals of 1in to $1^1/4$in (25mm to 30mm) and fitted with the saw cuts to the inside of the hull. The saw cuts will close together as the timber curves.

Clothes pegs holding timber strips to top edge of GRP hull preparatory to fixing deck beams in place.

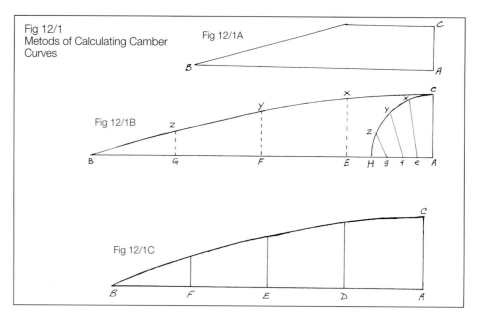

Fig 12/1
Metods of Calculating Camber Curves

Fig 12/1A

Fig 12/1B

Fig 12/1C

Care should be taken to avoid the adhesive reaching the top or inside faces of the timber.

Sheer and camber

Sheer is the curvature or rise of the deck forward and aft compared with amidships. Camber, or round of beam, is the curvature or round-down of the deck transversely. The hulls of most ships have both sheer and camber, although in recent years many ships have been built without sheer. In addition, they may have straight-line camber; that is, the central part of the deck is flat or level for at least the width of the hatchway, then runs down in a straight line to the ship's side (see Fig 12/1A).

The sheer of the deck is shown on the elevation or profile drawing. On external profiles this is the line of the deck at the side. On sectional profiles or elevations (*ie* those plans which show the ship as if cut along the longitudinal centreline), this will be of the deck at the centreline. On some profile drawings the line of the deck at the centre is also shown. The difference in height between two lines at any point shows the camber at that point. When a figure is given for the camber, this is at the

maximum beam of the ship. Obviously the amount of round-down will decrease towards the bow and stern as the sides of the ship curve in towards the centreline.

There are several methods of preparing a round-of-beam, or camber, curve. Fig 12/1B shows a graphic method.

Let AB represent the half breadth of the ship. At A erect a perpendicular AC the length being the maximum round of beam amidships. With centre A and radius AC strike an arc to cut AB at H. Divide AB, AH and the arc CH into the same number of equal parts. At E, F and G erect perpendiculars equal to ex, fy and gz. Draw a fair curve from B to C through X,Y and Z. This is the round-of-beam curve. Complete the curve by repeating on the opposite side of AC

Fig 12/1C shows another means of drawing the curve graphically.

Let AB represent the maximum half-breadth of the ship. At A erect a perpendicular AC, the length being the maximum round of beam amidships. Divide AB into four equal parts marking these points D, E, F. At each of these points erect perpendiculars, making the length of that at D equal to $^{15}/_{16}$ of the maximum camber, that at E $^3/_4$ of the maximum camber and that at F $^7/_{16}$ of the maximum camber. Draw a fair curve from C through the tops of each perpendicular to B. Repeat on the opposite side of AC.

Finally, the amount of round down of the deck at any point can be calculated by using the formula:

$$Y = (X^2 \div B^2) \times A$$

Where A = maximum round of beam
  B = Maximum beam of ship
  X = Beam of ship at the point at which the round of beam is required
  Y = amount of round down

The camber curve must be transferred to a suitable piece of plywood or timber to create a template for the beams which will be fitted across the hull to support the decks.

Deck beams

Before the deck beams can be cut and fitted it is necessary to mark the positions of the various access hatches, superstructures, deck houses etc. The deck beams must be fitted clear of these required openings and yet adequate support for the deck must be provided. Sometimes deck beams can be fitted and later, after fore and aft supports have been fitted, they can be cut away to provide the necessary access. Some of the photographs illustrate types of deck supports on a number of models. Where there is both sheer and camber on a model these need to be repeated on the support frames and beams. For example, a longitudinal support running down the centre of the hull must have a sheer curve to match that of the hull. If the longitudinal support is down the centreline of the ship, or part way between the centreline and the ship's

Three deck beams fitted to bow section of GRP hull. Note triangular pieces of scrap plywood reinforcing the joints.

Deck beams fitted to stern section of model, cutaway sections of the beams being needed to clear the operating rods between the tiller and the servo unit.

(Right)
Hull showing how beams have been cut away and coamings formed for detachable superstructure. This photograph is of constructional work for a New York harbour tug.

(Far right)
Deck beams attached to frames of a plank-on-frame hull for the twin screw coaster *Arran Mail*. The cutaway sections of frames to accommodate the propeller shafts are clearly visible.

(Below)
Deck beams and side framing with reinforcing triangles fitted to hull for model of *Keila*.

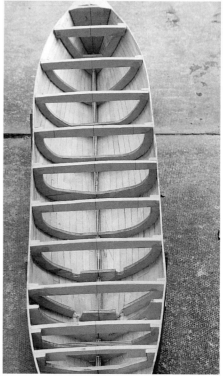

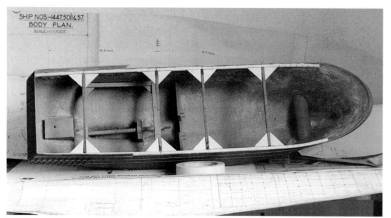

camber template, the required number of beams to fit across the hull from bow to stern can be made. Each should be measured carefully to ensure the centre top of the curve is on the centre of the beam and that it fits neatly between the side deck supports. Deck support beams should preferably be cut from $1/4$in (6mm) thick plywood or similar hardwood and glued to the side support frames with either epoxy or PVA adhesive. A stronger joint for athwartships beams can be obtained by gluing small triangles of scrap plywood between the beams and the side support timbers. This can be seen in the photographs. This method of attaching beams applies equally to all types of hulls, although small light hulls could have beams cut from thinner plywood or wood recovered from cupboard panels and the like. Once all the deck beams and side supports have been completed and the glue has been given time to cure, the entire timber frame-

side, it will not have the exact same curve as near the side of the ship due to the camber of the deck and care will be needed here.

When preparing to fit deck beams to the hull, particularly to a GRP hull, the width (beam) of the hull at deck level should be measured, for quite often a GRP hull will spread slightly round the top and will need to be drawn in to the correct beam and held in place until the deck beams have been firmly glued. Using the

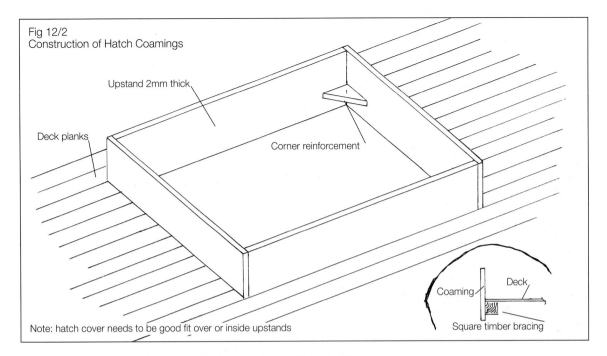

Fig 12/2
Construction of Hatch Coamings

Upstand 2mm thick

Deck planks

Corner reinforcement

Coaming

Deck

Square timber bracing

Note: hatch cover needs to be good fit over or inside upstands

work should be painted or varnished to render it all waterproof, since it will become inaccessible once the decks have been laid and fixed in place.

There are places where deck beams can be fitted and interconnected to fore and aft supports to form the shape of an access hatch, as shown in the picture of the herring drifter hull. When this is done, care must be taken to ensure that the camber and sheer curves are maintained. It is also possible to make and fit the hatch coamings before laying the deck, securing them to the beams and fitting the deck closely to the coamings to form a waterproof joint. Coamings, which are dealt with later in this chapter, are upstands of timber or similar material over which a hatch or superstructure will fit to create a water-resistant joint and at the same time secure the hatch or superstructure firmly in place on the model. Fig 12/2 illustrates coamings for a simple hatch.

Materials for decks

The material from which to make the main decks of the model is a matter of personal choice. If the hull is constructed of timber then the sensible choice will be to use plywood, such as good-quality marine plywood either $1/16$in or $1/8$in (1.5mm or 3.0mm) thick. The thinner material can be made to conform to the sheer and camber curves more easily. The underside of the deck must be painted before it is fitted to proof it against dampness, as it will become inaccessible once it is glued down. Select a plywood with a good surface such as a birch-faced ply. The better-quality materials will be more expensive but will be safer in wet conditions and they are almost always easier to work with.

An alternative to timber for the main decks is styrene sheet. This material is easy to cut and impervious to water but it is not suitable for the decks of a steam driven model as the heat will cause distortion and, moreover, styrene is inflammable if in contact with flame. One manufacturer of model ship kits does recommend that the underside of decks of steam-driven models be insulated against heat, but this is not necessary unless the section of deck concerned is very close to the direct source of heat. Styrene sheet comes in a variety of thicknesses from only a few thousandths of an inch to $1/8$in (3mm) thick. The modeller can therefore choose a thickness equivalent to that of plywood and get the same results. It is not necessary to paint the sheet on the underside when laying the main deck but it is necessary to roughen it in the areas where adhesive is to be used. Styrene sheet is normally joined using a liquid polystyrene cement. The two pieces to be joined must be held in close contact and a small quantity of liquid applied to the joint with a brush. Within a matter of seconds the parts can be released as the liquid welds one to the other. The joint should be left undisturbed for a few hours to cure. This adhesive is not suitable for joining styrene to timber or other material, and decks need to be glued with a two-part epoxy, preferably of the slow-cure type.

Laying decks

Whether the main deck is of timber or styrene, it will need to be held in place over the beams of the model until the adhesive has set firmly. This can be done using weights (small pieces of lead or similar heavy material), or the deck can be held down with brass pins which can be sanded away or removed when the glue has set. It is also important to know whether the decks of the prototype ship are planked or are of steel plates. Decks can be made from planks provided there are enough beams to which they can be fixed, or deck planking can be simulated with thin planks of timber glued over a solid underdeck. In the case of gluing thin planks over a deck, a plywood main deck is advisable as it is easier to glue thin timbers to timber than to styrene. If the prototype has some timber decks and some steel decks then styrene sheet may be the easier course, with the timber planks laid over the styrene using a contact adhesive. When simulating steel decks using plywood, the grain of the ply must be well filled and sanded to provide a very fine surface. Styrene already has a surface akin to steel.

Laying a timber deck using planks over an open framework of deck beams

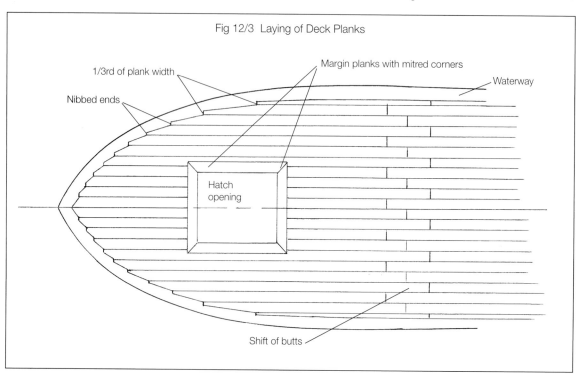

Fig 12/3 Laying of Deck Planks

1/3rd of plank width

Margin planks with mitred corners

Waterway

Nibbed ends

Hatch opening

Shift of butts

may have been the way such decks were laid in full-size practice, but this method is not recommended for a working scale model. It is unlikely that the modeller will be able to simulate caulking of such planks and render such a deck fully watertight for a model to be sailed in anything but very calm waters. Much more suitable is the method used by most expert ship model-makers of laying deck planking over a solid deck of plywood or styrene. Examination of a real timber deck will show that the lines of caulking have a somewhat ragged appearance as the pitch does not form straight even lines. There are also rules laid down by the Classification Societies governing the laying of deck planking, the staggering of butts and the finishing of planks at curves. The usual way that deck planks are laid are shown in Fig 12/3 which illustrates the conventional way of finishing the planks at curves and how butt joints are staggered. Deck planks were usually laid and held down with spikes where the beams were timber or bolts where the beams were steel and such spikes or bolts were sunk into the planks and the holes plugged with pieces of wood dowel and trimmed flush. Caulking the planks renders the seams and butts watertight and is done using oakum and pitch, which creates a clear black line between each plank. Details of the way in which timber decks were laid on a full size ship will be found in the book *From Tree to Sea* by Ted Frost (see Appendix 3).

Simulating deck planking

There are a number of methods of simulating deck planks on the model and the simplest is to draw the planks on the ply deck using a waterproof black ink with a drawing pen such as a Rotring. This is acceptable on a very small scale model where planks scale only $1/16$in to $3/32$in (1.5mm to 2.0mm) wide but is not good practice in larger scales. Most decks, full size, are laid in teak or pine and generally the planks are

some 5in (127mm) wide. The lengths of the deck planks can vary between 16ft and 25ft (4.8m to 7.6m) and decks are laid using such random lengths although the shipwright will try to keep his deck symmetrical. Deck planks can be made from thin strips of a variety of timbers but to simulate a teak or deal deck it must be remembered that ships' decks are frequently washed both by the sea and the crew and the teak or deal becomes almost white over a very short time. The material used for deck planks must, therefore, be almost white. Birch veneer or thin birch plywood (0.4mm thick) is ideal although it is possible to purchase ready-cut planks of lime or box which are only 1.0mm thick and of various widths. Whichever material is selected, care is needed to lay the deck correctly.

Caulking decks

Experienced modellers will use their own method of simulating the caulking when laying a timber deck. Gluing a thin strip of black tape or paper to the edge of a plank before fitting it is one accepted method. Leaving a thin groove between each plank and later filling the groove with black cord is a second, and a third is to run a black, permanent ink felt-tipped marker pen down both edges of the plank before it is laid. Each method has its merits and all work quite successfully. Whichever method is used, the finished deck will need to be sanded smooth and given at least three coats of matt varnish to seal it upon completion. The deck which is laid using black paper as caulking cannot be sanded, as the paper will tend to smudge and stain the planks using sandpaper over the surface. Paper-caulked decks should be scraped smooth along the length of the planks. A steel scraper which is very sharp and drawn firmly over the timber at an almost vertical angle will rapidly smooth out any imperfections and remove the edge of the paper without any problems. An alternative to a steel scraper is a piece of glass used on edge but this should only be used while wearing gloves to protect the hands.

To lay the deck planks properly draw a centreline down the length of the model and start to lay the deck planks at the centreline. Note carefully the way the planks are laid on the full-size ship – some have a wide central plank (a King plank) running the length of the ship against which all the thinner planks fit. Some of the deck machinery, winches, windlass etc, have timber or cast bases and have a margin plank round them in picture-frame fashion with mitred corners. Hatch coamings may also have margin planks similarly fitted. At the edges of the decks there will be waterways, some of which may be of timber and slightly proud of the deck planks and some may be just spaces left showing the steel deck below, while others may be cemented, which must be suitably painted. These features must be shown correctly on the model, bearing in mind that the ends of the deck planks must conform to the rules of the Classification Society. Fig 12/3 also

Customs & Excise cutter *Badger* showing stern with seat and guard rails.
RAY BRIGDON

Customs & Excise cutter *Badger* showing access hatch to tiller of rudder. Seat and hatch effectively conceal this access.
RAY BRIGDON

gives some details of fitting margin planks to machinery plinths and hatches.

There is little doubt that a working scale model merchantman will be enhanced by a well-laid deck. The modeller must be aware that a model is more frequently seen from above than from any other direction, so that decks are very conspicuous. Since a laid and planked deck must fit round deck fittings, machinery and hatches etc. some may prefer to leave the fitting of the deck planks until the model is more advanced. This is a good idea where the ship's bulwarks are to be fitted later but not so easy to do if the bulwarks form part of the hull at an early stage. This is a constructional decision which will have to be made early on, bearing in mind the complexity of the deck layout.

Hatches

Some of the ship's hatches will be those shown on the drawings but one or two may be needed to gain access to a section of the hull and do not form part of the

hatch system of the prototype. Starting from the after end, a working model will need a hatch above the rudder stock to provide access for the fitting the tiller and linkage to the steering servo(s). There will usually be some item of deck machinery on the after deck such as a capstan or warping winch and this can be used to help locate a hatch for rudder access. A detail of such a hatch and disguising cover can be seen in the photograph of the Customs launch *Badger*. Further forward, and depending upon the ship being modelled, there will be either a cargo hatch or the accommodation block, and this can afford easy access to the drive motor or steam engine, propeller shaft and coupling. Further forward will be other cargo hatches or another accommodation block which can be used to provide access to batteries, gas tank etc.

Types of hatches

Hatches fall into various categories; cargo hatches, fish hatches, access to accommodation, escape hatches etc. Cargo hatches are generally quite large openings and in

Model of coaster *Jonrix* showing Macgregor type hatch covers with side supports, chains and rollers. In this case the hatches open fore and aft.

Main hatch on model coaster *Arran Mail* showing tarpaulin cover made from linen handkerchief stained black.

Underside of hatch of *Arran Mail* showing construction.

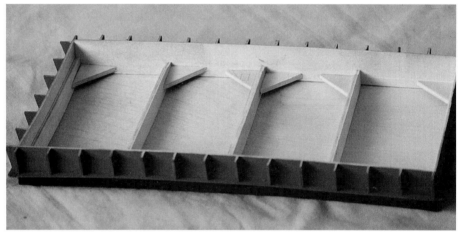

full-size practice are sealed in various ways. The earlier hatches were fitted with removable beams between which were placed timber boards after which the whole hatch was covered in a heavy tarpaulin held in place by long steel bars placed over the edges of the tarpaulin and in cleats secured to the hatch stiffener fitted along the coaming. The steel bars were secured in the cleats by wooden wedges. Modern ships are fitted with steel hatch covers which run on rollers and rails along the hatch coamings. These are drawn aside and stowed at each end or side of the hatch leaving a clear opening. Such hatch covers by MacGregor and other makers are now common on cargo ships and the covers are often strengthened to allow cargo or containers to be loaded on top of them. Making

model hatches and covers is not difficult and, despite fitting a reasonable amount of detail, the covers can be made removable to give access to the inside of the hull. The accompanying sketches and photographs will give the modeller some assistance. Model hatch covers carrying fine detail need to be handled with care when being removed at the pondside to avoid causing damage to the detail work. The earlier hatch with its tarpaulin cover is easily simulated by making the hatch in plywood or styrene sheet and covering the top with a piece of linen (a handkerchief is ideal), painted dark green or black. Such a hatch is shown in the photographs of *Arran Mail*.

On the forward end of the ship, the forecastle, there may be a small cargo hatch, a small access hatch or companionway, and there will be deck machinery such as windlass, anchor cable stoppers, bollards etc. As there is little need for access to the bow of the model other than to position ballast weight the forecastle deck can be fixed permanently. If, however, the bow is made into a feed water tank for a steam-driven model then a piece of deck machinery will need to be made into a small hatch and cover through which the tank can be filled.

Making hatches watertight

All hatch covers or accommodation blocks serving as hatch covers must be built to fit closely to their coamings, so that little or no water can enter and damage the electrics or radio gear inside the hull and to ensure they stay firmly in place in windy conditions on the pond. It is not unknown for a beautifully-made deckhouse to be blown off a model and to sink in the lake with resultant damage, all because the deckhouse was a slack fit on the upstand of the coaming. If there is any doubt about the way a hatch or deckhouse fits on its coaming then some additional means of fixing will be needed. If there is no weight problem with the model then a weight fitted under the hatch cover or deckhouse will help to hold it down. Some form of spring clip such as a Terry clip and bar could possibly be fitted under the edge of the hatch and cover so that a firm push will lock the unit down. Small screws that could be hidden in the edge of the hatch cover could be used to secure it. Whatever method of securing the item is used the best are those which work well and yet are almost invisible, for here again the model will be seen from above more often than from any other angle and any securing methods should be unseen.

Consideration of adjacent fittings

Another important point to watch for is the outfit of cranes and derricks. Frequently these are mounted on platforms adjacent to the hatches or on top of small deckhouses in which the winch motors or other machinery are located. These derrick platforms are not always located equidistant on either side of the ship's centreline so that careful measuring is needed to place them accurately. It is not unknown for a person seeking to find faults with a model to see offset derrick platforms and to comment thereon. Derrick platforms and mountings need to be considered along with hatches so that all can be fitted at the same time and be painted to conform to the ship's colour scheme. Derricks, cranes and their associated blocks and machinery are detailed in a later chapter.

Flush hatches

There will sometimes be a need for an opening to be formed where a coaming upstand cannot be used and where the hatch top needs to be flush with and part of the surrounding deck. This means that such a hatch must be sealed down in a manner which will keep the water out and yet allow the cover to be removed periodically. The easiest method of making such a hatch is to have a landing running right round the opening on to which the removable top will fit accurately. A fillet of silicon rubber bath sealant should be run round this landing, with a number of small screws to pull the cover down tightly to the seal. After a short while the sealant will form a rubber ring which will effectively keep out the water but which will not stick to the hatch cover. Some means of disguising the holding-down screws will be necessary. This method is good for a hatch which does not require frequent use and the rubber seal is good. However, a quick-lock method of fastening down the cover would be preferable for one which has to be removed frequently. If the hatch is small, a turn buckle or similar system could possibly be incorporated.

13
Superstructures

ouses of various kinds built on the decks of ships are commonly referred to as superstructures. They comprise the navigating bridge, cabin accommodation, engine and boiler room casings, crew accommodation and other deckhouses. In the case of the ship model this can be generally be taken as all the structures above the main or top deck of the hull.

All the various forms of superstructure cannot be covered in detail but the basic constructional methods are given. If they are looked upon as a series of boxes then the construction of a deckhouse becomes much easier. The more complex shapes can be reduced to a number of separate pieces and assembled after each piece has been completed and, if necessary, painted. The first consideration must be to decide from which material the superstructure(s) is to be made. If the model is to be steam-driven then the choice must be plywood or some form of timber. If the drive is to be by electric motor(s) then plywood or styrene sheet may be used. Styrene sheet is probably the cleanest and easiest of all materials from which to build the upperworks of a model ship. It has a fine smooth surface which accepts all paints, other than the cellulose based ones, and requires virtually no filling or sanding, except possibly at joints.

Materials

Whether the structure is made from plywood or styrene sheet it needs to be well-built and solid, particularly if it is to be detachable for access to the interior of the model. Frequent handling requires a solid construction. The thickness of the material should be selected to suit the duty and good quality $1/_{16}$in (1.5mm) plywood or styrene is suitable. A thinner 1.0mm-thick styrene is available and can be used for superstructure work, the nearest thickness in plywood being $1/_{32}$in (0.8mm). Both materials can be bent to form curved shapes, but very tight bends will need to be formed using some heat. Where the superstructure is a detachable unit it must be built to fit over the coamings on the model making sure that a good fit is obtained. The lower edges of houses must be cut to match the sheer and camber of the deck to obtain a close fit to prevent any water entering the hull.

Bridges

The deckhouse shown in Figs 13/1 to 6 is for a coaster, the twin-screw *Rovuma* and the sketches illustrate how the unit was constructed from thin plywood. The bridge of this ship is open, with an enclosed wheelhouse centrally located. Most older ships carried no protection on the open bridge, leaving those on duty there exposed to all weathers. Modern ships are almost all fitted with totally enclosed bridges and open bridge wings. Tugs now have totally enclosed wheelhouses and the latest split-funnel arrangement allows vision astern from the wheelhouse without the need for the master to move to the bridge wings. Some types of bridge and wheelhouse shapes are shown in the accompanying illustrations. On service craft such as tugs, oil rig support ships etc, a primary consideration is the provision of as much all-round visibility from the wheelhouse as possible. A bridge built for maximum visibility is illustrated in the photographs of *Scott Guardian*.

The photographs show methods of building the superstructures of model ships. When building the upperworks of the model, consideration must be given to the need for detailing the interior, particularly that of the wheelhouse and chartroom. These have large windows which will, in the larger scales, reveal the interior all too clearly. An empty wheelhouse will show up very poorly. It is not always possible to fit out a wheelhouse completely, so

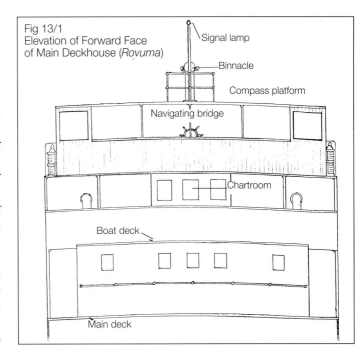

Fig 13/1
Elevation of Forward Face of Main Deckhouse (*Rovuma*)

Signal lamp

Binnacle

Compass platform

Navigating bridge

Chartroom

Boat deck

Main deck

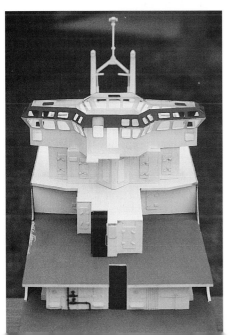

one fitted with a wheel, gypsy (if visible), compass, telegraph and seat is better than an empty space. A wheelhouse which has been neatly fitted out can be very effective and two of the photographs show such work.

(Centre left)
Close detail of bridge/wheelhouse of rescue ship *Scott Guardian*. Compare with model wheelhouse also pictured.
NEIL PATTERSON (IMT LTD)

(Lower left)
Wheelhouse under construction for model of *Scott Guardian*.

Construction

The corners and decks of the superstructure unit must be reinforced, particularly if the structure is to be detachable. Reinforcing blocks or triangles of ply or styrene glued carefully to the corners will strengthen the work and provide additional gluing surface. Where the corner of a superstructure is curved it may be necessary to build up extra layers of material to permit the curve to be sanded or carved to the correct profile. A piece of square stripwood can sometimes be used at a corner where a curve is needed but it needs to be rebated at each side to accommodate the side sheets. On the pilot's cabin of the cutter *Chimaera* the forward corners were

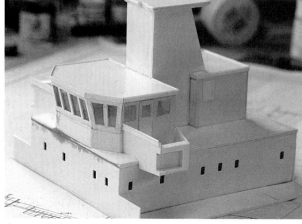

(Top)
Superstructure of model of *Jonrix* under construction using styrene sheet.

(Above)
Superstructure of *Jonrix* under construction showing front of unit.

(Right)
View of finished superstructure for model of *Jonrix*. The whole of the upperworks of this model were built from styrene sheet.

made from square stripwood and sanded to shape. This cabin was built from $1/16$in (1.5mm) plywood and decorated with veneer strips to simulate the panelling. The interior was fitted with a small table and two benches, a companion top rail and a table lamp which could be illuminated. It was finished in mahogany stain, varnished and the windows were provided with curtains made from scraps of crêpe paper. It will be obvious that the amount of detailing will affect the methods of building. A roof cannot be fitted before the interior is detailed, nor can working lamps be fitted without installing the necessary wiring. How the structure is to be assembled needs careful forethought, and space must be left for fittings and wires. The best way of tackling this part of the model is to make a list of all the parts to be assembled and to number the parts in the order in which they are to be fitted. Some of the parts and fittings will need to be painted or similarly treated before they are installed, and those areas where glue is to be applied must be kept clear of paint. The inside faces of the walls, floor and roof of superstructures should be treated with paint or other suitable finish before they are assembled, unless the structure has no large windows or ports through which the inside can be easily viewed.

Windows and portholes

A further and very necessary point relates to windows and portlights. It is difficult to paint a cabin accurately if the glazing has been fitted first unless the clear material has been masked off before the paint is applied. There are some products on the market which can be put on to the glazing and peeled away once the painting has been done. Often it is easier to paint the structure before the glazing is fitted, but this means that the roof or floor must be fitted later once the windows have been treated.

In the case of the wheelhouse/bridge of the trawler *Glenrose I* the interior was fitted out with control desk, benches and companion, together with most of the VDU displays. This was all made, painted and installed before the roof was fitted. The glazing, however, was fitted much later, each window being a separate piece of 2mm thick perspex cut to fit the appropriate opening and fitted after the window surrounds of 0.5mm styrene strips. These window surrounds were strips of styrene 3.0mm wide, glued so that they projected beyond the outside walls to form a frame to each window. With such thin material it was an easy matter to curve the strips to the shape of the window cutouts and to trim them to fit neatly.

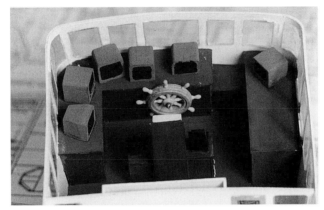

(Top)
Superstructure for model of the pilot cutter *Chimera* showing pilots' saloon minus roof to permit the interior to be seen. Note curtains of tissue, polished table and bench seat. The panelled exterior and door of mahogany veneer show clearly in this picture. The engine-room skylight with open tops and stays is left thus to supply air to the steam plant inside.

(Left)
Wheelhouse interior on model of the fishing boat *Denebula*. Scale 1:40.

(Lower left)
Wheelhouse window detail on stern trawler *Glenrose I* – full size. Note window surrounds and fabricated gooseneck vents.

(Above)
Interior of wheelhouse on model of *Glenrose I*. Scale 1:40.

(Left)
Interior of wheelhouse on *Glenrose I* looking aft. Note window surrounds fitted before glazing.

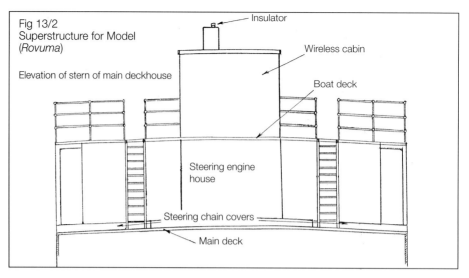

Fig 13/2
Superstructure for Model (*Rovuma*)

Elevation of stern of main deckhouse

Insulator

Wireless cabin

Boat deck

Steering engine house

Steering chain covers

Main deck

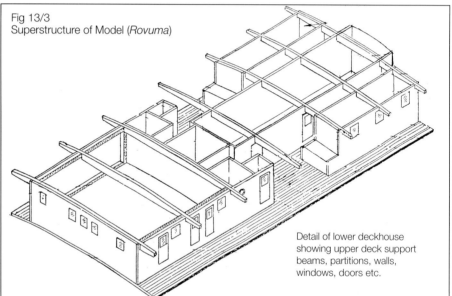

Fig 13/3
Superstructure of Model (*Rovuma*)

Detail of lower deckhouse showing upper deck support beams, partitions, walls, windows, doors etc.

Had this wheelhouse been made from timber then a similar exercise in window framing could have been carried out using thin veneer strips.

Finish

When making superstructures from plywood or similar timber it is always necessary to use a filler compound to fill and conceal the grain of the timber. Even if the unit is to show a timber finish, some filling of the grain is needed since that of the tim-

ber will be out of scale and thus require reducing. There are various grain fillers on the market in most countries. Some are specifically designed to enhance the figuring of the timber when the surface is sanded to a fine finish, while others are made just to fill and obscure the grain. Care is needed to select the most appropriate type. In all cases the final surface of the timber needs to resemble the material of the real ship, *ie* painted steel, painted timber, varnished timber etc. Most automobile accessory shops in the UK stock a product called

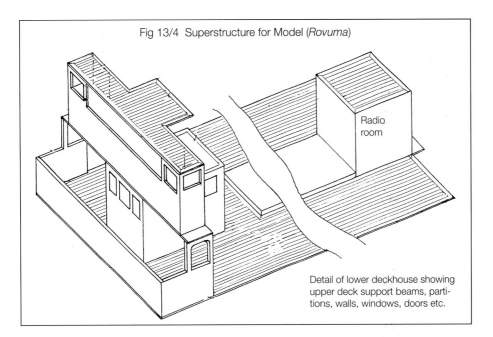

Fig 13/4 Superstructure for Model (*Rovuma*)

Radio room

Detail of lower deckhouse showing upper deck support beams, partitions, walls, windows, doors etc.

'spray filler', which will fill and conceal fine timber graining and small blemishes, leaving a good surface for subsequent painting.

As discussed earlier, some of the deckhouses or superstructures may need to show rivet heads, often on the casings over the boiler and engine-rooms of the ship. In these locations the rivets were not usually countersunk but had round heads and were very visible. Great care is needed when applying rivets and in larger-scale models it is wise to use small round head pins or real rivets glued into pre-drilled holes. The Classification Societies' Rules applied to these places too, and photographs of the real ship will help to ensure that the correct number of rows and spacing of the rivets is used. Some of the photographs show rivet detail on engine-room casings and a funnel.

Many cargo ships will be found to have small structures on either side of the

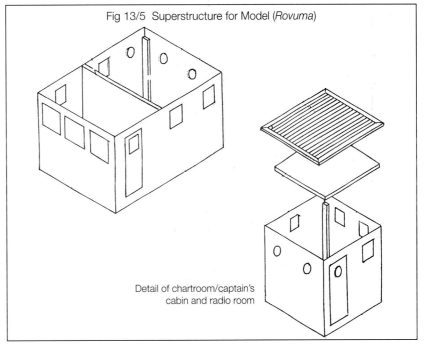

Fig 13/5 Superstructure for Model (*Rovuma*)

Detail of chartroom/captain's cabin and radio room

masts and derrick posts, on which derrick heel fittings were fitted. They could also give access to the cargo holds or accommodate switchgear etc. Such structures are easily simulated on the model with simple boxes. On some ships small cabins can be found built to the sides of the ship and

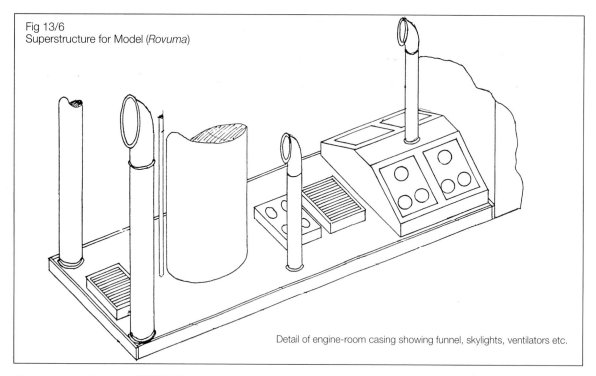

Fig 13/6
Superstructure for Model (*Rovuma*)

Detail of engine-room casing showing funnel, skylights, ventilators etc.

Pusher tug *Heron* built by Peter Backhouse of Doncaster shown here with the wheelhouse in the lowered position to allow movement through low bridges.

Heron shown with wheelhouse in raised position for good navigation.

were for crews known as Lascars who were men from Eastern countries such as China whose religion and upbringing dictated that they ate different meals to the Europeans and lived differently. Such small cabins kept them segregated and allowed them to live as they wished. An example of such accommodation is shown in the photographs of the coaster *Rovuma* where they are located on both sides of the ship fore and aft. The photographs show a number of types of vessels with their differing details but, unless the superstructure is very unusual, most can be built using the methods described.

Funnel of model of pilot cutter *Britannia*. Note rivet detail on funnel and on engine-room casing, typical of steam driven herring drifters. Twin smoke units were concealed in this funnel about 2ins (50mm) down from the top.

Elevating bridges

There is, however, one more type which should be mentioned, namely, that of ships known as low air draft vessels. These ships are designed to navigate to and from the sea up rivers and canals where there are fixed low bridges. On a number of these vessels the bridge can be lowered from its normal seagoing position along with the masts and associated rigging, to allow the ship to proceed to its unloading berth. In the lowered position of the bridge would not give adequate visibility at sea so it cannot be built with the bridge in the lower position permanently. While masts and rigging are easily lowered to deck level, the bridge is raised and lowered by a system of hydraulic rams. Steering and other navigational equipment is all electronic or hydraulically controlled. The photographs of *Heron* illustrate this type of ship in model form with the bridge in both raised and lowered positions.

Funnels

The most prominent feature on a merchant ship is the funnel or funnels mounted on top of the main superstructure. Very few ships have been built without funnels although a few were so built just after the last war. Being a distinctive feature, all

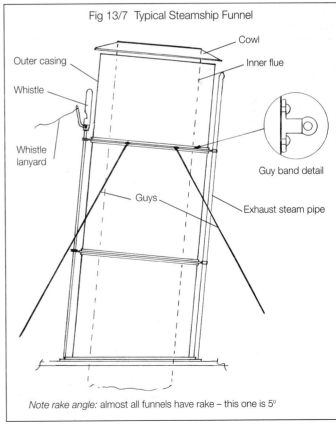

Fig 13/7 Typical Steamship Funnel

Cowl

Outer casing

Inner flue

Whistle

Whistle lanyard

Guy band detail

Guys

Exhaust steam pipe

Note rake angle: almost all funnels have rake – this one is 5°

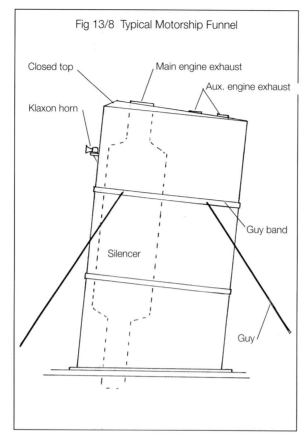

Fig 13/8 Typical Motorship Funnel

Closed top

Main engine exhaust

Aux. engine exhaust

Klaxon horn

Guy band

Silencer

Guy

needed to provide good draught for the efficient burning of coal or other fuels. Development of the steam-driven forced draught fan and furnace front air casings allowed funnels to be shorter as the fan provided all the air needed for good combustion. Just as the steamship funnel is needed to exhaust spent furnace gases, so a motorship needs a funnel or funnels to carry away exhaust gases from the oil engines.

The visible part of the steamship funnel is the outer casing, inside which is the exhaust trunking from the boilers. The outer casing is set so that there is an air space between it and the inner flue pipe and this effectively insulates the inner pipe. It is necessary to maintain the temperature of the flue gases above 320^0 F to prevent the formation of acid dew on the steelwork. These conditions dictate the way that the funnel is built on the steam-driven vessel.

The funnel of the motorship is designed to carry the exhaust also but, frequently, within the casing a silencer will be fitted and, very often, exhausts from auxiliary machinery is are also engine-driven. Thus the top of the funnel may well be closed off and have a number of stub pipes protruding. In the case of the larger merchant ship, the silencer in the funnel is a steam boiler where the heat in exhaust gases is used to generate steam while still silencing the exhaust noise. The steam is needed to heat the heavy oil used by the main engine. In some cases the funnel is also used to carry away waste air from the ventilation system.

The funnel of all ships is also used to carry the steam whistle or siren which is generally fitted high up on the forward face

owners use the funnel to indicate their ownership of the vessel by painting the funnel in a design or colour scheme that is of a particular style. For example, Cunard ships carry a funnel painted bright red with a black top section and with three narrow black bands spaced equally down the casing. Alfred Holt ships, known as the Blue Funnel fleet, have a tall funnel painted bright blue with a black top. The coasters of J R Rix of Hull have a funnel carrying the company's logo, as can be seen in the photographs of *Jonrix*. Many books carry illustrations of funnel designs and *British Steam Tugs* by P N Thomas (Waine Publications) has a page of eighty-eight different funnel designs and colours used by tug owners in the UK over some years. It follows that one's research into a working ship must include funnel detail which must be faithfully copied on the model.

In the early days of the steamship the funnel(s) were very tall, the height being of the funnel casing. Often there will be pipes running up the after side of the funnel from the boiler safety valves or from other parts of the ship. To give access to the whistle or siren, ladders are fitted up the funnel casing and sometimes steel platforms are fitted round the funnel near the top.

Ships having more than one funnel usually need the additional funnels to serve boilers located in more than one boiler room and these are usually large merchantmen or passenger ships. Motor ships with more than one funnel are also usually passenger liners. The second or third funnels are not always required for exhausting flue gas or oil engine exhaust but are used to conceal auxiliary machinery such as ventilation plant or air-conditioning machinery, the extra funnel being considered by the designers and owners to be a suitable feature of the vessel to make it distinctive and different.

There are a number of methods of making model funnels and the type of funnel will dictate which method to use. Where the model is outfitted with a steam plant the funnel will be required to contain the exhaust pipe from the boiler and it will

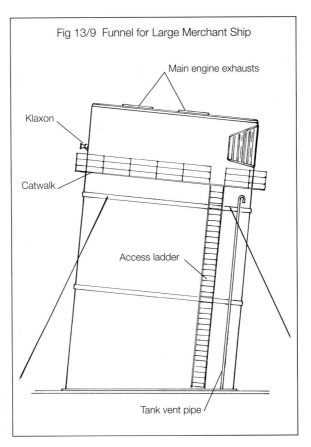

Fig 13/9 Funnel for Large Merchant Ship

Main engine exhausts

Klaxon

Catwalk

Access ladder

Tank vent pipe

need to be hollow. In the case of an electrically-driven model the funnel need not be functional and can be made differently. Where the model is of a steamship then the funnel must show a suitable cowl top, or if for a motorship then the funnel top may be closed and fitted with stub pipes. Some methods of making funnels are shown in the sketches Figs 13/7 to 8.

14
Masts, Derricks & Rigging

With few exceptions all merchant ships have masts, very many have derricks and all have rigging of one kind or another. Some of the older merchant ships were very reminiscent of the old square-riggers and had up to four masts, the later ships seem to have only one and that is often difficult to recognise as a true mast.

Today masts are generally installed to carry navigation lights and radio aerials and, sometimes, to provide a lookout platform at high level. Masts of wood have long since given way to tubular steel and the rigging, while providing support for the mast, no longer provides a ladder system to give access for crewmen to yards and sails. The more modern merchant ship is generally outfitted with a single steel mast (or perhaps two) and this is the system discussed here.

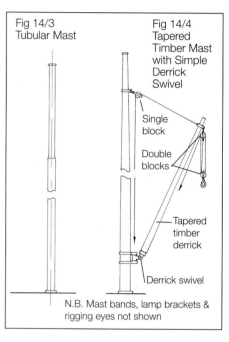

Fig 14/3
Tubular Mast

Fig 14/4
Tapered Timber Mast with Simple Derrick Swivel

Single block

Double blocks

Tapered timber derrick

Derrick swivel

N.B. Mast bands, lamp brackets & rigging eyes not shown

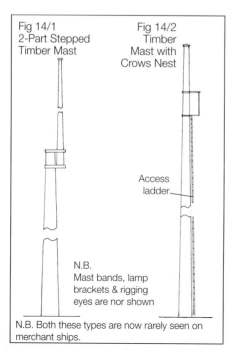

Fig 14/1
2-Part Stepped Timber Mast

Fig 14/2
Timber Mast with Crows Nest

Access ladder

N.B. Mast bands, lamp brackets & rigging eyes are nor shown

N.B. Both these types are now rarely seen on merchant ships.

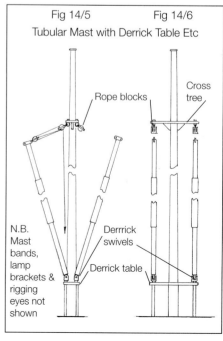

Fig 14/5   Fig 14/6
Tubular Mast with Derrick Table Etc

Rope blocks

Cross tree

N.B. Mast bands, lamp brackets & rigging eyes not shown

Derrrick swivels

Derrick table

(Far left)
Main mast of coaster *Timrix* showing navigation lights and access ladder etc. Note metallic cabling up mast under rungs.

(Left)
Main mast of model of *Denebula* made from brass tube and rod. Lights shown are operative.

(Below left)
Main mast of model of *Glenrose I* made from brass tube and styrene, still to be fitted with navigation lights.

Masts on a cargo ship provide supports for derricks and can carry lamps, radio equipment and radar units. Examples of various types of masts are shown in the photographs and details are also provided in the sketches Figs 14/1 to 6. The method of making masts for a model is up to the individual modeller. Some prefer to work totally in timber while others work with metal and/or styrene rod and tube.

Masts

Steel masts can be simulated using brass or aluminium tube, although styrene tube can be satisfactory. The styrene tubes can easily be distorted and they need to have a second tube fitted inside the correctly-sized tube to give the necessary rigidity. Both metal and styrene tubes create a steel-like surface for painting. Platforms for lamps and the eye plates, bands etc, for rigging need to be soldered to the metal mast, while liquid polystyrene cement is used to attach styrene fittings to the styrene tube.

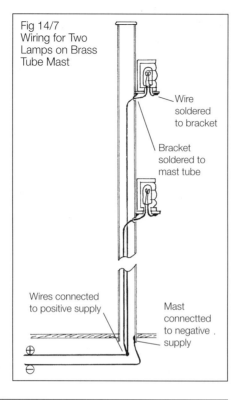

Fig 14/7
Wiring for Two
Lamps on Brass
Tube Mast

Wire soldered to bracket

Bracket soldered to mast tube

Wires connected to positive supply

Mast connectted to negative supply

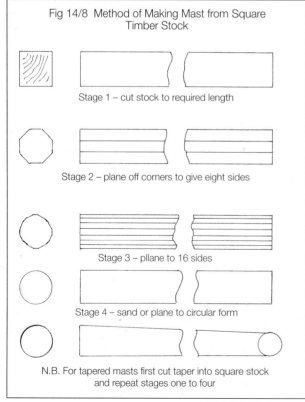

Fig 14/8 Method of Making Mast from Square Timber Stock

Stage 1 – cut stock to required length

Stage 2 – plane off corners to give eight sides

Stage 3 – pllane to 16 sides

Stage 4 – sand or plane to circular form

N.B. For tapered masts first cut taper into square stock and repeat stages one to four

If a mast is to carry lamps that are to be illuminated then brass tube is better since it can form the common return path for the lighting current; see Fig 14/7 which illustrates how a brass tube mast can be used for illuminated lamps.

Some care is needed to make wood masts accurately and good-quality timber must be selected from which to make them. Most model and DIY shops stock dowel of various diameters and of differing timber from which masts can be cut and sanded to shape. Birch, ramin, walnut and other hardwoods are all suitable for mast making and, where dowel is not available or of unsuitable size, square stripwood can be used. It is not necessary to own a lathe to turn and shape masts for a model ship. Fig 14/8 shows how pieces of square stripwood can be planed and sanded to correct form. Crosstrees, lamp brackets and eyebolts for pulley blocks can be fitted to the masts using an appropriate adhesive. Cyanoacrylate (Superglue) is suitable for fixing small metal parts to timber masts but larger metal pieces are best secured by a good epoxy and preferably also by small pins. The masts for a model should be painted and the detail picked out in the correct colours before they are installed and rigged. It is very difficult to paint such slender cylindrical parts after they are fixed to the model.

Derricks

The heel fitting of a tubular steel or timber derrick was mounted either on a swivel attached to the mast itself or on a similar swivel mounted on a derrick table at the base of the mast. Various derrick mountings and swivels are shown in Fig 14/9. The timber derricks fitted to the earlier cargo ships and fishing boats are easily made from dowel. Bands to carry eyes for attaching blocks etc, can be simulated by gluing thin strips of cartridge paper round the dowel. Such bands can also be formed from thin strips of brass glued to the derrick with epoxy or Superglue. Tubular steel derricks can be made from brass or aluminium tubes. Brass tubes can be soft-soldered and fittings attached in the same manner. Aluminium units can also be soldered but it is easier and better to assemble them using Superglue or epoxy. Tubular steel derricks are normally made up of several lengths of tube of diminishing diameter, the outside diameter of one piece being equal to the inside diameter of another so that they slot together for welding.

Once the derricks have been made a decision must be made about the way in which they will be fitted on the model. Derricks were only used in port. At sea they were stripped of the blocks and fittings which were stowed away and each der-

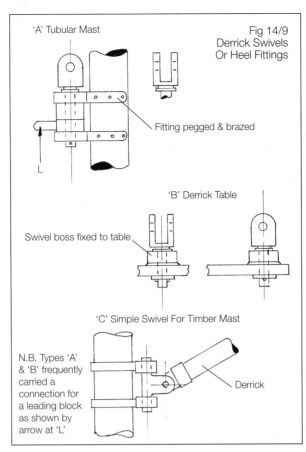

'A' Tubular Mast

Fig 14/9
Derrick Swivels
Or Heel Fittings

Fitting pegged & brazed

L

'B' Derrick Table

Swivel boss fixed to table

'C' Simple Swivel For Timber Mast

N.B. Types 'A' & 'B' frequently carried a connection for a leading block as shown by arrow at 'L'

Derrick

(Below)
Timber bulwark rail with single ball stanchions on model herring drifter built by David Deadman. This model took a gold medal and the kit class trophy at the Model Engineer exhibition at Wembley.

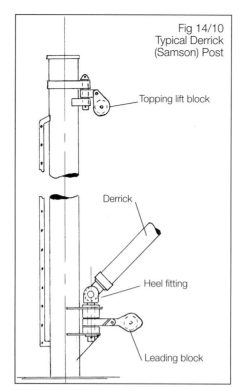

Fig 14/10
Typical Derrick
(Samson) Post

Topping lift block

Derrick

Heel fitting

Leading block

(Below)
Main mast and boom of
model herring drifter
Formidable to scale
1:24 showing lashing to
deadeyes.

(Bottom)
Fore mast of *Chimaera*
showing booms and
rigging to bottle screws
(rigging screws). Note
single stanchions on
timber bulwark rail with
cord simulating wire
rope.

rick was secured firmly into a crutch. If the
model is to depict the ship at sea then
blocks and much of the ropework would
not be visible. If the model is to show the
ship approaching a port then the derricks
could be shown fully-rigged.

In the case of a modern ship outfitted
with cranes in place of derricks, these are
mostly fully rigged at all times. Such cranes
are sited at various places on deck adjacent
to the hatches and have jibs which can
extend at least halfway across the hatch
opening. Such cranes are electrically or
hydraulically driven and usually have a
cabin in which the crane operator sits.

Where there are a number of hatches
on a ship, some derricks are mounted on
short masts specially fitted for cargo handling, known as sampson posts (see Fig
14/10). Details of the winches used for
cargo-handling are described in the chapter
on deck machinery.

Rigging

The rigging plan of a ship shows the sizes
and types of all rigging and blocks. If one is
not available, then recourse has to be made
to photographs of the prototype and possibly illustrations of similar ships. Early ships
were rigged with ropes of various sizes,
mostly hemp or sisal cordage. The size of a
rope is designated by its circumference,
whereas steel and similar wire ropes are
usually sized by the measurement of the
diameter. Ropes are a specialised subject
which needs to be studied more carefully
and requires more space than is available
here. There are a number of articles and
books on the subject for those who wish to
study it more fully. A suitable book for
gaining information on ropes and rope-
making is *The Complete Book of Knots and
Ropework* by Eric C Fry published by
David and Charles in 1996 but it would be
more sensible for the researcher to ask the
rope makers or manufacturers in the relevant country for details of their products.
Most manufacturers are generally happy to

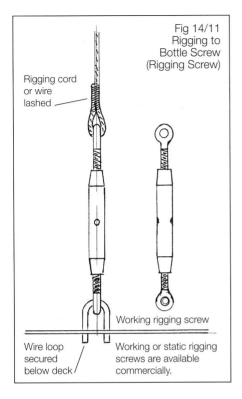

Fig 14/11
Rigging to
Bottle Screw
(Rigging Screw)

Rigging cord
or wire
lashed

Working rigging screw

Wire loop
secured
below deck

Working or static rigging
screws are available
commercially.

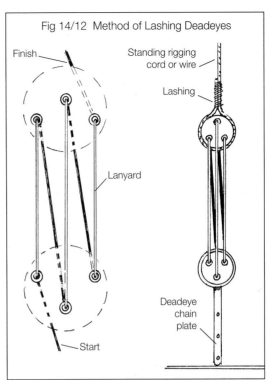

Fig 14/12 Method of Lashing Deadeyes

Finish

Standing rigging
cord or wire

Lashing

Lanyard

Deadeye
chain
plate

Start

give details of their products and a polite request may even result in an invitation to view the rope-making process.

Normally the ropes of the standing rigging (*ie* those that are used to support the masts and permanently fixed, as distinct from those which are used and move through blocks), are of steel and are tensioned with rigging screws or with deadeyes and lanyards (see Fig 14/11). Ropes used for cargo-handling are usually of steel wire, but those used for mooring a vessel are of hemp or, today, made from polypropylene or nylon fibres, which are more flexible and stretch whereas wire does not. On the older ships hempen rope was used for all work apart from the standing rigging. Today much use is made of the synthetic fibres, which do not rot or rust as do the hemp or wire ropes, from which mooring hawsers are made, fishing nets are woven and some lashings are made.

When selecting cord from which to make up the rigging for a model it is wise to buy finely-woven material. Some rigging cords have a furry finish which shows badly on the finished model. These fine hairs can be laid if the cord is treated with wax or gently drawn through PVA adhesive and then through the fingers. Apart from these there are many other types of cord, thread and rope which are of use to the model-maker. Stranded stainless steel trace wire, as used by anglers and available from angling shops, makes excellent standing rigging but needs care when securing the ends. It is available in a number of sizes. Nylon fishing line and that of dacron and similar synthetic material, also available from angler's shops, can be obtained in a range of sizes and used for modelling rigging. None of these suffer from the fine hair condition mentioned above but all will need to be painted to the correct colour needed for the ship. Being of synthetic material they are difficult to dye.

The rigging cords available in many different sizes from the ship model shop usually come in either beige or black, although very occasionally white can be found. A good finish to rope work is essential and simple knots are not always acceptable or even correct. Most ropes on board ships are bound at the ends as shown in Fig 14/12 and fine thread carefully wound round the rope ends and secured with a drop of Superglue is much more attractive and in line with full-size practice.

Where standing rigging is set up (tensioned) by either bottle screws or by deadeyes and lanyards, great care is needed to ensure that the mast is not pulled from its correct position. The standing rigging should be tensioned so that it is only just tight. Rigging cord that is to be used for standing rigging should be pre-stretched before it is used. This can be done by hanging lengths of the cord from hooks at high level with fairly heavy weights attached to the lower end, then left for some days to stretch to the maximum possible. The length of fibre cords can vary due to atmospheric conditions such as dampness or dry heat, so it is better to use stranded wire for standing rigging. A simple stranded wire is easily wound from three or four of the fine copper wires found in domestic electric cables. Drill three or four small holes in a piece of ply or similar material and secure the three or four

strands on one side of the ply with each length of wire through a single hole. Draw the wires into the chuck of a hand drill. Place the ply with wires attached into a vice or clamp it to the side of the work bench. Holding the drill so that the wires are fairly tightly stretched, wind the drill handle. In a short time the strands will twist together to form a 'wire rope' and the ends can be prevented from unwinding by a spot of solder before cutting the finished wire from the ply and the drill. This wire will, of course, need to be painted and, as the ends are best secured to the model by soldering, such painting will need to be done after the wires are fitted.

As with all jobs on the scale model, rigging needs care and attention because it is a highly visible part of the model ship. Small mistakes, such as poor knots or lashings, will be easily spotted. Practice knotting and lashing the cordage away from the model until some degree of competence is achieved. Whenever a poorly finished rope is found, cut it away and do it again. It is best to fit all the standing rigging before attempting any of the running rigging. The standing rigging will then support further work and the running rigging will not foul it. Blocks are discussed in greater detail in a later chapter.

15
Deck Fittings

At an early stage in the construction of a model it is a good idea to make an itemised list of all the deck fittings that will be needed. This will show what has to be made or perhaps purchased and also if any need to be completed and fitted at a particular stage of construction before access to their position is lost through something else being fitted. A further advantage of such a list is that it can be extended to show when an item has been made, whether it has been painted or if this is to be left until it has been fitted, and when it was so fitted. In this way there is little chance of a small item being omitted.

Guard rails

All ships, with few exceptions, have guard or other rails of one kind or another. Those with steel or timber bulwarks will have cap-

ping rails along the top edge and these are often of timber where there are steel bulwarks. Such rails are simply simulated using strips of hardwood, shaped to conform to the curves of the bulwarks and secured with adhesives. Rails of mahogany or teak are very decorative, mahogany being the preferred material in full-size practice. Some of these rails, in full size, were surmounted by small stanchions supporting a wire rail for additional safety where the bulwarks are low. An example of this is shown in the photographs of the herring drifter *Formidable*, which also show the timber top rail quite clearly. Figs 15/1 and 2 show the construction.

Most rails consist of a number of bars or tubes supported by stanchions, as can be seen in many of the photographs in this volume. The average height of the top of the top rail from the deck is 3ft 6in

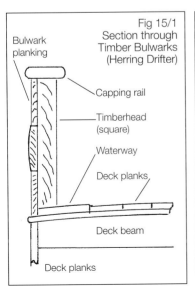

Fig 15/1
Section through
Timber Bulwarks
(Herring Drifter)

Bulwark planking

Capping rail

Timberhead (square)

Waterway

Deck planks

Deck beam

Deck planks

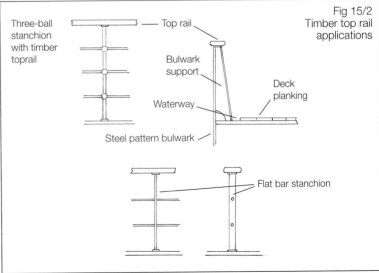

Fig 15/2
Timber top rail
applications

Three-ball stanchion with timber toprail

Top rail

Bulwark support

Waterway

Deck planking

Steel pattern bulwark

Flat bar stanchion

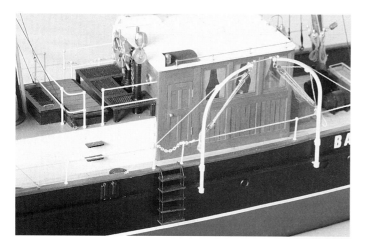

(Above)
Midships view of *Chimaera* model showing single and double stanchions with chain section in way of boarding ladder.

(Right)
Partly completed shelter deck on model of *Glenrose I* showing flat bar stanchions. Note top rail of larger section than lower rails and some sections with wire rope in place of rod.

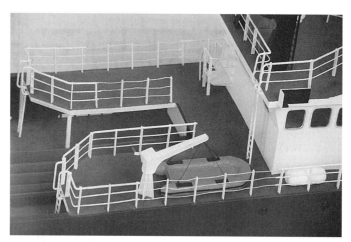

are not unusual, with the top (tube) rail being a larger diameter than that of the lower rails. The top rail is sometimes formed from varnished timber. Where access through the rails is needed for boarding or other reasons, portable sections of rail, which could be lifted out, were fitted. Sometimes a length of light wire or chain would be put across the opening as a temporary safety measure. Sometimes light chain would be used to close a space between two stanchions where the boarding ladders were fitted and here the chain would carry hooks for easy disconnection. Fig 15/3 shows a number of different types of stanchions.

On the more modern ship, stanchions are mainly made from flat bar, either drilled to accept the lower rails or to which they and the top rails are welded. In some instances rails are made from standard size steel tubes to which screwed bends and fittings of standard design are attached – an example of this can be seen in some of the photographs.

Stanchions for rails on a model ship must be correctly spaced, aligned and truly vertical. Where stanchions are positioned close to the edge of a deck, it is better to leave off fitting the rails until the model is almost complete to avoid having to stretch over them. It is also better to paint sections of rail in the final colour finish before installing them in holes drilled along the edges of a deck. However, flat bar stanchions, such as those seen in the pictures of *Glenrose I*, were not glued into the styrene deck but were heated and pushed into small pilot holes, the heat melting the styrene round the stanchion and sealing each one in place. Obviously

(1.05m) but on some passenger ships the rails are higher. Two, three or four rails are the usual kinds to be found although, again on some passenger ships, five or more rails

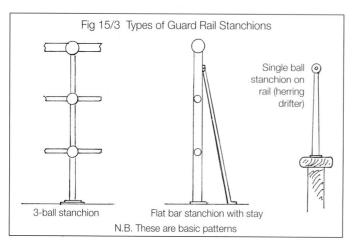

Fig 15/3 Types of Guard Rail Stanchions

Single ball stanchion on rail (herring drifter)

3-ball stanchion   Flat bar stanchion with stay
N.B. These are basic patterns

the top rail needed to be soldered with care using a small heat sink on the stanchion to prevent the heat from the iron reaching the deck. In this instance the rails could not be painted until after they had been installed. This method is recommended only for a model built to a large scale where stanchions and rails are reasonably substantial. A ship's rails must be made and fitted accurately, for they are a prominent part of a model and poor rails will detract from an otherwise fine vessel. Take time to step back and view the rails from various angles and always ensure that the stanchions remain straight and vertical. On very small scale models an effective way of making horizontal rails is to use fine cord drawn fairly tightly through the stanchion holes and secured at intervals with Superglue. Once painted such rails look quite well and, if accidentally bumped, will not usually distort.

Ladders and companions

Ladders and companionways are an integral part of a ship's fittings. A number of commercial firms produce laddering in brass, metal, plastic and wood, but very often the commercial product is not to the same scale as the model and there is no alternative but to make one's own (something which the purist will do anyway). Plain laddering is not difficult to make either from styrene rod and strip or from brass, but it will be necessary to make a jig like that

(Above)
Stern of model of *Arran Mail* showing companion ladder. Each tread is formed of two lengths of brass rod and the sides are of styrene strip and the handrails of brass rod.

(Left)
Stern view of *Jonrix* model showing two companion ladders and other relevant detail. Scale 1:75

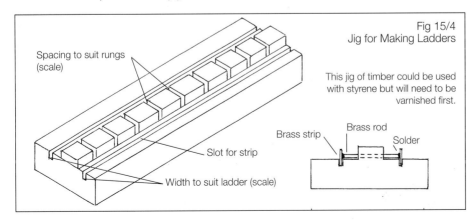

Fig 15/4
Jig for Making Ladders

Spacing to suit rungs (scale)

Slot for strip

Width to suit ladder (scale)

This jig of timber could be used with styrene but will need to be varnished first.

Brass strip

Brass rod

Solder

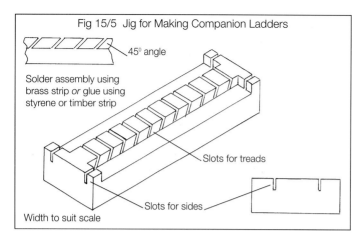

Fig 15/5 Jig for Making Companion Ladders

45° angle

Solder assembly using brass strip *or* glue using styrene or timber strip

Slots for treads

Slots for sides

Width to suit scale

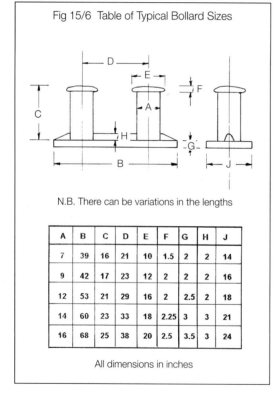

Fig 15/6 Table of Typical Bollard Sizes

N.B. There can be variations in the lengths

A	B	C	D	E	F	G	H	J
7	39	16	21	10	1.5	2	2	14
9	42	17	23	12	2	2	2	16
12	53	21	29	16	2	2.5	2	18
14	60	23	33	18	2.25	3	3	21
16	68	25	38	20	2.5	3.5	3	24

All dimensions in inches

ber and metal are available from sources shown in Appendix 2. For the small scales they can be bought as brass or nickel etchings and folded up into the correct shape. Such etched companions are shown in the stern view of the coaster *Jonrix*. The handrails, made of brass wire, were added using Superglue and the units were painted before being fitted on the model. A jig, such as that shown in Fig 15/5 is needed when making companion ladders, whether in brass, timber or plastic. Certain rules need to be followed: for example, the rungs of standard ladders are normally set at intervals of 9in (225mm)whereas the treads of a companion ladder are usually set at 7in (175mm) spacing. Companion ladders slope at about 45° from the vertical and almost always have handrails. Standard ladders are usually vertical or nearly so and quite often have no handrails.

General Arrangement drawings normally show the position of ladders and companions, but on some ships a companion from the deck below is shown only within a small housing, with access doors on the weather or main deck. These small companion tops are easily made from plywood or styrene. On older ships they were quite decorative, with nicely executed panelling, stained and varnished. Panelling can be made from small strips of veneer glued with a contact adhesive and stained and varnished. Door furniture can be simulated from small brass pin heads or nail heads, while small pieces of brass can be used for hinges. Alternatively it may be possible to find decorative real brass hinges in model shops or those shops catering for the doll's house enthusiasts.

Bollards

There are many fittings on the decks of ships and in some cases their size and construction are governed by the rules of the Classification Societies. Bollards are a prominent fitting, generally used to tie the ship to the quayside or for similar purposes,

shown in Fig 15/4 to ensure uniformity. Some of the photographs show plain ladders from various sources. An excellent source of good ladders in small scales comes from the producers of brass and nickel etchings and sometimes these can be found in shops specialising in model railways where the ladders are used for signals.

Companion ladders are a little more difficult to make. Many sizes in plastic, tim-

and their size depends upon the size of the ship and the purpose for which they are used. A GA drawing will show the positions of the bollards and often indicate the size and type. A table of bollard sizes is given in Fig 15/6. Plastic or aluminium knitting needles are an excellent source of accurate round rod from which to make bollards. Today the sizing of knitting needles is metric, thus a needle marked 5 will be 5mm diameter and one marked 6.5 will be 6.5mm. By gripping a length of needle in the chuck of an electric drill it is easy to cut off short lengths using a fine saw. They can be glued to the base using Superglue or epoxy, with a thin cap cut from plastic sheet fitted to each top. For angled pattern bollards the needle must be cut at an angle to suit.

Fairleads

Fairleads are used to guide ropes over the ship's side to the bollards, capstan, winch etc. They vary in type and size, and some are shown in Fig 15/7. These can be bought from some model shops but can be easily fashioned from small scraps of brass or styrene using small files. Again the position of such fittings is normally shown on the drawings, but in the absence of a detail drawing have a look at photographs or, as a last resort, use common sense to place the fairlead where it will obviously be needed. Some fairleads are simple castings with rounded corners where the ropes run, others are more complex and have rollers on vertical spindles to guide the ropes.

Ventilators

Around most ships' decks are a number of ventilators from the deep tanks and other compartments, often of the type shown in Fig 15/8 and known as 'gooseneck vents'. Pipes with small hinged covers, known as sounding pipes, which allow rods to be inserted to check for level of water, fuel, etc. These are shown in the sketches. Often photographs will show such fittings more clearly than drawings. They do give an authentic atmosphere to a model when fit-

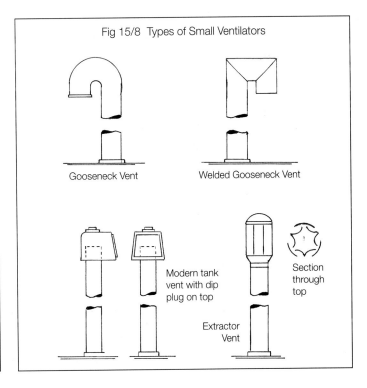

Fig 15/7 Types of Fairleads

Standard cast pattern 'A'

Panama pattern 'B' deck or bulwark mounting

Roller Pattern 'C' Roller fairleads can have closed tops and three sheaves

The standard pattern 'A' can be purchased from most specialist model shops in various sizes according to scale. Patterns 'B' & 'C' are not readily available in model form.

Fig 15/8 Types of Small Ventilators

Gooseneck Vent

Welded Gooseneck Vent

Modern tank vent with dip plug on top

Extractor Vent

Section through top

Aft deck of
Scott Guardian, model
under construction.
Note small vents
surrounding stores
hatch in centre and
cargo lashing rails.
DAVID MILTON

direction. Examples of cowl ventilators can be seen in some of the photographs and in Fig 15/9. In the case of a model fitted with a steam plant it may be wise to make such cowl vents functional. Many of the model manufacturers mentioned in the appendices have cowl ventilators in their range of fittings, some being of brass, some of resin and some in white metal. Cowl ventilators are not too difficult to make and they can be formed in styrene sheet in a manner similar to vacuum forming. A wooden plug or former must first be to made to the shape of the cowl but to less than the finished size by the thickness of the styrene sheet that is to be used. Having made the plug as shown in Fig 15/10, a circular hole just larger than the maximum diameter of the plug should be cut in plywood of 3 to 4mm thick and about 1in (25mm) larger all round than the hole. Cut a piece of thin styrene sheet to cover the plywood and secure it to the ply with adhesive tape – masking tape is ideal. Using an electric paint stripper gun or similar heat source, gently heat the styrene until it can be seen to soften in the area of the hole in the ply. Quickly push the former into the

ted. An example of such vents is shown in the photograph of the stern deck of the rescue ship *Scott Guardian*, the stores hatch in the picture is surrounded by ventilators.

The most common type of ventilator has always been the cowl ventilator and it is to be seen on vessels of all types. Its purpose is to supply fresh air to the ship and also extract (foul) air when necessary. The former is done by turning the cowl to face the direction in which the ship is travelling and the latter by turning it in the opposite

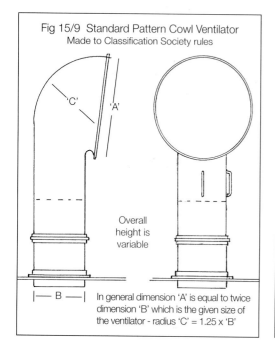

Fig 15/9 Standard Pattern Cowl Ventilator
Made to Classification Society rules

'C' 'A'

Overall
height is
variable

|— B —| In general dimension 'A' is equal to twice
dimension 'B' which is the given size of
the ventilator - radius 'C' = 1.25 x 'B'

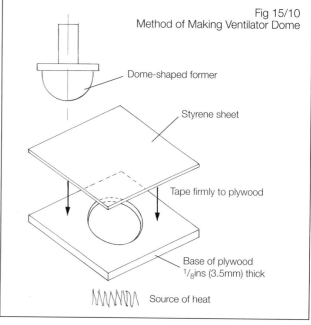

Fig 15/10
Method of Making Ventilator Dome

Dome-shaped former

Styrene sheet

Tape firmly to plywood

Base of plywood
$1/_8$ins (3.5mm) thick

Source of heat

Large cowl ventilators ahead of the funnel on *Kingston Peridot* made from styrene sheet as described in this chapter. These ventilators were made functional to feed air to the Cheddar Models steam plant.

Engine-room casing and pilots' cabin of Tyne pilot cutter *Britannia*. Model to 1:24 scale. Cowl vents on this ship were tall and slender.

styrene squarely over the hole until it meets the ply and allow the styrene to cool. The resultant cowl can be carefully cut away from the sheet and trimmed to its final form. The stem of the ventilator can be made from a length of dowel or from plastic tube or rod. Details such as the handles used for turning the ventilator into or against the wind and the flanges of the stem can be simulated card or styrene sheet.

Other types of ventilator used for air supply or extraction, some known as mushroom vents, can be seen on many ships, and come in a very large range of sizes from only a few inches or centimetres to as much as 6ft (2m) in diameter (see Fig 15/11 overleaf). Some ventilators differ where they are intakes for mechanical ventilation systems and are often large trunks shaped similarly to a goose neck. Many of these mechanical units are marked as 'Thermotank' units, this being the name of the company who made them. Similarly, on some vessels, there is shown a 'Thermotank' room, which contains several such units. The air supply for the latter and, indeed, for other units elsewhere within a house or

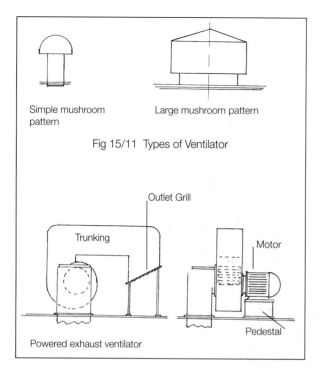

Simple mushroom pattern

Large mushroom pattern

Fig 15/11 Types of Ventilator

Outlet Grill

Trunking

Motor

Pedestal

Powered exhaust ventilator

casing, is obtained through large grilles set high up in the house/casing side.

Coaling hatches

Coal-fired steam ships will have coal hatches on the main deck on either side of the boiler room or engine room casing. These are generally circular in shape, with covers which lock into rings set in the deck. They can be made from thin ply or styrene and set into the deck planking so that they come flush with the top surface of the deck. The area around such hatches on a wood deck is frequently stained by the coal dust which becomes ingrained into the timber.

Access hatches

Access hatches for stores, shaft tunnel escape etc, are also sited on the decks. Some are plain with simple hinged covers on a low coaming and easily constructed from scraps of timber or styrene. Others are more complex, with the locking handwheel on top of the hinged cover. The

photographs of *Scott Guardian* clearly show such a hatch which was made from small pieces of styrene and fitted with an etched brass handwheel. The amount of small detail in the way of fittings which can be included on a hatch will depend largely upon the scale of the model. Small hatch covers are often secured by tightening butterfly nuts on swivel bolts, but escape hatches have to have a means of quickly releasing the locking system from both sides and this is usually done with a handwheel.

Anchors, chain stoppers etc

Cleats, frequently fitted round the rails or bulwarks to which ropes can be secured, are simply made from thin brass wire bent to shape and secured in place with five-minute epoxy or Superglue. The hawse pipe covers and chain stoppers are prominent parts of the forward deck of any ship. They can vary quite a lot and some types are shown in some of the photographs. The types of anchor that are found on ships vary and one of the commonest and most widely used is that known as the 'Hall'

(Right)
Bow of *Jonrix* model showing 'Hall' anchor drawn up into hawse pipe.

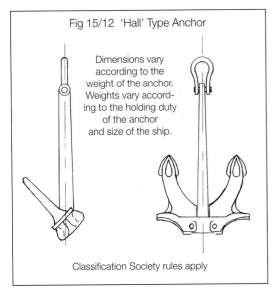

Fig 15/12 'Hall' Type Anchor

Dimensions vary
according to the
weight of the anchor.
Weights vary accord-
ing to the holding duty
of the anchor
and size of the ship.

Classification Society rules apply

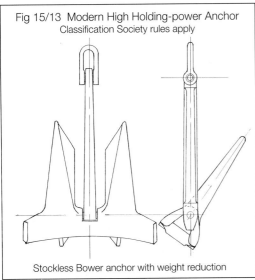

Fig 15/13 Modern High Holding-power Anchor
Classification Society rules apply

Stockless Bower anchor with weight reduction

similar heavy-duty type as seen in the photograph of *Keila* and in Fig 15/13. As can be seen, anchors come in various sizes and are fitted to ships according to the ship's size and to comply with the rules of the appropriate Classification Society. An assessment of size can be gained from the GA drawings, which often show a stowed anchor, and by examination of photographs. If the drawings do not illustrate an anchor then consultation of the Society rules and reference to their tables will assist the modeller to fit an anchor of about the right size.

Anchors of many types are available from a number of specialist model shops and mail order outlets, some being available in brass and others in white metal. It is necessary to select the correct size and most of these anchors are sized by the length of the stock (shaft). By referring to the calculations given in the appendices, the modeller will be able to select the required anchor by comparing stock length with the other given dimensions.

Anchor chain – more correctly called cable – is normally of the stud link pattern (see Fig 15/14), and such chain cable was not available from the model shop at the time of writing. An excellent range of chain of many different sizes is, however, available off the shelf at most good model shops or from mail order suppliers. It is usually sold by the metre or foot and it is sized according to the number of links in

anchor, which can be seen in the photographs of *Jonrix* and in the sketch 15/12. Some of the most modern ships are now fitted with anchors of the Danforth or

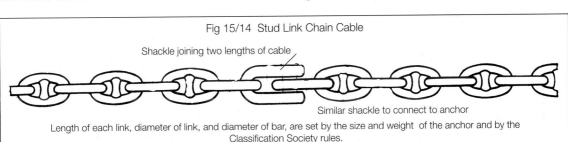

Fig 15/14 Stud Link Chain Cable

Shackle joining two lengths of cable

Similar shackle to connect to anchor

Length of each link, diameter of link, and diameter of bar, are set by the size and weight of the anchor and by the Classification Society rules.

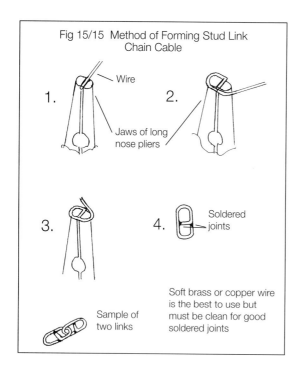

Fig 15/15 Method of Forming Stud Link Chain Cable

1. Wire — Jaws of long nose pliers

2.

3.

4. Soldered joints

Sample of two links

Soft brass or copper wire is the best to use but must be clean for good soldered joints

Stud link chain cable can be made from thin brass wire. Each link will have to be soldered as it is formed. This is not so difficult as it sounds but does require patience and time. A pair of round-nosed pliers are needed to shape the links, starting at the stud bar and bending the wire into the required shape shown in Fig 15/15. A small soldering-iron will close the link at the end. The next link needs to be shaped with the wire running through the previous link and closing the joint with the soldering-iron needs to be done with care. Once the first few links have been made successfully it becomes easier to proceed. As little of the anchor cable is visible on the average merchant ship, only a short length of chain will be needed.

Hawse pipes and anchor stowage also differ. On some ships the hawse pipes terminate in a simple flange over the plating near the bow, whereas on others a box is built into the hull plating into which the anchor almost disappears. Whilst some of the smaller modern merchant ships carry only one anchor stowed ready for immediate use with a second fitted on deck but without chain cable attached, most vessels have two anchors stowed ready for immediate use, with the chain cables running over the windlass. Sometimes a third anchor is carried as a spare. On a working

each inch. It is usually in plain brass finish but can also be bought finished black or even silver. Little of the chain cable will be seen on the merchant ship where it appears from the hawse pipe, runs through the chain stopper and over the windlass to disappear through the deck into the chain locker. Where it is visible it may be a rusty colour or on some vessels it may be white or black.

Detail view of herring drifter by David Deadman showing steam capstan, net floats, rigging to deadeyes etc.

model, hawse pipes must be sealed to the hull at top and bottom to prevent any water from leaking into the hull. Brass tubes are the best material to use for forming the hawse pipes as this material is easily soldered and can be firmly glued in place with epoxy or similar adhesives. The bore of the tube should be sufficient to allow the chain to slide through it freely and, of course, the ends of the tubes need to be trimmed to fit the ship's side and the deck. The GA drawing will usually show the line of the hawse pipe which, when fitted, will show an oval aspect. It is also usual for the hawse pipe to accept the stock of the anchor so that the flukes will lie tightly against the side plating of the ship when the anchor is drawn up and locked in place with the chain stopper.

It is rare to find a ship today with an anchor of the common stocked kind, although herring drifters carried such anchors which were raised and lowered by the capstan and secured over the ship's side by lifting with a small anchor davit not unlike a lifeboat davit. The capstans of such ships were fitted with a cable lifter below the warping drum round which the anchor cable was passed to raise or lower the anchor. A drifter capstan is shown in a number of the photographs.

Navigation lights

Navigation lights, whether working or static, are prominent features of any ship model and, once more, they must conform to the rules of the Classification Society which are also the rules used universally for all lights at sea. Basically the merchant ship under way at night must show a white light from the foremast visible over ten points of the compass on either side of the centre line of the ship. A second light, of the same range and mounted 15ft (4.5m) higher than the first, is normally mounted slightly further aft. Most ships also carry a stern light visible over six points of the compass on either side of the centreline. On the

port side of the ship there must be a red light so arranged to show an unbroken light from straight ahead to two points abaft the beam and on the starboard side a similarly-arranged light showing green. These port and starboard lights are usually fitted into light boards which are today painted black and which are arranged to restrict the visibility of the light to the rules. Prior to the mid-1970s such port and starboard light boards were painted to match the colour of the light – green for starboard, red for port. There are also regulations which govern the display of lights to indicate when a vessel is towing or under tow, when it is not moving or not under command etc. When modelling a tug or a fishing vessel both have a 'Christmas tree' of lights at the main mast and of various colours to be illuminated when necessary to indicate what they are doing. Such lights need to be shown correctly. To be precise regarding lights one needs to consider the period during which the selected ship is in service, since the regulations laid down by the Board of Trade, Lloyd's etc have been altered over the years. Most GA drawings will give details of the mast lights and many of the model magazines and those devoted to full-size ships carry articles from time to time which give details of the current regulations. It is necessary for the modeller to seek out such information from some of the sources already given in Chapter 3. A request to one of the still-working shipbuilding companies mat result in a copy of a drawing giving details of the 'Christmas Tree' fitted to a recent ship which will provide valuable information.

The earlier ships' lamps were oil-lit and the rules required that two of each lamp must be carried at all times. Later, when electricity became the norm, ships were required to carry standby oil lamps which were frequently mounted above the electric units. Today ships have standby lights which are battery-powered in addition to the main units. It can thus be seen that most ships will show two lamp units in pairs above each other, the more modern being totally electric, the earlier being one of each. There is a good range of both plain and illuminated lights available from the specialist model shop, many of which are made from brass and are of good quality. The range also covers a number of sizes and types from which the modeller can select the lamps best suited to the period of his/her model. Making suitable lamps is a task needing a little care and an electric drill. Clear plastic rod (perspex or similar) can be chucked in the drill and gently turned using small files to give the required shape of the lamp. A small hole drilled part way through the base of each lamp will allow the inside to be given a coat of red or green paint or will permit a small coloured bulb to be fitted. The base and backing for the lamp can be made from small pieces of brass or styrene after which it can be mounted in the appropriate position on the ship. Details of wiring to illuminate the lamps is given later.

Casting in white metal and resin

Where there are a number of identical small parts on the scale model, it is much easier to make one very accurate master of the fitting and to use this master to make a mould in silicon rubber in which the required number of the fitting can be cast. The process of casting in either white metal or in resin is a simple one but the moulds and the masters need to be made with care. The two processes differ as detailed below.

There are several types of white metal for casting, all rated according to the chemical makeup of the component metals. The most commonly used contain a mixture of lead and tin or lead and bismuth. Finer flowing and higher quality metal contains lead, tin and antimony and the finest is pewter which is an alloy of tin, antimony and copper. All have different melting points and they are used for making all manner of parts for various trades including jewellery. Metals known as No 3 and No 4 sold by Alec Tiranti Ltd (see Appendix 3) are most suited to making parts for a model ship and this company also produces a beginner's outfit for casting in white metal. As just mentioned the first job is to make a master of good quality and without any flaws or scratches, for these will also be reproduced in the castings. The master can be made from wood, plastics or brass as the moulding material does not generate heat to damage the master but a good surface finish is essential. Next a box must be made of thin ply or styrene, deep enough to contain sufficient moulding material to allow the master to be sunk in it to half of its depth, and with 8 to 10mm of moulding rubber all round the master. Fig 15/16 and the photographs illustrates the box.

The silicon rubber moulding material comes as a very thick, red-oxide coloured compound to which a catalyst must be mixed in exact proportions. It is necessary to weigh out the quantity of rubber using a good set of (kitchen) scales. To assess the quantity of rubber needed to fill the mould box, fill the box with water to the brim, pour it into a plastic cup, mark the level of the water on the cup, empty it and then dry the cup thoroughly, then pour in the rubber up to the same mark. Add the required number of drops of catalyst specified in the mixing instructions and stir well. Stand the mix in a very warm place for at least half an hour to allow all the entrapped air to be released. This is a slow process but

(Below)
Two halves of rubber mould for a small deck vent with sample of casting shown.
DAVID MILTON

(Bottom)
Both halves of mould for a tugger winch rotor with the master of the rotor turned from a plastic knitting needle shown alongside
DAVID MILTON

even in a very warm atmosphere the rubber will take at least twelve hours to cure and set. Fix the master firmly into the mould box supporting it on thin wire or in some way that will keep half of it above the top of the box. Pour the catalysed rubber carefully into the box until it reaches the top, taking care and trying to avoid covering the master above the halfway mark with rubber. Place the mould box in a warm place for at least twelve hours. In winter the best place is the domestic airing cupboard or the top of the central heating boiler. In summer the sill of a south-facing window is adequate. Note that the silicon rubber will not cure if the temperature is less than 70^0 F (20^0 C).

On the next day, test that the rubber has solidified and clean the top edges of the box. Spray the top of the rubber with a thin coating of silicon polish and build another box over the first in which to pour the second half of the mould. Seal the top section to the bottom to prevent the rubber from leaking through. Mix a second batch of rubber with catalyst, pour it into the box to the top edge and set it aside to cure as before. Do not attempt to dismantle the mould box until the rubber has had an adequate curing time which, for safety, should be about twenty-four hours.

Take the mould box to pieces very carefully and gently pull the two halves of the mould apart. If they have been treated with silicon polish or wax they will part fairly easily. Remove the master and examine the two halves for any flaws. The next task is to provide a pouring spout in the rubber and to cut any air-release ways and this can be done as shown in the sketches using a very sharp craft knife. It is also wise to fit the mould halves with some form of locating pins so that they always go together correctly. Cut two pieces of 3.0mm plywood to fit the sides of the rubber parts and, after dusting the two halves with talcum powder, clamp them together using strong rubber bands and, if available, the spring clip that comes in the beginner's

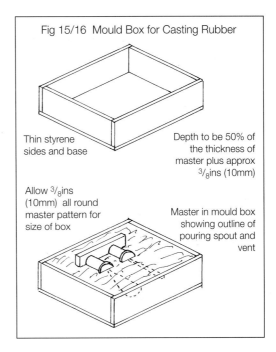

Fig 15/16 Mould Box for Casting Rubber

Thin styrene sides and base

Depth to be 50% of the thickness of master plus approx $3/_8$ins (10mm)

Allow $3/_8$ins (10mm) all round master pattern for size of box

Master in mould box showing outline of pouring spout and vent

casting kit. Melt one or two small pieces of the alloy in a suitable container (the small melting pot from Tiranti is ideal), and test that the molten metal is at the correct heat by putting the end of a matchstick into the melt. If the stick chars, the temperature is correct for pouring. Carefully pour the metal into the mould until it is full and gently tap the sides of the mould to release any trapped air. Allow a few minutes for the mould to cool and the alloy to set before opening it up and checking the casting. It is more than likely that the first one or two attempts will be unsatisfactory but the metal can be returned to the pot and reheated. Where there are parts of the mould into which the metal does not flow, it will be obvious that air is being trapped and thus a thin slot needs to be cut into the rubber to allow such air to escape. The small stalks of metal and rough seams that sometimes show can be removed quite easily with a sharp knife and the casting trimmed with small files. Before painting the finished casting it is best to burnish it with a small wire brush such as is used for cleaning suede.

Casting in resin is very similar to the

above but the rubber can be of a different composition. Strand Plastics provide a rubber compound suitable for making moulds for resin casting and the compound rubber called 'Gelflex', which melts and is re-useable, is also suitable. In the case of Gelflex the masters will need to be made from metal as the rubber is only molten when heated and it must be treated differently. This product has not been detailed here since the user needs to seek detailed instructions from the suppliers. The other rubber compound is pourable at room temperatures and thus the masters can be made from materials other than metal. Resin will not run into fine small spaces so one should confine the casting to fairly large parts with very little undercut (see Fig 15/17).

For casting in resin begin by making a mould box in the same way as before allowing at least 10mm of solid rubber space all round the master. Secure the master into the mould to half of its depth as before. Mix and pour the rubber in the same manner and allow a minimum of twelve hours curing time. Build up the upper box, treat the lower mould surface with dusting of talc or silicon wax and pour the second batch of rubber. After full curing time part the mould and examine carefully. Note that most suppliers of the rubber compounds can provide rubber in paste form for carrying out repairs to moulds which have been damaged. Make a pouring spout and airways as before and then prepare the resin mixture.

The polyester resin suppliers all stock casting resin in one or two forms. Ordinary lay-up or gelcoat resin is not suitable for casting. Normally, casting resin is clear so that a powder needs to be added to make opaque castings. Such powder is readily available from the suppliers. Mix up the required quantity of resin with powder and finally add the necessary catalyst, after weighing the mix to assess the correct quantity of catalyst to be added in accordance with the maker's instructions. Once the resin has been catalysed, allow only a few minutes for the trapped air to escape before pouring it into the mould. Resin gets quite hot due to the chemical action that occurs during the curing process and the mould should be left for an hour or two before it is opened and the casting removed. Resin castings need to be left for a short while in a warm place to dry out, as the surface is sometimes tacky until it has been exposed to air for a short period. One pleasing aspect of resin casting is that metal powders can be added to the resin before it is catalysed to simulate the metallic appearance of the metal used in the prototype. For example, brass filings used correctly by quantity will give the resin casting the appearance of brass.

White metal and resin castings available commercially have usually been produced with a centrifugal casting machine fed from temperature-controlled metal melting crucibles. Alec Tiranti Ltd supply a small centrifugal casting machine and metal melting pots for the modelmaker but these are rather expensive if only a few parts are needed. It is, however, a feasible purchase for a model boat club where its cost could be shared among the members who could then buy the necessary materials and produce castings in greater detail.

White metal, silicon rubbers, resins etc, are all materials which carry some warnings regarding use and in relation to health. Such warnings should not be ignored and sensible precautions as laid down in the user instructions should always be followed. They are not intended to frighten the user away but simply to advise how he or she can safely make good use of the material. A well-ventilated workplace is the principle criterion.

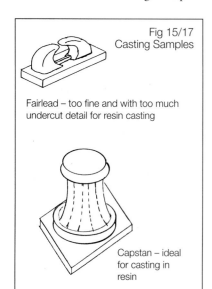

Fig 15/17
Casting Samples

Fairlead – too fine and with too much undercut detail for resin casting

Capstan – ideal for casting in resin

16
Lifeboats & Davits

All ships must carry lifeboats of one kind or another and also self-inflating liferafts (dinghies) stored in canisters. Lifeboats are carried on the upper decks and are handled by a system of davits, which are small cranes specifically designed to lower and raise lifeboats. Some ships today carry a totally-enclosed lifeboat mounted on a slip at the stern from which the lifeboat can slide rapidly into the water in an emergency. A smaller merchant ship often carries only one semi-inflatable lifeboat big enough to accommodate the whole crew and which can be lowered into the water by a small hand-operated crane. One is shown in the photographs of the coaster *Timrix*.

still being mostly clinker-built, some being fitted with small engines and propellers, whilst others were fitted with a system of levers which when operated by those on board drove a propeller. Development and research brought in lifeboats made from aluminium, steel and moulded glass-fibre, the latter being the most commonly used today.

The lifeboats are an important part of a model and, if not well-researched and

(Left)
Stern of model *Timrix* showing semi-rigid inflatable boat and hand-operated crane. With a crew of only seven men this is an adequate lifeboat arrangement. Scale 1:75.

(Below)
Davits under construction on model of steam trawler *Kingston Peridot*, scale 1:48. Note superb model lifeboat from Quaycraft.

Lifeboats

The earliest lifeboats were clinker-built of wood and propelled by oars. They had no buoyancy aids and were little more than large dinghies of the type that can be seen on the lakes near the sea. Progress and safety measures demanded that the lifeboat be made into an unsinkable unit and buoyancy tanks were fitted at bow and stern and also along the sides. Following the disaster of the *Titanic*, all ships were required to carry sufficient lifeboats to contain the entire complement of the ship's passengers and crew plus a safety percentage. Newer lifeboats appeared, those of wood

correctly made, will mar its final appearance. A saving grace from most modellers' point of view is that almost all lifeboats when stowed are fitted with a canvas cover which effectively conceals the interior of the boat. Lifeboat covers are usually supported from inside the boat by a timber framework so that it assumes a tentlike shape to shed water. Sometimes the cover support is of rope stretched between the bow and stern. In both cases the canvas tends to sag and is not very tightly drawn. It is sensible for the modeller to observe the lifeboats of full-size ships to gain an indication of how such covers lie. Fitting a model lifeboat with a cover does eliminate the need to spend many hours fitting ribs, thwarts, knees, oars etc, to the inside of the boat. The covers are easily made from scraps of tissue tensioned with cellulose dope as used by the model aircraft modeller, or in the larger scales made from scraps of thin cotton. Even if the lifeboat is modelled with a cover, it is necessary to fit hand ropes to match the full-size detail.

The lifeboat, its size, type and construction fall under the control in the UK of the Department of Trade (formerly the Board of Trade). Within its publications can be found tables listing sizes and requirements for ships' lifeboat. General arrangement drawings usually indicate the number, size and type of lifeboats fitted to a ship and their positions.

If the model ship carries more than one or two boats, it is a good idea to make a suitable mould from which a number can be formed. In the same way that a completed model hull can be used for making a GRP mould so can a model lifeboat hull be used (see earlier detail in Chapter 8). It is not necessary to make a production mould in two halves as a single mould will generally be adequate. The method of working does not differ from that described before except that only small quantities of materials are involved. Thin glass tissue can be used instead of glass cloth when moulding the small hull which will result in a lightweight construction.

It is also possible to mould the model lifeboat in the GRP mould using *papier mache* instead of resin and glass cloth. Small squares of newsprint soaked in thinned PVA adhesive should be applied to a well-waxed mould and laid over each other until a reasonable thickness is built up. After allowing a fairly lengthy period for the *papier mache* to dry out, the shell can be removed, treated with a sanding sealer and then painted and varnished. Such lifeboat shells are light in weight and, if necessary, can be fitted out with ribs, thwarts, rowlocks, oars etc.

The method used by the author to produce a lifeboat master is to cut the shape of the keel, including bow and stern, and the whole shape of the ship to the sheer of the topsides from thin plywood. This can be checked by placing the shape over a scale drawing. Two blocks of balsa or jelutong are next cut and each roughly carved to the shape of one half of the boat. These blocks are then glued on either side of the keel and the assembly laid to one side until the glue has set. Using templates as guides to the hull shape at various points along the keel, the blocks are carved and sanded to the final shape, after which the whole plug is sealed and painted before being waxed and used for making a mould. If the lifeboat is to be of clinker-built form then, before painting the plug, it is necessary to fit thin strips of card or veneer to simulate the clinker planks.

Where only one, or perhaps two, lifeboats are carried on the ship being modelled, they can be constructed in a number of different ways depending upon how they are to be displayed. For boats to be shown complete with covers then the method described above will suffice. If fully-detailed boats are required, then shells will need to be made and outfitted. The method described above to make the plug is still the best way of producing a suitable shell which can be formed over the plug using thin ply, veneer or even plastic sheet in strips. For this, however, the keel needs to be part of the shell and thus the plug or former must have a groove in which a suitable keel can be

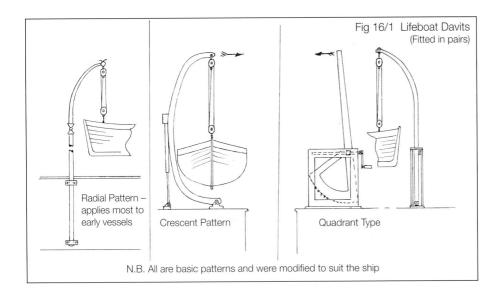

Fig 16/1 Lifeboat Davits
(Fitted in pairs)

Radial Pattern – applies most to early vessels

Crescent Pattern

Quadrant Type

N.B. All are basic patterns and were modified to suit the ship

set and to which the shell can fixed. Such lifeboat shells are quite delicate when removed from the former and need the ribs and thwarts to stiffen them and make them more firm.

On covered clinker-built boats the planking is visible only on the outside, but if the lifeboat is to be shown without a cover then it will be visible on the inside as well. Where the boat is to be used as a plug for moulding then the clinker planks will have to be fitted and secured before the master mould is made so that all moulded boats will carry the same clinker planking. Since the lifeboat is broadest amidships it will be obvious that the planks will need to taper to both bow and stern in order to fit correctly. Full details of making open boats is given in the book *Model Open Boats* by Ewart C Freeston, which, although now out of print, may be obtainable through libraries.

Davits

Lifeboat davits have changed over the years. In the earlier days of the powered ship they were simple swivel cranes mounted at the sides of the ship and between which the boat was slung. Later developments brought the quadrant type davit, the crescent and 'Lum' davits followed by the gravity type

units. All these types are illustrated in Fig 16/1 and the photographs. The ship's side below each pair of davits (lifeboat station) has to be kept clear of any obstructions which may hinder or prevent the boat being placed safely in the water. For example, a boarding ladder would not be positioned beneath a lifeboat station.

The radial davit, the commonest and earliest type of davit, can be made from brass rod. The rod should be tapered towards the top using a fine file until the correct shape is reached. The ball end at the top can be formed from the rod but can also be made from a suitable bead. The sketches show how such a davit would be rigged. Crescent

Radial davits and lifeboat (covered) on model of the Clyde passenger steamer *Duchess of Fife*. Note small cowl ventilators on top of the midships cabin.

(Below)
Starboard side of North Sea ferry *Norland* providing detail of gravity davits and boats. Note that none of the boats have covers.

(Bottom)
Further detail of lifeboats and davits on *Norland*. Note the tall guard rails with three intermediate bars and companion to upper deck.

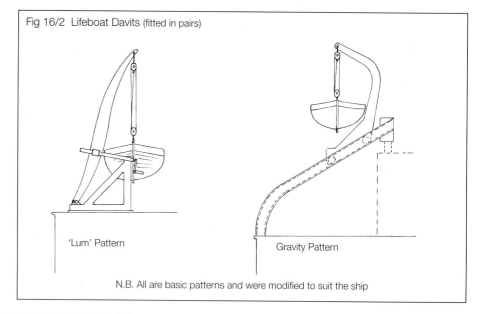

Fig 16/2 Lifeboat Davits (fitted in pairs)

'Lum' Pattern

Gravity Pattern

N.B. All are basic patterns and were modified to suit the ship

and 'Lum' type davits need to be made from sheet material such as styrene, brass or other sheet and the material used will govern how each is made. They are more complex than the early units and will need care to build accurately. Where a number of sets of davits are fitted it will be possible to make a master of the principle part of the davit and use it to make a mould in which further parts could be cast in white metal.

The standard type of gravity davit is fitted on the open boat deck. As will be seen from the illustrations, the boat in its cradle slides down the davit until it is suspended over the side of the ship, whereupon it can be lowered by the blocks and ropes (generally referred to as 'falls') into the water clear of the ship's side. Gravity davits can be a constructional exercise in themselves. Each trackway of a gravity davit is made up of two heavy channel bars, open parts facing each other, and between which the cradle runs with its rollers (wheels) on the lower flange of the channels. The two channels are held apart by tie plates fitted on the underside of the lower flanges. The inboard end of each track is secured either to the top or side of an adjacent deckhouse, or where there is no deckhouse, by an 'A' support. The outboard end is secured to the boat deck by

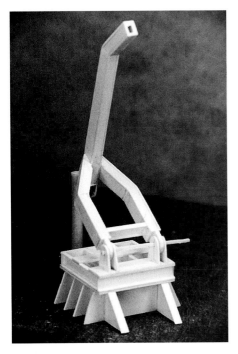

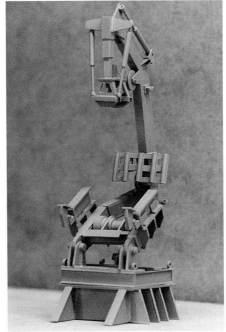

large triangular brackets. The track does not extend below the boat deck. If there is a promenade deck below the boat deck then heavy plate stanchions are fitted between the two decks in line with the foot of the track-way. The outboard end of the trackway, where it changes to the vertical, is either curved or angled depending upon the manufacturer. The cradle is normally of box form with a smooth outer surface on which the sheaves to take the falls are fitted. It is fitted with a bracket or chock to support the keel of the boat. Fig 16/2 shows some constructional details of the gravity davit. Suitable girders of channel and 'H' section can be found in the ranges of plastic mouldings now available at most model shops. Bending such sections needs care but can be achieved by warming the pieces in hot water and gently curving them while they are warm. The small rollers that carry the boat carriage and the finishing of the carriage can be seen clearly in the pictures.

Lifeboat and davit fittings

The falls (blocks and ropes) which lower the lifeboat to the water and recover it when necessary usually comprise triple-sheaved blocks having steel or, in earlier days, cast-iron frames with bronze sheaves. The ropes are normally of hemp or of plastic or nylon fibre. They are rarely hauled mechanically but the more modern forms of davits do have winches which can be electrically-driven or hand-operated. Skill is needed by the seamen using hand-operated falls to ensure that both sets are operated simultaneously. Fig 16/3 shows in diagrammatic form the way the ropes run between the sets of blocks.

Ships' blocks are a feature that is often

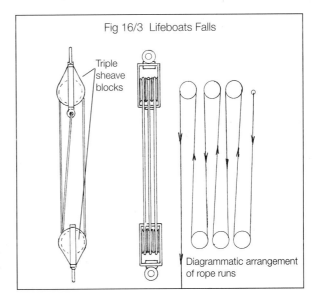

Fig 16/3 Lifeboats Falls

Triple sheave blocks

Diagrammatic arrangement of rope runs

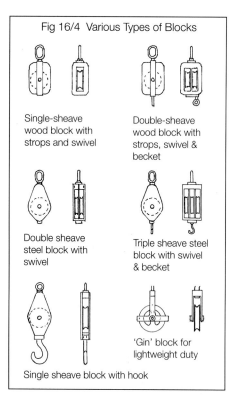

Fig 16/4 Various Types of Blocks

Single-sheave wood block with strops and swivel

Double-sheave wood block with strops, swivel & becket

Double sheave steel block with swivel

Triple sheave steel block with swivel & becket

Single sheave block with hook

'Gin' block for lightweight duty

incorrectly interpreted. In early times the blocks were made from timber and rope-stropped, *ie* they were hung using ropes. Later they were made from cast iron or steel and each is distinctive. Sheaves of the wooden blocks were usually of hardwood, then came sheaves of bronze or stainless steel. The sheave is the part of the block over which the rope runs, and which revolves with the movement of the rope. It is often called a pulley being similar to the pulleys of a car engine. Fig 16/4 illustrates a number of blocks. The average model shop will carry a range of timber blocks which are little more than small pieces of hardwood, grooved to indicate the sheaves and drilled for the cords, with additional grooves for the strops that attach the block to the relevant part of the ship. The steel or cast block in use today is rarely seen in the model shop and very few manufacturers make a range of such blocks.

The method of making blocks used by the author is shown in Fig 16/5. The sheaves are made from short pieces of plastic or aluminium knitting needle chucked in the electric drill and grooved before being cut off. The cheeks and straps are simply cut from sheet styrene and glued together with liquid poly. A small brass pin or length of brass rod forms the pin of the sheaves and, with care, the sheaves will be free to turn within the framework of the block. The pin is glued to the cheeks using Superglue, taking care to allow the sheaves to remain free to turn. According to the number of sheaves and how the block is mounted, the rings required for fixing the block to the mast or other piece of equipment are fixed to the strapping of the block. The attachment for the upper part of the block generally needs to swivel to allow the block to turn. While block-making can appear complex, it is really only necessary to work carefully and with patience to produce good blocks. Always allow adequate time for liquid poly and Superglue to cure fully before putting the block into service, particularly if it is to form part of a moving feature on the model.

As previously mentioned, a merchant ship at sea may well have most of the working blocks, save those of the lifeboats, dismounted and stowed away, so there will be many fewer blocks to make for a ship so depicted than for one shown approaching a port. It is possible that there are some items of fittings not mentioned in this section and just possible that some fittings are special to a given ship. Whatever the unusual fitting may be or whatever form it may take, it is more than likely that it can be made using one of the methods described or by fabricating it from specific shapes of material available from many sources. The unusual boat davits shown in the photographs of *Scott Guardian* are a typical example of such a fitting, but careful examination of the pictures will show that they could be made from standard styrene sections available from most model shops.

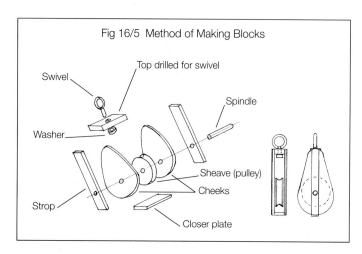

Fig 16/5 Method of Making Blocks

Swivel

Top drilled for swivel

Spindle

Washer

Sheave (pulley)

Cheeks

Strop

Closer plate

17
Winches, Windlasses & Capstans

The winch, windlass and capstan are all appliances designed to haul heavy weights but in different ways. The winch has a drum upon which rope can be wound, the windlass is specifically designed to handle the ship's anchors and the capstan is a similar unit but with its rope drum mounted on a vertical shaft. A chain cable lifter is rather like a capstan, but is fitted with a horizontal cable holder (that is, a shallow drum with indentations to take the links of the chain), round which the anchor cable passes. It is sometimes combined with a capstan head. It is fitted instead of an anchor windlass on some ships.

Winches

Winches on the very earliest steam-powered ships were simply rope drums geared to a handle which was turned manually, but few of these will be encountered by the merchant ship modeller. Steam-driven winches come in a considerable number of sizes, depending upon the load they have to handle, the smallest being found on the coaster and used with a derrick to lift, load and discharge cargo. All derricks and cranes have to be tested and certified for particular duties. On a heavy-lift ship the steam-driven winch would be quite large. Most winches have one or more drums of convex shape on the end(s) of the main shaft and used for hauling rope. When two or three turns of rope

(Top)
Winch on forward deck of North Sea ferry *Norsea* with capstan in foreground. Rod with bands is reading 100mm intervals to permit scaling off picture.

(Centre)
Windlass with rope drum on foredeck of *Norsea*. Note the anchor cable and the mooring warps of fibre.

(Lower)
Further view of the port windlass on *Norsea*. These units are driven by hydraulic power. The ventilation louvres in the superstructure are air intakes to the accommodation.

Model winches on *Arran Mail*, scale 1:32. Both units were made in timber.

Winches on *Arran Mail*. Both serve only one derrick. Handles control speed and operate the magnetic brakes.

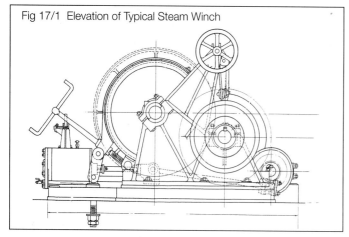

Fig 17/1 Elevation of Typical Steam Winch

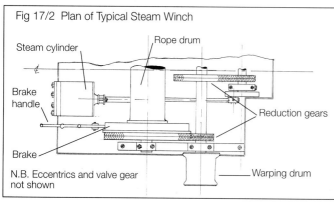

Fig 17/2 Plan of Typical Steam Winch

Steam cylinder

Rope drum

Brake handle

Reduction gears

Brake

Warping drum

N.B. Eccentrics and valve gear not shown

are wound round the drum (known as a warping drum) the revolving drum will haul the rope which can be guided by the winch driver. All winches have a braking system which is usually a band round a special section of the winch drum that can be drawn tight by a handwheel on a worm-drive shaft. This is designed to hold the winch against its load weight.

Initially, steam ships were fitted with electric dynamos supplying current at 110 volts DC which, at first, was only used for lighting. As they developed, dynamos became larger and provided current for driving small motors which in turn drove deck machinery. Until comparatively recent times many merchant ships, tugs, fishing boats etc were fitted with 220 volts DC dynamos which provided current for all the deck auxiliaries including winches. The development of turbine and subsequently diesel-driven alternators revolutionised some of the larger ships' machinery and such alternators provided current at 440 volts, 3 phase 60 cycles (Hertz). This is in contrast with shore-based alternating current which is normally 440 volts, 3 phase 50 cycles (Hertz). The difference between the two is found in the speed of the electric motors using such current. A two-pole motor running on a 50-cycle supply will turn at 3000rpm (2900rpm in service), whereas a two-pole motor on a 60-cycle supply will run at 3600rpm (3500rpm actual). The number of poles fitted to the motor dictate its speed. The more poles the slower the motor speed, for example a 4-pole 60 cycle motor will run at 1750rpm, a 6-pole motor at 975rpm and so on.

Winches today are driven mainly by an electric motor running at a speed commensurate with the work the winch has to do and its designed gearing. As an alternative to electric winches, many owners now fit hydraulically-powered winches and other

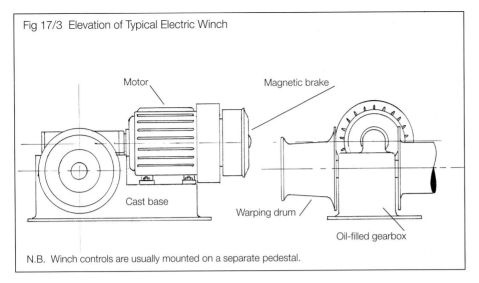

Fig 17/3 Elevation of Typical Electric Winch

Motor

Magnetic brake

Cast base

Warping drum

Oil-filled gearbox

N.B. Winch controls are usually mounted on a separate pedestal.

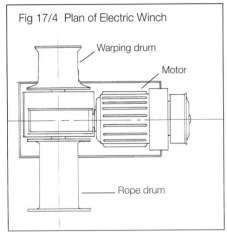

Fig 17/4 Plan of Electric Winch

Warping drum

Motor

Rope drum

auxiliary equipment. The hydraulic pumps are either shaft-driven from the main engine or electrically-driven and located in a special pump room below decks. Examples of both electrically driven and hydraulically-driven winches can be seen in the accompanying photographs, Figs 17/1 and 2 give some details of steam winches whereas Figs 17/3 and 4 show electrically-driven units. In addition, on many merchant ships there are a number of small winches for various duties such as handling stores and baggage, raising and lowering accommodation ladders and the ship's boats. All must be researched and built.

None of the winches are really complex, even those that are steam-driven and

the modeller can often find suitable kits of winches in the specialist ship model shops. A lathe will ease the job of making a model winch from scratch but is not essential. Warping drums and rope drums can be turned by chucking the material, whether it be brass, wood, aluminium or plastic, in the electric drill and shaping the parts using small files and abrasive paper. The winches shown in the photograph of *Arran Mail* were made from wood in an electric drill and each is assembled from four main pieces. Although there is only one derrick, two winches are needed, one to raise the load and the other to slew the derrick from side to side, *ie* from over the hold to the quay or over the ship's side. The main point when making a model winch is to note, from the sketches and pictures, how it is assembled and

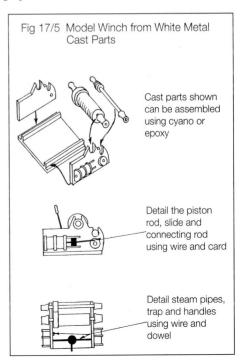

Fig 17/5 Model Winch from White Metal Cast Parts

Cast parts shown can be assembled using cyano or epoxy

Detail the piston rod, slide and connecting rod using wire and card

Detail steam pipes, trap and handles using wire and dowel

to take care to build the model in the same way. Side frames and the base can be made from small scraps of plywood suitably drilled to accept the shafts and drums. Steam cylinders can be made from small pieces of dowel or knitting needle, whilst connecting rods and controls can be formed from brass or copper wire and other details from thin card. Finally the finished winch can be painted carefully with the details of control knobs etc, picked out in contrasting colour. The result will be astonishingly good if the work is done with care and attention to detail. Fig 17/5 shows construction of a small model winch from white metal parts.

Towing hooks

As mentioned previously, American-built tugs tow from 'bitts', but in Europe and most of the rest of the world tugs use towing hooks and towing winches. There is little variation in the hooks found on tugs. They all have a locking device over the open top of the hook, with a means of releasing the towing hawser easily and quickly. Two

Fig 17/6 Towing Hooks

Latch arrangement

Shock absorber box

Heavy spring

Main body

Liverpool Pattern

Latch with lever

Mounting bracket with pin

Shock absorber box

Circular Pattern

types are generally found and are as shown in Fig 17/6. All towing hooks carry some form of shock absorber, usually a very strong and heavy spring which is arranged either to absorb the shocks on compression or, in reverse, on tension. Most towing hooks are mounted at the after end of a section of the tug's superstructure, which is specially strengthened for the purpose, and the hooks also run on a semi-circular rail for additional support. In most cases two hooks are fitted, with one being slightly smaller than the other and each used according to the required duty. Towing hooks are a feature of most tugs but very large ones, such as deep sea towing tugs and salvage tugs, have towing winches. Hooks need to be carefully made and fitted. A few model ship kit makers offer towing hooks in their range of fittings, some being made of plastic and some of white metal. Where a model tug is to be used for towing in competition, the tow hook must be strong enough to draw the weight required and it is therefore best to make it from brass.

Brass rod from which to make the tow hook must be annealed (softened) by being heated to a cherry-red colour and allowed to cool naturally. The rod can then be bent fairly easily, although it may be necessary to repeat the annealing process as the material work-hardens. Once the curved shape has been achieved, the attachment end can be flattened and drilled to fix to the rest of the unit and the other end shaped to the curved point. The latch arrangement can be simulated from thin brass strip and wire and the shock absorber box and spring formed from strip. When the hook is to be functional, the superstructure mounting the hook fixing must be strengthened to take the towing weight. The shock absorbing section of the hook will of course not be required to be functional.

Windlasses

The windlass, usually found only on the forward deck of the ship, is, if anything, simpler to build than the winch, as there is no rope drum and only the chain cable lifter to make in addition to the warping drum or drums. Some large ships have two windlasses, one for each anchor, but generally two cable lifters will be built into one windlass to serve both anchors. Many of the latest small ships such as trawlers and tugs are fitted with only one ready-use anchor, handled by a small windlass. As with the winch, earlier windlasses were steam-driven and on some of the larger ships a steam engine was fitted below the forecastle deck and drove the windlass through shafts. Later windlasses are either electrically-driven or use hydraulic power.

Making the model windlass is a similar exercise to making the winch, with a few differences of detail. The windlass shown in the photograph of *Jonrix* was made from wood using the electric drill and it was detailed using brass wire and card. The photographs of *Norsea* and of *Scott Guardian* show very different types of windlasses, the former on a large North Sea ferry, the latter on an oil rig rescue and standby ship. It can be seen

(Top)
Windlass with warping drum fitted to stern trawler *Glenrose I*. Note hydraulic pipes and motor housing. All deck machinery on this ship is hydraulically operated.

(Upper centre)
Trawl winch fitted below shelter deck on *Glenrose I* with hydraulic motor clearly visible on the right.

(Centre)
Steam windlass with warping drums on forward deck of model of Tyne pilot cutter *Britannia*, scale 1:24. Once more construction is of timber with card and wire decoration.

(Lower centre)
Windlass on foredeck of model of *Jonrix*, the small size of which can be judged from the 2-pence coin. This unit was made entirely from wood with brass wire for handles.

(Bottom)
Windlass on forward deck of *Scott Guardian* showing control handles and chain cable stopper with polypropylene warps on both warping drums.
N PATTERSON

that their duties are different. The size of a windlass is governed by the dimensions of the chain cable and the size of the anchor that is to be handled. A windlass incorporates a brake in the same manner as the winch. This is designed to hold firm only until the chain stopper can be fixed tightly and then it is released so that there is no tension on the windlass when it is not running. When building a model windlass the gearing, countershafts and electric motor or steam cylinders and coupling rods need to be carefully fitted.

Capstans

Capstans vary in size and duty in the same manner as do winches and windlasses. The earliest capstans were operated by fitting long lengths of timber, called capstan bars, into square holes set round the circumference of the capstan near the top and having members of the ship's crew turn the drum by pushing the rods. Round the base of the

(Below)
Forward deck of *Chimera* model showing capstan, anchor davit, fairleads, stock anchor on deck etc. The capstan is a manually operated unit.

(Right)
Capstan and bollards on stern deck of coaster *Timrix*. Note that the capstan is driven from beneath this deck.

(Lower right)
Capstan on *Scott Guardian* mounted on the motor casing with controls on casing.
N PATTERSON

capstan was a series of pawls which slipped over a ratchet (toothed ring) to prevent the capstan from running backwards. The upper portion of the capstan was, in effect, a warping drum of large size but fitted with shallow vertical bars (whelps) shaped to the curve of the drum. On some capstans the lower part was fitted with a chain cable lifter section, It must be made clear, however, that not all capstans were fitted with chain cable lifters. It is sometimes possible to see a hand-operated capstan on very old small ships where the drum is rotated by crank handles and gears fitted on top of the capstan head.

Capstans were first steam-driven and then, latterly, also driven by electric or hydraulic power. Invariably, the powered capstan is driven from machinery located below the deck, leaving only the drum and chain lifter, if fitted, visible, with the operating controls on an adjacent pedestal. The model capstan is much simpler to build than either the winch or the windlass as it requires little more than the ability to turn suitable material into the warping drum shape with the addition of the chain lifter below (see Fig 17/7). The photograph of *Chimaera* illustrates a capstan of the hand-operated type. On some modern ships the capstan is fitted purely to handle warps when docking and is a simple warping drum as shown in the pictures of *Scott Guardian*.

However, the capstans fitted to herring drifters were different. They were mostly manufactured by Elliot & Garoods and known as the 'Beccles' patent capstan. This was fitted with a small steam engine on top of the capstan under a sheet metal cover, the steam and condenser pipework being led up the centre of the unit. The whole arrangement allowed the drum and chain lifter to revolve while the engine and pedestal system remained fixed. The capstan carried pawls and a ratchet round the base and the pawls could be heard to click as the drum

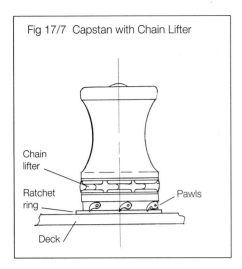

Fig 17/7 Capstan with Chain Lifter

Chain lifter

Ratchet ring

Pawls

Deck

Miniature piping and valves on model of *Scott Guardian* made as described in the text. These serve the fire-fighting system on the full-size ship.
DAVID MILTON

revolved. The engine also drove a small warping drum which was fitted horizontally on one side of the engine casing. There are excellent illustrations and a description in the book *From Tree to Sea* (see Appendix 3) and a model of this capstan is shown in the photograph of the herring drifter built by David Deadman.

Pipework

When modelling the winches or windlass, the steam supply and condenser pipes often form a significant part of the equipment and must, therefore, be incorporated on the model. The steam pipes can easily be simulated from pieces of rod, tube and even wire of suitable size. The range of styrene extrusions available from most model shops today and produced under the names 'Evergreen' and 'Plastruct' (the former originating in the USA and the latter in the UK), cover a good range of tubes and styrene rod. Valves for steam pipes can be made from such material as shown in Fig 17/8 with the addition of etched brass handwheels. Once painted these valves can be very effective, as can be seen in the accompanying photograph of a pipe system for fire duty on a model of *Scott Guardian*, the small size being clearly indicated by the two-pence coin. Within the Plastruct range there are a number of ready-made valves

but of fairly large size. Etched brass or nickel silver handwheels are available from a number of specialist suppliers. It will be noted that the valves thus made or bought are almost invariably similar to globe valves in full-size practice and that gate valves, with taller spindles and deeper base sections, are rarely seen. In very small scales the difference in valves is barely visible but in larger scales the gate valve can be shown by fitting a longer spindle under the handwheel and using filler to simulate the deeper valve body.

When adding pipework to a model make sure that the pipes are correctly fitted with the brackets which support them from the deck or bulkhead and also ensure that insulation or wrapping is simulated where necessary. Frequently the steam pipes on deck were lagged with asbestos sections covered with bitumen or tar-impregnated sheets for waterproofing and secured with wire net mesh. In many cases, of course, wear and tear destroyed the insulation and left sections of bare pipe. Details of this kind can elevate an otherwise plain model.

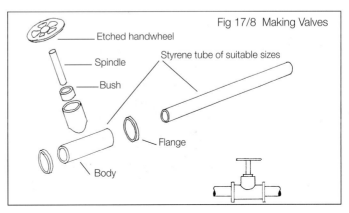

Fig 17/8 Making Valves

Etched handwheel

Spindle

Bush

Styrene tube of suitable sizes

Flange

Body

18
Radio Control

Remote control of model ships has been commonplace for many years and each year the controls become more sophisticated and, thankfully, more reliable. Just as the computer is improved and developed so are radio control systems. The simplest and probably most used outfit is the two-channel system offering control of two functions, for example, speed both ahead and astern and steering. There are more complex forms of radio control system and these will be described later.

Radio control equipment

Radio controls for model ships in the UK are set to operate within two frequency bands, 27 Megahertz and 40 Megahertz, and the number of individual frequency channels within these two bands is detailed in Appendix 4. Use of other frequencies, such as 35 Meg used by model aircraft, is illegal. In other parts of the world different frequencies are used and the operator in each country must adhere to set bands. Within each frequency band there are a number of channels. In the 27-Meg band these are colour-coded whereas in the 40-Meg band they are given three-figure numbers. The control crystals in both transmitter and receiver are set to one of these band channels so that more than one model may be sailed at one time provided each model uses a different channel within the chosen band. For example, on the 27-Meg system one model with a yellow crystal and a second with a red can sail together quite safely without interfering with each other. Were both to attempt to sail using the same colour band, they would be in conflict and could not be correctly controlled. It is important when visiting the sailing pond to ensure that the crystal set in use does not conflict with any other. If it does, then either change the crystals in the radio outfit, or wait until the other user has completed his sailing and switched off his system. Most model boat clubs have a radio control board displayed by the lake side indicating, by means of coloured and numbered spring clothes pegs, the number of channels in each band. An individual user obtains the clothes peg relating to his/her coloured or numbered channel and clips this to the transmitter aerial. The fact that a peg is missing from the control board indicates that that particular channel is in use and must not be used by anyone else until the peg is returned. This is the accepted and universally-used system among model boat clubs in the UK and similar systems are in use in other countries.

Returning to the simple two-channel radio control system, this comprises a transmitter (usually referred to as a Tx), a receiver (the Rx), two servo units, a receiver battery holder and a switch harness. In addition there are usually a number of different horns and discs to fit the servo drive shafts. The types of horns and discs used with servo units are shown in the photographs, each type designed to provide a different drive from the servo to the appropriate operation (rudder). The Tx requires batteries which slot into the casing and generally seven or eight AA-size dry cells are needed unless the unit is fitted with rechargeable Ni-cad batteries. On the front

of the Tx are two control sticks or levers. The left stick usually moves up and down and the right stick moves left and right. Both sticks are self-centring but can be fitted with ratchets to hold them in any set position. The left stick is thus designed to control the model ahead and astern and the right stick to control the rudder to steer left or right. Also positioned on the front of the transmitter is an on/off switch and a meter or coloured light system to indicate the current charge state of the Tx batteries. The Tx crystal is generally located in an easily-accessible position as is the charging socket for those which are fitted with rechargeable batteries. Note that the crystal fitted to the Tx will not fit the Rx and that crystals are only obtainable in matched sets. They should only be changed in set pairs and always matched with an appropriate coloured or numbered flag indicating the frequency being used.

The receiver supplied with the two-channel outfit has three sockets at one end, one to accept the battery connection and two to accept the leads from the servos. There is a single long aerial cable usually exiting from the opposite end to the servo connections. Some receivers have aerial

leads that measure about 3ft (1m) and some have aerials that only measure about 18in (50cm). In neither case must the aerial leads be shortened or lengthened as they are supplied to match the signals from the Tx and interference with the length can affect the operation of the system. It is possible to use a portion of the rigging of the model as an aerial, if the rigging is made from wire, provided that the total length of aerial lead and wire rigging matches the original aerial length. Using a section of wire rigging allows the aerial to be effectively concealed. In normal conditions it is possible to place the aerial round the top of the hull of the model just below deck level, where it will usually be fully effective. The Rx needs to be protected from water and, particularly in the case of a steam-driven model, should be encased in a plastic box or similar damp-proof container with the aerial and servo leads running out through protective sleeves. The battery pack associated with the Rx usually comprises four AA-size cells in a suitable case but this can be replaced with a rechargeable battery pack. The battery pack is connected to the Rx by a small wiring harness incorporating an on/off switch and, in the case of a rechargeable battery pack, a charging socket to accept the supply plug of the battery charger unit.

As previously detailed (Chapter 10), the electric motor(s) needs to be controlled for speed and direction. In the latter case the control board attaches to one of the

(Left)
Servo unit with a selection of horns and discs used in various ways to connect up operating features in a model.

(Below)
Two-channel radio system with electronic speed controller in model of *Britannia*. Note Yuasa lead acid battery in secure cradle and Marx Luder Decaperm motor. Sockets on radio tray are for connecting up battery chargers.

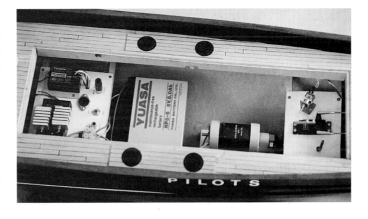

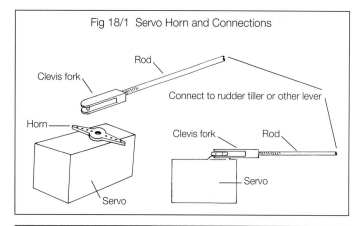

Fig 18/1 Servo Horn and Connections

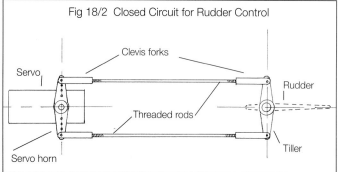

Fig 18/2 Closed Circuit for Rudder Control

18/2 so that the system is always in balance and the levers both pull and push simultaneously.

By far the largest range of radio control equipment is offered by the Japanese manufacturer Futaba and the majority of model boaters seem to use Futaba equipment. There are other very reputable makers such as Sanwa and Acoms from Japan and there is the Digifleet system from UK makers Fleet Control Systems which is competitively priced and very reliable. Within the USA, there are a number of makers of radio equipment one of whom supplies a unit specifically designed with the model shipbuilder in mind. The great majority of radio control systems are designed initially for the model aircraft industry and changed internally to suit the frequencies of the model ship, thus almost all the instruction leaflets that are supplied with the radio outfits refer to ailerons, flaps etc. This can be somewhat disconcerting but easily translated to model ship terms.

The more sophisticated outfits are needed when the model has twin screws and needs independent control of each shaft and where there is a bow thruster or similar auxiliary. The requirement then is for a four-channel outfit, which generally comes complete with two, three or four servos depending upon maker and price. In the case of a four-channel outfit the differences are small. The Tx sticks operate in gimbals so that both can revolve and move in any direction. This allows each stick to control two functions. Moving a stick forward or backward could control speed and direction and moving it sideways could control rudder movement, whereas the second stick moving forwards and backwards would control the second motor and bow thruster. There are two channels on each stick.

There will be times when the radio control equipment must be installed in a section of the model where the access needs to be watertight and the hatch over the Rx gear needs to be secured more firmly. In this

servos, but in the case of the electronic speed controller it replaces one servo. It is essential to ensure that the speed controller be fitted with a plug to match the receiver. The servo comprises a small electric motor within a casing containing a reduction gear, set with limit controls and including the necessary circuitry to accept signals from the Rx that cause the motor to run in one direction or another and to stop at the position dictated by the signal from the transmitter. All servos are proportionally controlled through the Rx and they will run to the position demanded by the Tx. The gearing of the servo allows the small motor to drive the rudder from one position to another or to control the throttle of a steam engine or similar function. The drive is transmitted by the use of servo horns secured to the drive shaft and wire rods with clevis forks or similar fittings as shown in Fig 18/1. Where the model has a large rudder it is wise to make up a closed-circuit rod and lever system as shown in Fig

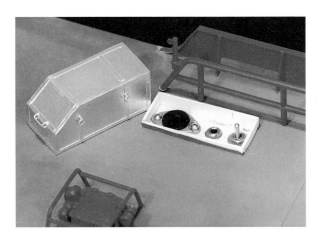

(Left)
Section of stern of *Scott Guardian* with rubbish skip removed to reveal on/off switch for radio system and charging sockets for batteries. This arrangement allows minimal removal of main superstructure which carries delicate detail.
DAVID MILTON

case it may be necessary to fit the on/off switch, or to fit an operating rod for the switch, so that it can be operated without removing the hatch over the radio gear. It can also be the case that the superstructure of a model will be delicate and quite complex so that constant removal and refitting is undesirable. In both cases the fitting of the Rx switch and the charging sockets in a position that does not require major removal of superstructure or hatches is desirable. An example of this is the fitting of such equipment under the rubbish skip on the stern of the model of *Scott Guardian*. This skip is made from styrene sheet and to full-scale. It fits tightly over an upstand on the deck and covers the switch for the Rx and its charging socket, together with a charging socket for the main drive batteries. The hull itself is adequately ventilated at high level so that there is no risk involved in charging batteries with the superstructure in place, but the superstructure is very complex and could suffer from frequent handling at the pondside.

In a similar manner it may be necessary to make the radio aerial detachable so that the Rx can be removed without it. In this case the length of the aerial must always be maintained but it can be cut and a small plug and socket fitted to allow it to be fixed firmly to the model yet permitting the Rx to be disconnected. The method shown in Fig 18/3 allows the aerial wire to become an integral part of the rigging of

the model, but it is necessary to remember to connect the Rx to the aerial when it is replaced in the model. This method of fitting the aerial to a model also allows the Rx to be used in a number of different models each having an aerial with a plug to mate with the Rx socket.

As will be seen in a later chapter, it is possible to control numerous other functions on a model. For example, it would be possible to raise and lower the anchor, swivel a crane and raise and lower a boat. All of these auxiliary functions require to be operated from the transmitter and it is now possible to add switching operations to radio systems having four or more channels. This does, however,

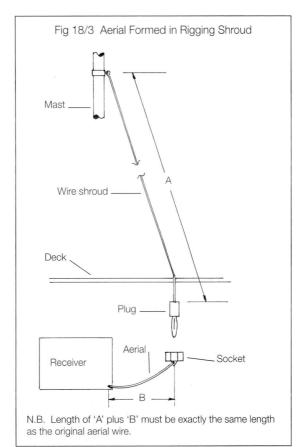

Fig 18/3 Aerial Formed in Rigging Shroud

Mast

Wire shroud

A

Deck

Plug

Receiver

Aerial

Socket

B

N.B. Length of 'A' plus 'B' must be exactly the same length as the original aerial wire.

increase the cost of the radio system and requires more space within the model for the relays and switches needed for the functions to be operated. It is necessary to consult the expert radio man to ensure that the correct wiring and switches are used for auxiliaries, a subject which is beyond the scope of this book as it would take more space than can be spared for such a complex subject.

Wiring

Wiring and cabling up the model internally and interconnecting radio, motor(s) and batteries etc, requires care. Cabling is generally divided into two kinds known as 'dirty' and 'clean'. 'Dirty' wiring is that which carries current from main batteries through speed controllers to motors, whilst 'clean' is that which carries the signals between radio receiver, servos and speed controllers. It is essential to ensure that no item of electrical equipment can create radio interference. Almost all motors will create 'noise', that is radio noise, through sparking brush gear etc, and it is sensible to give the radio equipment and motor installation very thorough tests to ensure that there is no unwanted interference. It is possible to purchase interference-suppressing kits for most motors used in model ships. In the author's experience, provided the clean and dirty wiring is kept as far apart as possible and good-quality guaran-

teed motors etc, are used, there is generally little to worry about. For example, run the electric cables feeding from the batteries to the speed control to the motor down one side of the hull and the radio control cables down the other and keep the radio receiver and the drive motor(s) and also the main drive batteries as far apart as possible. Screening, the fitting of an earthed plate between radio and electrical gear, will not be needed except possibly when the model is of all-metal construction.

The cables which carry the current from the main drive batteries to the speed controller and from the speed controller to the motor(s) should be of fairly high current-carrying capacity, that is to say, larger in section than the average domestic 13-amp cable. The reason for large-section cable is to ensure that there is only a small voltage drop between battery and motor and also to ensure that the cables will remain cool at all times. Passing fairly large currents through small-section cable causes the cable to heat rapidly and even to burn. Large currents mean high amperage such as 15 amps which may be needed to start or even run the selected motor. Keep all main cables as short as possible for the same reasons as given above. Preferably solder the cable ends where they are required to slot into screw-down terminals or solder them into spade or slip-on connectors. Good soldered joints will ensure that the current-carrying capacity of the cable is not impaired. Clip the main cables together and make the cable runs as tidy as possible. Use different-coloured cables for positive and negative connections between batteries and speed controllers and between speed controllers and motors, or at the least use

Two-channel radio system and Decaperm motor in model of Customs & Excise cutter *Badger*.

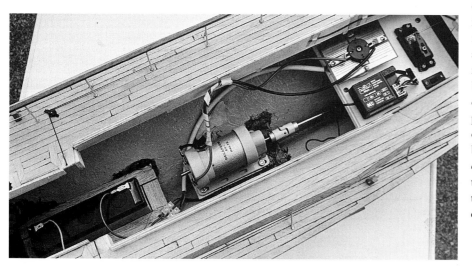

coloured tags on each cable to show their function.

The wiring between the radio receiver and the various servos and/or speed controls is usually provided as an integrapart of the servo or controller but, in some cases, it will be found that the cable provided is not long enough to reach between the Rx and the servo etc. Most radio equipment makers have extension cables available and these can be bought from good model shops. It is not wise for the individual to cut and insert extensions into servo leads unless one is competent with a soldering-iron and has a supply of suitable cable and shrink-wrap covering. A suitable test meter is also needed to check that home-made cable extensions are in good order.

As for the mains cables, the radio cables need to be clipped together to form a neat wiring harness and need to be fixed with suitable clips to the hull. One sample of radio control board is shown in the illustration of *Keila*. Here the entire radio installation is fitted on one plywood panel mounted above the propeller shaft and the radio wiring is thus almost completely divorced from the main cables. The items shown comprise the 4-channel Rx, the battery pack, on/off switch, servo connecting the rudder, resistance speed board controlling the bow thruster and electronic controller for the main motor and, tucked between the Rx and the electronic controller, the socket for coupling up the battery charger can just be seen. On test both in and out of the water this installation worked perfectly without any suppression equipment being fitted to either of the two motors.

Testing the equipment

Of all the stages of building a working model ship, it is possible that the fitting of the radio equipment is the one requiring the most care. It is all too easy to fail to plug in a lead correctly or to make a dry joint when soldering and then find that the

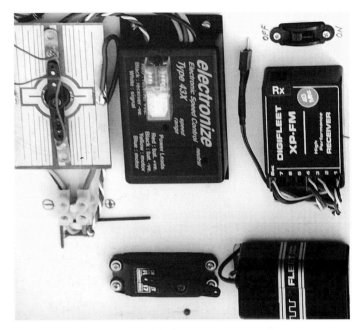

system fails to operate. Take care with all soldering, and check all connections not just once but several times. Before visiting the pond take the model outside, switch on the entire system (note that the Tx must always be switched on first and the Rx second), walk at least 200ft (70m) away with the Tx and have someone check that the system works as one operates the control sticks. A well set-up system should work without any of the servos twitching or any one part interfering with another. If twitch occurs, check that the batteries are fully charged and that the radio receiver aerial is well clear of any possible source of interference. Check too that the Tx aerial is fully extended and, of course, that there is no one near operating a system on the same crystal or even operating a CB radio close at hand. Double check that all connections are sound and correct those that may prove faulty. If the system still twitches after all has been checked then it will be necessary to seek the aid of someone with experience or even to return some part that may be faulty to the makers.

With a steam-operated model there will be no 'dirty' wiring unless the model is fitted with auxiliary features which are driven

Radio tray for model of *Keila* comprising, clockwise from top right: on/off switch, radio receiver, Nicad battery unit, rudder servo, connection block, Bob's board controlling bow thruster and electronic speed controller for main motor. Loose wire with plug is to connect to battery charger.

Four-channel radio outfit installed in steam-driven model of *Chimera*. Note how the rudder servo is mounted at a different height to permit the tiller to be cord operated. There is insufficient space in the stern of the model to permit rod operation under the decks.

by electric motor. Testing out of doors can be confined to checking that the radio controls do function correctly, *ie* that the rudder turns, the throttle moves and the ahead/astern lever operates. Once these have been seen to work, all will be well. Do check that the radio receiver cannot be flooded with condensate or steam and, if the Rx is fitted into a box, place a small bag of alum crystals in with it to keep it as dry as possible. Of course before the model is placed in the water, the steam outfit will have been lubricated and charged up with suitable water and fuel.

Once the model ship has been adequately checked then a visit to the pond is in order. Sailing a finished model for the first time is always an event of some excitement and, of course, the camera should be ready to record the moment of truth. A number of photographs are shown here depicting how some radio controls, steam outfits and motors are installed in various models. Each model will need to have the control system tailored to suit and most modellers will fit such controls in their own individual way so that hardly two models will be the same. For the beginner the best advice that can be given is to follow the maker's recommendations whenever possible.

When starting to build a working scale model merchant ship for the very first time, avoid the multi-channel radio systems, stick to the simple 2- or 4-channel outfits, and learn by experience how to handle the controls and how best to install them in the model. Remember to recharge the batteries when the sailing is over for the day and remember that Ni-cad batteries need to be fully discharged before being recharged. Do not use the car battery charger to charge sealed lead-acid batteries but obtain a correct charger from the model suppliers. Always stick to the simple rules and, as experience grows, so will the enjoyment of this hobby. Some model shipbuilders get great pleasure out of the building of the ship but little from sailing, others get their pleasure from the sailing and not the building, but the majority seem to get pleasure from both. There is always something new to learn and experience in the model world and the world of model ships is no exception.

19
Auxiliary Working Features

Whilst the well-built and detailed working model is a fine sight on and off the water, the ship which really attracts attention is often the one which is fitted with working auxiliary features. Such features usually fall into two categories, those that can be switched on at the lakeside before the model is placed in the water and those which are switched by remote control while the model is sailing. Among the former are the ship's lights, an engine sound system, radar scanners etc, whereas the latter include cranes, fire monitors, etc.

Lighting

The most popular auxiliary function is the ship's lights. The port and starboard navigation lamps and the masthead lamps have been described in the chapter on fittings and they would normally be switched on at the start of a sailing session in the evening, or they could be controlled remotely if so desired. The deck floodlights and the lights within the hull used to illuminate the accommodation would also normally be switched on at the pondside. Suitable light units can be found within the ranges of fittings offered by a number of suppliers and they can be purchased with working lamps already fitted and wired with small tails of cable. Take care when buying such commercial fittings to ensure that firstly they are of the correct scale size for the model and secondly that they are of consistent voltage. Some illuminated fittings from European makers are fitted with 3-volt lamps, some with 6-volt lamps and some

with 12-volt lamps. It is obviously not wise to attempt to connect units of differing voltage together. It is also possible to buy suitable lamps and to build the light units to suit the model exactly.

Miniature filament-type lamps in small glass envelopes can be found in most model shops for they are used not only for model ship illumination but for lighting model railways and other models. They come in a variety of sizes and the most common voltage is 6 volts. The smaller the lamp the more expensive it can be but the lamps are available with envelopes coloured red and green as well as clear. The only real problem with the glass lamp is that, quite often, it needs to be fitted in a location that is difficult to reach and where the lamp is sealed in place so that replacement is impossible without dismantling a section of the model. The life of the lamp then becomes problematic as cutting away detail work to change a light bulb is obviously undesirable. The best method of extending the life of a filament lamp is to run it in a circuit at a lower-than-listed current, for example a 6-volt lamp can be run quite satisfactorily on 4.8 volts with very little difference in intensity but with less chance of burning out rapidly.

Many modellers today solve the problem of fitting easily-damaged filament lamps by using light-emitting diodes (LEDs), which can be found within the ranges of lamps offered by the electronics stores such as Maplins, Tandy, Radio Shack etc. The only snag found so far is that they do not have a clear or white lamp in the range. Red, green, yellow and blue seem to

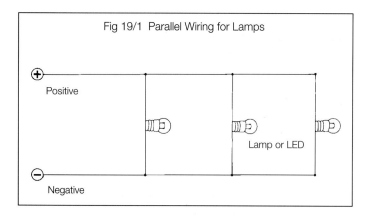

Fig 19/1 Parallel Wiring for Lamps

Positive +

Lamp or LED

Negative −

of long life and can be safely used in awkward locations. Some are even intense enough to be used for floodlights or searchlights.

With all model lighting always wire the lamps in parallel as shown in Fig 19/1 and compute the current required in watts or amps to ensure that the supply battery will have sufficient charge for the duration for which the lights are required. For instance twelve lamps each rated at 0.5 watts on a 6-volt circuit will require a total of 6 watts or 1 amp. If the battery feeding the circuit is rated at 6 volts and 2 ampere-hours then the lamps will remain lit for slightly less than two hours before the battery will need to be recharged. The reason for stating less than two hours is simply that the lamps will go dim near the time that the battery reaches its limit and they will not then be visibly lit. Note that the wiring diagram in Fig 19/1 indicates positive and negative connections clearly as is necessary if LEDs are used in place of the filament lamps shown.

be the colours available and thus the yellow must be used in place of the white or clear. LEDs must be wired correctly with the positive terminal connected to the positive lead. They will not operate with the current reversed and will not actually pass any current when fed wrongly. This ability to block current is used in many electronic applications and is a feature of the diode. Yet again they come in a range of sizes and current ratings but with 6 and 12 volts being the norm. They are very robust units

(Upper)
Smoke unit made for model of *Duchess of Fife*. Graupner smoke unit is contained in tank (see one connection). Chimney tube has base holes to allow small fan to drive smoke up the chimney.

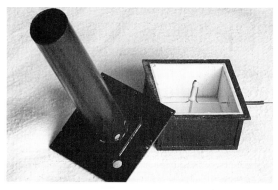

(Lower)
Operating gear for smoke units on *Britannia*. Lever on rudder servo will push switch at extreme of control movement. Switch works on basis of push once for on and push again for off.

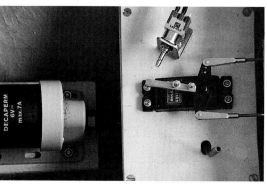

Smoke units

A smoke generator is another visible feature which can be fitted, since all steam ships and most motor ships will discharge smoke at some point. Smoke units can be bought from most model shops and they are not expensive. In fact the cost far outweighs the problems of making a suitable unit in the home workshop. They come in two forms. The first comprises a small open-ended tube with wire tails exiting from the bottom to be connected through a suitable switch to a supply of 6 to 9 volts DC. The tube is filled with smoke oil to the marked depth and when the current is switched on it causes an element to heat the oil which gives off white smoke. The second type, manufactured by the German company Graupner, comprises a small element within a glass tube which must be fitted into an oil container built by the modeller and fitted with a chimney which can be located in the funnel of the model. This unit operates best at between 9 and 12 volts but, as the oil reservoir can be built to hold much more oil than the tube of the first type, it can give off smoke for longer.

When fitted to the funnel of the model, both types of smoke unit will benefit from the inclusion of a small fan cabled in parallel with the unit and able to blow the smoke gently up through the funnel so that it exits the model correctly. The smoke unit can, of course, be switched on manually at the start of each sailing session but, as most ships do not emit smoke continuously, it is wise to incorporate some form of remote switching either from the radio system or by a 'push on/push off' switch operated by the tiller being set hard over with the trim also full over. Returning the trim to the midships position will prevent the switch from being operated by normal rudder movement. An example of this form of switching is shown in the photograph of the pilot cutter *Britannia*, where two small smoke units were fitted into the funnel. Details of the Graupner smoke unit fitted into the funnel of the paddle-steamer *Duchess of Fife* are also shown in the photographs.

Radar scanners

One of the most obvious fittings to automate on the model ship is the radar scanner or scanners, which revolve slowly and continuously even when the ship is moored alongside the quay. When motorised on the model ship they add realism. It is an unfortunate fact that many scanners are positioned on platforms extending outwards from masts and obviously designed for the purpose of carrying the radar units. This positioning makes driving the scanner from

a motor hidden within the model difficult and sometimes impossible. A flexible drive can be used if the bends of the casing are kept to a suitable limit but sometimes it is necessary to use small gears as shown diagrammatically in Fig 19/2. On the other hand, driving a scanner which is located on a pillar above the wheelhouse of a model is straightforward and relatively simple.

To drive a scanner, use a small motor and suitable gears. Motors rated at 3 or 4 volts can be bought from a number of suppliers and many such suppliers can provide simple nylon gears to give the required speed reduction. Motors and gears are listed in the catalogue of Trylon Ltd (see Appendix 2). As the scanner is to operate at all times while the ship is sailing, it can be switched at the start of each session and there is no need to use remote control. In all cases the motor and gear set for the scanner(s) must be mounted out of sight within the superstructure or below decks. A suitable motor/gear set for a scanner drive can be found in the servo unit which is no longer worked by the radio control

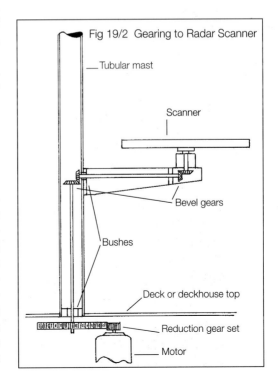

Fig 19/2 Gearing to Radar Scanner

Tubular mast

Scanner

Bevel gears

Bushes

Deck or deckhouse top

Reduction gear set

Motor

system. Disconnecting the control board and connecting the servo motor to the battery supply will give a beautifully-geared unit to drive the scanner.

Fire monitors

Fire monitors spraying water to quite long distances are a fascinating operating feature for a model tug, oil rig rescue ship or fire boat. There are a number of makers who supply working model fire monitors but they are usually confined to scales larger than 1:50. Pumps for delivering water to the monitor are also listed among the fittings available from the same makers but are not affected by the scale as they will be concealed inside the model. To fit a working monitor it is necessary first to make and fit a skin fitting from suitable copper or brass pipe and to drill a hole in the hull below the waterline to accept it. The fitting needs to be sealed firmly to the hull to prevent leaks. A suitable skin fitting is sketched in Fig 19/3. Note that the copper pipe of the skin fitting is provided with a small soldered ring over which the flexible pipe will

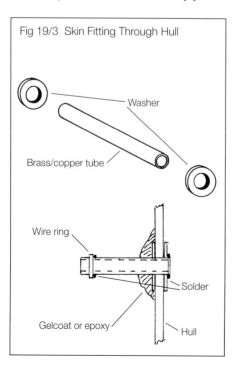

Fig 19/3 Skin Fitting Through Hull

Washer

Brass/copper tube

Wire ring

Solder

Gelcoat or epoxy

Hull

fit tightly and prevent any water from leaking into the hull. The water pump will need to be fitted below the waterline as it is usually necessary to ensure that the pump inlet is always flooded with water. Such small pumps do not usually have a suction capacity. Flexible silicon rubber pipes can be used to connect between the pump and the skin fitting and from the pump to the monitor and such pipes need to be a very tight push-fit to avoid any leaks.

Anchors

To raise and lower an anchor of a model ship requires the anchor to be weighted to keep the chain cable taut and all parts of the hawse pipe, including the entry and exit places, to be adequately smoothed to allow the cable to run freely. It is much easier to run the anchor cable on to a drum below decks than to attempt to build a working windlass. The windlass can then be used to guide the chain through the deck to the drum. To drive the chain cable drum, a small motor suitably geared will be needed and, unless the modeller wishes to control the anchor totally from the transmitter, a pair of limit switches will be needed to stop the motor when the anchor reaches the end of the required travel. This arrangement needs only a simple switching action from the Tx. To have the anchor reach the bottom of the pond or lake and to hold the model against the wind or current is not really feasible and the raising and lowering of the anchor is only intended to give realism to the working model. Fig 19/4 gives a diagrammatic arrangement of a suitable anchor drum system to guide those modellers who wish to incorporate a working anchor on their model.

Vehicle ramps

Raising and lowering a vehicle ramp on a model ferry is somewhat simpler than the anchor handling system. The method illustrated in Fig 19/5 requires only a small

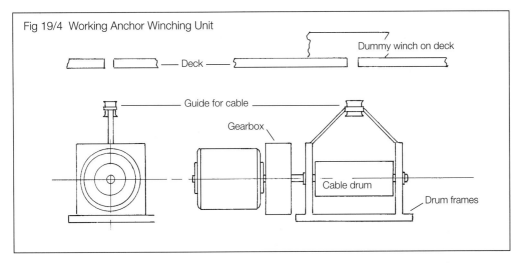

Fig 19/4 Working Anchor Winching Unit

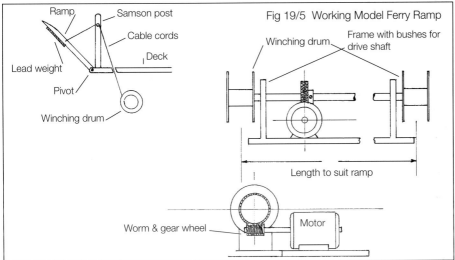

Fig 19/5 Working Model Ferry Ramp

motor, a worm and wheel gear set, brass rod, some scraps of sheet brass or aluminium and a small changeover relay. Using small pulleys and cord this system will work well, particularly if the ramp has sufficient weight to hold the cords fairly taut. Remote operation from a simple switch on the transmitter is all that is needed to control the ramp.

Cranes etc

Cranes and/or grabs on cargo ships and on dredgers offer opportunities for the modeller to fit remote operation. If the crane or grab cabin is carefully fitted on a balanced base, preferably on a spindle with a suitable bearing as illustrated in Fig 19/6 overleaf, then it can be made to revolve using a servo, as illustrated also in Fig 19/6. The servo travel of about 120^0 each side of centre should provide sufficient movement of the crane or grab from side to side. Remote raising and lowering of the hook or grab is similar to the anchor movement described previously, except that the cable drum and motor can be fitted into the crane or grab cabin and the wiring led through the centre of the cabin pivot. In the event that the scale is such that the drum and motor must be fitted below deck, the cord system will have to run through the central pivot of

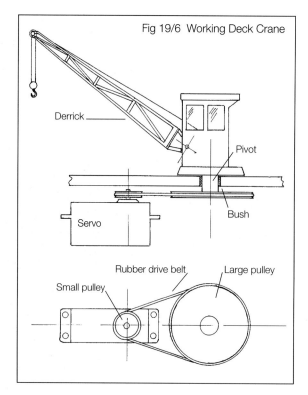

Fig 19/6 Working Deck Crane

Derrick

Pivot

Bush

Servo

Rubber drive belt

Large pulley

Small pulley

the cabin. In either case the system described for the anchor can be applied.

Water discharges

The full-size merchant ship has a number of water discharge pipes, usually just above the waterline and situated by the engine-room. Such pipes discharge water that has been used for cooling the engines or from the condenser systems and can be seen on all merchant ships whether steam- or motor-driven. A scale model can readily be fitted with such a feature. A small electric pump such as is used on the windscreen washer system of a car and which can be obtained from scrapyards is very suitable for providing a water circulation system. Two skin fittings are required in the model's hull, one below the waterline for the suction to the pump and the other above the waterline at the desired position of the water discharge. The pump should be located low in the hull in the same way as the pump for the fire monitors and connected to the skin fittings with silicon rubber tubing. If the screen wash pump is operated on a current of between 6 and 9 volts it will give a low-pressure output ideal for the simulation of water discharge from an engine. The model of *Scott Guardian* illustrated in the photographs will have four water discharge pipes in the stern, two of which will be operational when the model is completed. Coupling two discharges to one pump requires only a 'Y'-piece in the pipework. The photograph shows one discharge operating with the vessel alongside the quay. Always ensure that the pipes of water systems are well secured to prevent leakage of water into the hull and subsequent damage to costly radio and electrical equipment. The water pressure provided by the pumps of the fire monitor system will normally be much too high for a simple cooling water discharge system.

Sound systems

One of the accessories available for the model ship which can prove attractive is a sound system. Sound systems are made by a number of manufacturers and can be found in a number of forms. The diesel-engine sound module is very popular and can be obtained to give the noise of a single-cylinder engine as may be heard on a small fishing boat, or the sound of a multi-cylinder engine. In both cases it can be coupled to

Stern of *Scott Guardian* in dock at Hull illustrating cooling water discharges, two for main engines and two for auxiliary engines – one auxiliary engine in service.

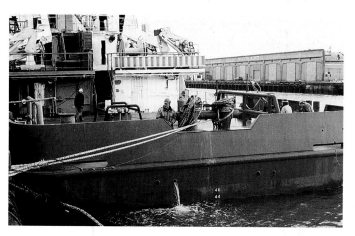

the speed control to provide the sound of the engine idling when the ship is at rest and then speeding up as the ship moves away. Such modules come as a circuit board with connections for the supply current from the battery and to accept a loud-speaker which should usually have a resistance of 8 ohms. A simple switch in the circuit from the battery to the module and the necessary connections to the speed system will allow the module to operate.

Modules for providing the sound of a ship's siren, a steam engine and other noises are also available. It is wise to provide a power source for these systems separate from the main motor drive battery. The loudspeaker needs to be mounted within the superstructure of the model ship and fairly high up. One or two windows will need to be left unglazed for the sound to be emitted and a false floor of fine cloth can conceal the speaker itself if it is fitted into a cabin area. The hobby magazines regularly feature articles on self-building sound effects modules and

some makers offer the sound units in kit form. Appendix 2 lists some suppliers of this type of equipment.

The features described above are all capable of being operated by remote control from the radio system using either the multi-switch modules which can be fitted to transmitters and receivers, or by means of a rotary switch operated by a servo under radio control. A rotary switch for servo drive is shown in Fig 19/7. The latter system is not easy to operate and can be somewhat 'hit and miss', requiring practice on the part of the operator to achieve competence. It is however a considerably cheaper alternative to the multi-switch.

There are other, quite often more complex, auxiliary working features to be found in some of the more expensive ship model kits, such as the ability to launch and recover a small boat, to flash Morse code type messages by lamp etc. The experienced modeller will find details of more complex and exotic systems within the specialist catalogues, whereas the newcomer to marine modelling will be wise to first gain experience with the simpler types.

Photo of puffer built by David Deadman and shown on the water at a regatta at Windermere, with its smoke unit in operation. The model is to 1:24 scale and is electrically driven.
DAVID DEADMAN

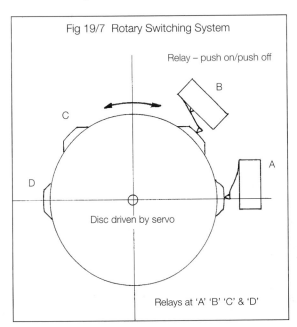

Fig 19/7 Rotary Switching System

Relay – push on/push off

B

C

A

D

Disc driven by servo

Relays at 'A' 'B' 'C' & 'D'

20
Unusual Drive Equipment

The majority of power-driven ships today use conventional propeller drives, although some have fixed or steerable Kort nozzles. Many ships are fitted with variable-pitch propellers which eliminate the need for fitting reversing gear to the engine. This permits direct control from the bridge and, if need be, allows the engine-room to be left unmanned. The engineers on these ships are employed with the auxiliary machinery and make only periodic visits to the main engines.

Kort nozzles

The Kort nozzle is a means of obtaining greater efficiency from the propeller as it acts as a venturi to accelerate the movement of the water. The steerable or rudder nozzle was a natural development from the original fixed nozzle. Model Kort nozzles with matching propellers can be purchased in a number of sizes from E Radestock (see Appendix 2) and are made of good-quality brass. Kort nozzles can, however, be made in the workshop from styrene sheet, using a timber former around which to wrap thin sheet and to build up a suitable thickness. Although this method will produce an acceptable nozzle which will perform correctly, the aerofoil shape can only really be obtained by machining suitable stock in the lathe.

Bow and stern thrusters

Shipowners are always looking for ways to reduce their ships' running costs. One way is to reduce berthing costs at those ports where the ship trades regularly by fitting the ship with the means of entering or leaving the berth, quayside or dock without

Scott Guardian in drydock at Hull. Note the deep anchor recesses and prominent rubbing strips: size can be compared to men working in dock bottom.
DAVID MILTON

the assistance of tugs. A simple answer lies with the installation of thruster units near the bow and sometimes also near the stern of the ship.

Bow and stern thrusters are simply tubes placed across the hull in which propellers are fitted. These can be driven in either direction and thus can move the bow or stern of the ship sideways in one direction or another. The advantage of such thrusters means that the ship can be turned very accurately, moved sideways to lie against a quay, or be placed in the correct position to enter and leave a restricted space such as a lock entry to a dock.

Bow and stern thruster units in model form are produced by a number of model ship kit makers such as Graupner, Robbe and Marx Luder. Each is made to a standard size and tube length and the model shipbuilder needs to cut the necessary holes in the hull of the model and cut the tubes to fit across the hull. Care is needed to seal the tubes to the hull sides and ensure that water cannot leak into the hull. The propeller drive system is usually arranged to fit over rubber 'O'-rings and to be watertight when clamped in place. As the standard tube size for such thruster units will almost certainly be out of scale, the holes in the hull will need to be to the correct scale size. This means that the holes in the hull will usually be smaller in diameter than the thruster tube and thus air can be trapped in the top part of the thruster and prevent the propeller system from working correctly when the model is placed in the water. In full-size practice, air release pipes are normally led from the top

(Above)
Port azimuth thruster of *Scott Guardian* showing anti-corrosion anodes and how closely the propeller fits the nozzle.
DAVID MILTON

(Left)
Detail of azimuth thruster looking towards the stern. The rings welded to the hull are needed to put the thruster into place. The thruster can revolve through 360°.
DAVID MILTON

of each side of the thruster tubes to a position well above the ship's waterline – the main deck or higher – and terminated in goosenecks, for the express purpose of ensuring that air can not be trapped in the thruster system. The same system can be adopted for the model with small-bore pipes being led to above deck level from the thruster tubes. It is of course necessary to seal the air-release pipes to the thruster tubes to prevent any water leaking into the hull. Where the thruster tubes are of plastic, then polystyrene cement will suffice but, if the tubes are of metal, epoxy cement of the slow cure type will be needed.

It is possible to make bow and stern thrusters by using pre-formed plastic tube or even copper tube such as may be used for water pipes in the home and which is available from DIY stores in short lengths. A small propeller which is a fairly close fit in the tube is needed together with small bevel gears and a drive shaft with bearings to which a small motor can be attached. The main problem which will be found with model bow thrusters is the fact that they will be sited and sealed into the bow of the model very low down and thus access becomes extremely difficult.

Once the thruster or thrusters have been installed and appropriate drive motor(s) have been selected and fitted, it remains only to cable up the unit(s) to suitable speed controls or switches which can be radio-controlled from the transmitter of the model. The model of *Keila* illustrated in the photographs is fitted with a Marx Luder bow thruster to simulate that of the full-size ship and it is controlled from one channel of a four-channel radio system. It works well and can turn the model in its own length. Some of the large cruise liners and larger ferries have more than one thruster at both bow and stern to provide maximum thrust for turning and berthing the ship and where the modeller is building a model of such a ship then research will indicate where and how many thruster units are needed.

Schottel drive

Some of the more specialised ships, such as oil rig support vessels, rescue ships and some tugs, are fitted with Schottel drives or Azimuth thruster units which are propeller drive systems where the whole propeller unit, fitted with a Kort or similar nozzle, is driven through a gear system with the drive unit sited vertically below the ship's hull and

where the whole unit can be turned to provide directional thrust. Such units can be seen in the photographs of *Scott Guardian* in dry dock at Hull. Schottel drive units are capable of being revolved through approximately 240°, *ie* 120° each side of the centreline, whereas Azimuth thrusters can be turned through a full 360°. *Scott Guardian* is fitted with three Azimuth thrusters, each independently driven and with the single forward unit capable of being retracted into the hull when not in use. The advantages of such thrust drives is very obvious as they allow the ship to be moved in almost any direction – sideways, backwards and in circles if necessary, without altering engine speed or direction. Vessels so fitted are operated by joysticks from the bridge, these joysticks being very similar to the units used to play computer games in the home. Obviously the control system is very sophisticated in the full-size ship.

Model Schottel drives are available from Marx Luder and are finely made in plastic and nylon. They incorporate a 2:1 reduction gear and are carefully arranged so that a standard servo movement will turn the drive through 240°. Although they are excellent value, they unfortunately come only in one size, approximating to 1:50 scale, which severely restricts their use. It is possible to build such units but the use of a good lathe will be needed together with the ability to turn parts and assemble them with the necessary gears.

Voith Schneider drive

One unusual drive which is fitted mainly to tugs is the Voith Schneider system (models of which were, at one time, available from Graupner who produced a kit which used such a drive). The Voith Schneider drive comprises a system of blades of aerofoil section set into a top disc that are driven by a vertical shaft from the engine or motor within the hull. The angle at which the blades are set as they revolve round the shaft dictates the speed and direction of the

(Left)
Model of Schottel drive unit by Marx Luder fitted to *Scott Guardian*. This is almost identical to azimuth thruster but can only move through 240°. It is scale size for the model in question and fully operational.

thrust provided. This drive system can therefore drive the ship in any direction at any speed with the engine running at a constant speed and with the ship moving to the dictates of the control in the wheelhouse. The system can be likened to that of the helicopter blade control where the angle of the blades dictate whether the craft rises or descends or moves fast, slow or stands still. The revolving Voith Schneider drive can also be set so that the ship stands still.

At the time of writing there does not appear to be a Voith Schneider model drive unit on the commercial market and to make such an item at a small scale would be very difficult without very good workshop facilities and without suitably dimensioned drawings.

Miscellaneous

Over the years there have been a number of unusual drive systems tried by some of the more enterprising shipbuilders and owners, ranging from computer-controlled wing sails acting as boosters to main engines to gas-turbine and nuclear-powered merchant ships. Few have proved commercially successful in the long term but they offer the modeller the opportunity to build a model somewhat different to the norm. The US ship *Savannah* was built with a nuclear reactor providing the power for the turbines and it was in service for a number of years with some success, but the running costs proved to be too high and a number of countries and ports refused to allow the ship to berth in case of radioactive contamination which led, ultimately, to her being decommissioned. An attractive ship, she would be a suitable candidate for a small-scale model with electric motor drive and radio control and there is little doubt that research would soon produce data and drawings to permit an accurate model to be built. Taubman's Plan Service International (see Appendix 2) list drawings of the *Savannah*.

One might suppose that the hovercraft that cross the English Channel and other waterways carrying passengers and cars would fall under the banner of the merchant ship and probably quite correctly. They certainly have unusual drive equipment which both inflates the skirt and provides the power for the propellers but they are more like aircraft than ships and they are very highly specialised vehicles running both over land and over the sea. They are, therefore, not included in this volume and the prospective modeller must seek advice elsewhere.

21
Painting & Finishing

It is an unfortunate fact that all too many fine models are spoilt by poor paintwork. Good paintwork can only follow good preparation. The surfaces to which the paint is to be applied must be well prepared and free from blemishes and flaws. Any marks left by tools and knives will show through the paint layers and mar the finished surface. Even the smallest fitting needs to be examined carefully and prepared properly for painting. Once the paint has been applied then it should always be protected by two or three coats of quality varnish. Although the paint in itself is a good finish, matt or satin paints will show fingermarks if they are not treated with varnish and a matt or satin varnish will give the necessary protection.

There is no precise point in the building process when paint should be applied to a model, but it is sensible to paint it as far as possible as the work proceeds and each section is completed. Obviously there will be parts which must be painted before they are fitted since access will not be possible when construction is more advanced. Furthermore, it is wise to paint small fittings before they are fixed to the model and interior surfaces which will be visible through windows etc, before the areas are sealed up.

Paints

There are a number of manufacturers world-wide who specialise in producing paints for the modeller. Each has a range of colours in matt, satin and gloss finishes and usually a clear varnish in the same finishes.

The paints produced by an individual maker are usually compatible one with another, but not all paints by differing makers can be intermixed. The cellulose-based paint produced for cars cannot be used over enamels and acrylics as the cellulose will attack the other coatings. Cellulose paint will also attack styrene and ABS plastics. However, enamels and acrylics can be used over the cellulose-based paints once they have dried.

Many paint manufacturers supplying the modeller include both enamels and acrylics in their range. The enamels are spirit-based paints which can be mixed together to produce differing colour shades but the maker's own type of thinners must be used to dilute them. Some will accept turpentine substitute or white spirit as a dilutant but the maker's own thinners is best. The acrylic paints are water-based and can be thinned with clean water, but the paint when dry is waterproof and hard. Acrylics cannot be intermixed with enamels. Both acrylics and enamels can be used in an airbrush when suitably thinned down.

Painting the hull

The first part of a model to be painted is the hull, once the propeller shaft(s), bilge keels, rudder post etc have been fitted permanently in place. The whole surface of the hull should be examined and all imperfections made good before any paint is applied. A wooden hull should first be given two or three coats of 'spray filler', a yellow compound available in spray cans from most car accessory dealers. It will fill small blemishes and effectively conceal the grain of the timber. Each coat should be allowed to dry thoroughly for at least four hours in a warm atmosphere and then be lightly rubbed down with a 400-grit abrasive paper used on a block. The final filler coat should be left for at least twenty-four hours before further coats are applied.

A hull made from GRP should be washed with warm water and detergent and rubbed all over with 400-grit paper to key the subsequent paint coats. For the best results, the hull should be given two or three coats of etching primer. This can usually be purchased in spray cans from a specialist paint supply company which supplies the car trade. Some of the mail-order suppliers may also be able to supply etching primer. As with the timber hull, the GRP hull needs to be carefully examined and any imperfections made good before the final etching coat is applied.

Having thus prepared the hull, it must be given two or three coats of primer. The spray cans from the car accessory shop are probably the best to use for this. Matt paint from the model shop bought in small tins and suitably thinned can be used in an airbrush but the quantity involved for a hull of reasonable size will probably cost more than the spray can. Many ships have a red oxide-coloured anti-fouling paint below the waterline and, if the whole hull is sprayed with red oxide, the bottom need not be further treated except when varnishing. If the hull is white or a very light colour, then it will be best to apply a light grey or white primer. As for the earlier paint coats, allow a sensible period of time for each coat to dry well and then rub down with progressively finer grades of abrasive paper used wet and on a block. Do not rub down with the paper held in the fingers as this does not give a consistently even cover and will result in hills and hollows appearing in

the paintwork. Allow the model to stand for at least forty-eight hours before proceeding to the next stage.

Modern automotive paints are normally used in a conditioned atmosphere provided by a 'low-bake oven'. In this the car, after being prepared, is spray-painted at a steady temperature of around 70^0 F after which the operator leaves the oven and brings the oven and the car up to a temperature of approximately 160^0 F. The car is baked for a period of some forty minutes after which the paint has been conditioned and is completely hard. If the car is painted outside of such conditions a period of three weeks must elapse before the paint reaches the same degree of hardness. Longer is required if the temperature is lower than 60^0 F. It can thus be seen that the automotive spray paints do need a warm dry atmosphere when used and a lengthy drying period in warm conditions to allow the volatiles in the paint to evaporate. Similar times are also needed for alternative paints such as enamels and acrylics to dry out properly.

Having allowed the hull time to dry, the lower part of the hull must be masked off while the upper section is painted. The masking must, of course, follow the waterline which rarely follows the same line as the keel and a clear line to which the mask-

Method of marking off the waterline of a model using a soft pencil clamped to an adjustable square. The hull of the model must be firmly fixed and truly vertical to ensure accurate marking on both sides of the hull.
DAVID MILTON

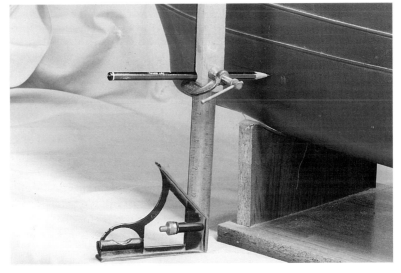

ing must meet is needed. This can be done in two ways. In the first, the hull is placed upside down on a flat surface and propped up to bring the waterline shown on the drawings parallel to the base. The waterline can then be drawn round the hull using a soft pencil fastened to a block or a square as illustrated. The second method is similar to the first but this time the hull is mounted on its stand and then propped up to

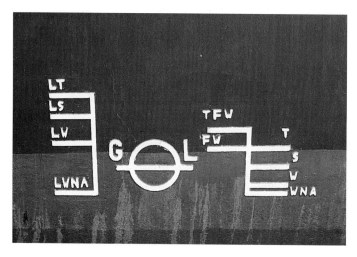

(Above)
Detail of Plimsoll Line on coaster *Lizrix* in King George Dock, Hull.
JOHN ORRISS

(Right)
Depth marks on bow of coaster *Lizrix*. Note how deeply the anchor is concealed and protected in the deep anchor pocket.
JOHN ORRISS

bring the waterline parallel to the base. The line can be marked in the same way as before using a soft pencil. With either method it is vital to see that the hull is vertical in the fore and aft direction so that the line, when drawn, is the same on both sides, *ie* is equidistant from the top of the hull on both sides at equivalent points.

Masking a model hull to allow a different-colour paint to be applied is easy provided a few simple rules are followed. Most commercially-available masking tapes are impregnated with strong adhesive that can leave a film on the finished paint surface and which can be so hard to remove that it lifts the paint previously applied. To avoid this problem, first rub down the tape on a sheet of glass or other smooth surface. This will reduce the adhesion of the tape and permit easier and cleaner use. When laying the tape to the drawn waterline, rub down the edge with a thumbnail to seal the tape to the hull. Where the line follows the curve of the hull and the tape will not curve to suit, darken the pencil line and lay a length or two of tape over the line. The dark line will be visible through the tape and the tape can be cut to the line with a sharp scalpel or craft knife. The remainder of the hull below the masking tape must be covered. Old newsprint can be taped to the masking tape and round the area to be kept clear.

When using a paint spray, whether a pressurised can or a spray gun, move the spray in a continuous action from one end of the hull to the other. Each run of the spray should overlap the previous run by about 50 per cent and the spray or gun should be held not less than about 9in (200mm) from the hull. Do not expect to gain good coverage of the surface in one run and do not try to apply full coverage too quickly as this will result in the paint collecting in runs and pools. Apply at least three coats of paint and examine each coat carefully for any blemishes or imperfections. Each coat should be lightly rubbed down with fine wet-and-dry abrasive used wet, after allowing at least twelve hours drying time.

Allow the final coat to dry for at least twenty-four hours and then remove the masking tape gently by drawing it back over itself in a rolling action. Do not just lift the tape away from the hull but roll it away. This will prevent any part of the tape pulling paint from the hull where it may not have fully dried. In general, where the masking is removed, the edge of the paint will have a raised line. Allow a few days to elapse to permit the paint to harden fully before gently drawing a sharp blade held almost vertically to the surface over the raised paint line. With care this will remove the excess paint without damaging the main layers, it is also possible to remove raised paint using 600-grit abrasive paper used wet and fixed to a small block.

Before varnishing the hull after it has been painted, the draught marks, Plimsoll Line and marks and any other hull details should be added, along with the ship's name in the appropriate places on either side of the bow and on the stern, together with the port of registry. Most of these can be applied using rub-down letters such as 'Letraset' and it is also possible to buy depth marks and thruster detail markings in the form of waterslide transfers. Rub-down letters can be applied to any good surface but the waterslide transfers must be affixed to a high-gloss surface. If the waterslide transfers are fixed on a satin or matt surface, the carrier film will show clearly regardless of how carefully any subsequent varnish coats are applied. It is much safer to place the transfers on to a gloss surface and to flat this down with matt or satin varnish later. Examples of the foregoing can be seen in the photographs one of which shows the Plimsoll Line and its associated markings on a ship lying in the port of Hull.

There is some controversy over whether a model should be finished in a matt or in a satin varnish. In general, full-size ships seen from a short distance have very little shine even though the paint used may have been of high gloss. The sea air and salt water very quickly reduce any glossiness to a dull matt. However, if a model is built to be displayed permanently within a glass cabinet (*ie* never sailed) then it is possible that a slight sheen such as given by a satin varnish will enhance it. For the sailing model the water on the sides of the ship will provide all the shine and matt varnish will prevent the paint surface from being spoiled by finger marks and dirt which can be easily wiped away. Almost all the models built over the years by the author have been finished with matt varnish, the only exceptions being some models of small steam launches, where the original launches were finished with highly polished brass fittings mounted on beautifully-varnished mahogany decks and the models were in similar fashion.

Painting superstructures etc

Painting the upperworks and superstructures on the model can follow the same procedure as the painting of the hull except that here the areas involved may be quite small and will not lend themselves to spray-painting. Although the airbrush is a valuable tool for applying paint it is also a fairly expensive unit, and using it for small areas of different colours means frequent dismantling and cleaning. Good watercolour brushes can be bought from most model shops and artists' supply stores. It is wise to buy good-quality brushes and to take care of them, the best being those made from Kolinsky Sable. They are available in sizes from OOO to 12. The OOO is very thin having but a few hairs and capable of producing a very fine line, whereas the 12 is very thick and is, of course, the most expensive. Sizes OO, 3, 6, and 8 are adequate for most modelling use, coupled with one or two flat brushes $^1/_2$in and $^3/_4$in wide (13mm and 20mm).

When finished with a brush, gently squeeze the remaining paint from the bristles using a paper towel, wash the brush in thinners, or water if the paint is acrylic, and finally clean the brush in warm soapy water until all trace of paint is gone. Stand the brushes in a jar with the heads upwards. Never lie them down or leave them in a jar of thinners as this will certainly damage them. Whenever possible keep the same brush for the same paint colour to avoid any possibility of cross-contamination. By taking care, some of the brushes currently used by the author are upwards of ten years old and are still serviceable.

When painting very small parts, whether by spray or by brush, they can be handled more easily if they are attached to a piece of wood using double-sided adhesive tape. Such double-sided tape is also useful for holding small parts while they are otherwise worked upon. There is no golden rule for painting, nor is there any magical means of selecting the quality of paint. Buy model paints in the colours you require from a reputable source, a good model shop or similar outlet. Whether enamels or acrylics, they must always be stirred well to ensure that the pigment which has collected on the bottom of the can or jar is fully mixed in. To get a really good finish, thin down the paint using up to 50 per cent thinners and apply a number of thin coats in preference to one thick coat. The thin coats will produce a much better finish and there will be virtually no visible brush marks when the paint dries.

Never forget that it takes some weeks for the paint, regardless of type, to dry properly, so a newly painted model must always be covered to prevent dust from spoiling the surfaces. When painting by whatever method work, if possible, in dry, warm and dust-free conditions. When placing the model on its display stand protect the hull at the points where it meets the stand with bubble wrap or similar padding until the paint has really dried hard. The usual felt covering of the stand is not adequate enough to protect the paint until it has had the necessary few weeks to dry. Those who have access to a conditioned, low-bake paint spray booth can, of course, place a model on its stand immediately after it has been baked.

Some ships display bands of contrasting colour at the waterline or at deck level etc, and many modellers use adhesive coach lines available from the car accessory shop. These are quite good but tend to be of a material too thick for use on a scale model. Many model shops carry a better-quality adhesive line system in a range of colours and which are on much thinner stock and therefore more suitable. It is possible to paint the band on the hull using enamel or acrylic paints if the area is first masked off, or if a suitable lining brush is used. The lining brush demands a steady hand and great care but the result is very satisfying. Lining brushes can be bought from specialist paint shops and some artists' suppliers.

Some of the kit makers include decals (transfers) with their kits. These are self-adhesive and waterproof and can be simply stuck to the model once the backing paper has been removed. It is doubtful if any of these products will be of use to the scale ship modeller but it is always handy to know that such are available if there is a need for them.

As with so many aspects of ship modelling, painting needs care and attention to obtain the required results. A well-painted model will always attract attention and seeing it oneself gives great satisfaction.

22
Ballasting & Sailing Trials

When a model has been completed and an adequate amount of time has been allowed for paint and varnish to dry and adhesives to cure, the time has come for it to be tested. The prototype ship is subject to what are called 'basin trials' when it is nearly ready to leave for its first trip. These trials are carried out with the ship secured in the fitting-out basin. The main engines are run up, propeller(s) and shaft(s) are checked, auxiliary machinery is run up and tested under varying loads and virtually everything on board is tested in one way or another. The domestic bath or the garden pond are suitable locations for such tests.

Ensure that the model is completely fitted out with drive and radio gear and that all is connected up and that the propeller shaft or shafts have been packed with grease. Take care when placing the model in the water for the first time, for those with high superstructures or carrying a fair degree of weight above decks can easily capsize when there is no ballast on board. First note how the model lies in the water. Most will have a list to port or starboard and this is easily rectified by careful placement of ballast. Unless particularly heavy drive equipment and batteries are installed it is unlikely that the model will float to its load waterline and suitable ballast will need to be installed.

Ballasting

At this point it is necessary to decide whether to sail the model in a laden or an unladen state. If the ship is 'tender', in other words reluctant to recover when given a list of more than 45⁰, then there is no alternative but to ballast it so that it floats to the load waterline. But if the ship proves to be stable, then it can be ballasted to indicate it is not carrying any cargo. However, as the bath or garden pond do not provide waves or currents which may be experienced on the lake, it will be sensible to err on the side of safety. Assume the model is tender if there is even a slight reluctance for it to recover when a list is imposed on it.

The best ballast is thin lead sheet such as is used by builders for flashing on roofs. It can be purchased from most DIY stores and supermarkets in rolls and it can be cut easily with a strong sharp knife or tin snips. Other heavy weights can be used but they will have to be positioned in the bottom of the hull over the keel to be of benefit and this is not always the best practice. Unless the model is very tender, the lead sheets should be cut to fit up the sides of the hull from the keel almost to main deck level. Placing the lead thus and spreading it along the hull to put the weight where it is needed will bring the model down to the waterline but also allow it to roll slowly and realistically. A tender model will require the weight to be placed as low in the hull as possible with the same result.

Putting ballast only over the keel will make a model very stiff in the water, so that when it rolls it will right itself with a sudden jerk and look strange. Real ships roll quite slowly even in very heavy weather. It must be born in mind that, while the model is a scaled-down version of a full-

size ship, the water cannot be scaled down and the waves found at the lake can be equated to full size as follows; a wave some 4in (100mm) high is equivalent to a wave 16ft (5m) high to a model built to a scale of 1:48 but it is 32ft (10m) high to a model scaled 1:96. Waves 32ft high are very heavy seas indeed, and were the waves on the lake increased to 6in (150mm) high then the small scale model is facing storms up to Force 7 or 8 with waves up to 50ft (15m) high. Waves on the lake of 4in (100mm) high are little more than large ripples.

When the model has been fitted with ballast, this should be firmly secured to the hull to ensure that it cannot move when the ship is on the water. Shifting ballast can cause serious problems and even sink a ship. Polyester resin or epoxy should be used to fix the lead to the hull and plenty of curing time left before proceeding further.

Basin trials

When the model has been ballasted and is still in the bath or pond, the radio controls and drive gear can be test-run. Run the motor or steam plant up to full speed in both directions and test the movement of the rudder and any other radio-controlled items. If the model is of a tug or oil rig support ship, the 'bollard pull' or towing capability can be tested by attaching a spring balance to the stern or tow hook of the model and to a fixed part of the pond or bath. When the model is run full ahead the indicator of the balance will read pull in ounces or grammes.

To test the radio equipment the services of an assistant will be needed to observe how the functions of the model perform. Place the model on its stand on a table or bench out of doors, switch on all controls and ensure that the motor(s) or steam engine are ready to run. Instruct the assistant to observe the operation of propeller, rudder etc, while the radio transmitter is operated progressively from distances up to 200ft (60m) away. With the transmitter aerial in the extended position there should be no problems. It should also be possible to operate the controls with the aerial in the closed position from a few feet away. If there are some problems, such as the rudder twitching or other controls not working correctly, check that all the electrical connections are sound. It may be that the electric drive motor(s) is causing interference and needs to be fitted with suppressers similar to those sometimes needed in a car to correct radio interference. Such suppressers can be bought in packs from selected specialist model ship outlets.

The maiden voyage

Once the basin trials have been completed and all is satisfactory then the model can be taken to the lake for its maiden voyage, a real event and, quite often, a time of special excitement. When this day arrives, make sure that the model is fitted with fully charged Ni-cad batteries or alternatively new dry batteries and that the steam plant is lubricated and the boiler and gas tank are filled. Take a few small tools to cover any minor problems that may require rectification and be certain that the propeller(s) is tightly fitted to the shaft(s). Give the model a run on the stand at the waterside before placing it on the lake. Operate the controls gently and observe how the ship behaves before opening up the throttle and giving it a full-speed run. It is possible that the sticks of the transmitter operate in the wrong direction and this can be altered by a simple switch on or inside the transmitter case. It will be found that the ship is easily

guided when sailing away from the operator but remember that, when it is turned to come back, the controls appear to work to the opposite hand.

Careful observation of the model when sailing will allow the radio controls to be adjusted after each short session, so that the ship behaves more precisely when they are operated. Make adjustments a little at a time until they do exactly as is required and then each sailing session will be pleasurable. When removing the model from the water, examine it carefully for any faults that may have developed in the hull or paintwork. Blemishes should be made good in the workshop and any faults found, such as water leaking through the stern by the shaft, should be sealed and the model tested in the bath once more. Sometimes a shaft leak will develop when the model is run astern. This is caused by the shaft seal at the propeller end, which is usually only a thin washer, not being close to the shaft. If the shaft has end float in the outer casing, this will allow water to find its way up the shaft even though it is packed with grease. The solution is to reduce the end float of the drive shaft in the outer casing to the point where it almost grips and stops the shaft from turning. The adjustments for

Smit Duitsland, a high-quality model tug by Eric Austwick pictured at the National Scale Regatta finals at the Dome, Doncaster in 1994.

end float will be obvious when the shaft is examined.

Sailing trials are always interesting and most will find them a challenge. Ships with single-screw propulsion will sail quite well ahead but frequently will be found to be difficult to turn when running astern. This phenomenon is a feature of almost all single-screw ships, including full-size ones. It is sometimes necessary to increase the fore and aft dimensions of the rudder to allow the model to perform well even when running ahead. Long slender models tend to have large turning circles and they will need to have their rudders extended to reduce this turning circle. Single-screw ships fitted with Kort nozzles will usually be found to be a little more manoeuvrable but the ship fitted with a steerable Kort nozzle is the best of the single-screw ships. These models will be found to steer well both ahead and astern and to turn very quickly almost their own length.

Twin-screw ships, especially those fitted with independent control of each screw, will perform well both ahead and astern but it will need practice on the part of the operator in using the two sticks controlling the motors. Some twin-screw ships are fitted with only one speed control, operating both motors simultaneously. In effect, this is running the model as though it were fitted with only one screw. If such a model has twin rudders it will steer reasonably well when running astern but not so well if only a single rudder is fitted. There is really very little point in having a twin-screw ship operating on one control except for the fact that two speed controllers and a four-channel radio system is considerably more expensive than one controller and a two-channel one.

When it comes to twin-screw ships and steam drive then there will be serious considerations regarding finance. Twin steam engines fed from one boiler dictate a large boiler and the cost will prove to be very high compared to electric drive. It is possible to drive twin screws from one steam engine using a purpose-made gearbox but usually this needs the services of a lathe and some precision working. The remarks on controlling the twin-screw steam-driven model are similar to those for an electrically-driven model.

One point that must be made relates to wooden models. Exposure to water may cause the timbers of the model to swell if they are not well-protected from such dampness. This is not a problem while the model is wet but, when it dries, the planks will shrink and draw with the result that the hull will develop cracks through which water can penetrate and aggravate the situation. If this should happen then the hull needs to be dried well, if necessary using a hair drier, until all trace of dampness has been lost. Cracks or spaces between affected planks must be filled with a suitable filler and then the hull will need to be treated both inside and out with protection. On the inside of the hull the best protection is a coating of polyester resin brushed well into the timbers, whilst on the outside a number of coats of good quality paint will suffice. Obviously such treatment should be done when the hull is built and before it is fitted out with equipment.

Upon returning from the lake after a sailing session, always remove the batteries from the model and also remove the radio receiver if possible and put all in a dry place after charging the batteries. Never store batteries, whether Nicads or sealed lead acid units, in a discharged state as this will reduce their life and require early replacement. Always ensure that the inside of the model is dried out. Often small quantities of water will collect inside when the model ships water in choppy conditions. If this water is not removed it will cause parts of motors or engines to rust.

If due care has been taken through all stages of building a model ship then the first sailing experience will generally be one of joy. Take a camera and record the great event. A model magazine may even print the photograph, if it is a good shot.

23
Building & Sailing for Competitions

Most model ship competitions and regattas are run under the auspices of the Model Power Boat Association (MPBA) in the UK In most other countries there are similar associations which have come together to form Naviga, an international association of model boat clubs. Details of the MPBA scale section and the nearest model boat club can be obtained by contacting the scale section secretary or other officers. Further details will be found in Appendix 2.

Classes of model

Under the MPBA rulings, scale model ships are divided into five classes, and a model must be placed in its correct class when entered for competition. Regattas for scale models are held throughout the summer by many model boat clubs, usually on Sundays and members sail competitively. To enter most sailing competitions, the entrant has to be a member of the MPBA in the UK and thus to be adequately insured against public liability, loss of a model, etc. Membership of the MPBA is open to all members of a *bona fide* affiliated model boat club on payment of an annual fee. Individual membership as a Countrywide member can be obtained from the Countrywide section for those modellers who do not live near a model club and prefer to remain an individual competitor. The fee for countrywide membership is usually twice that of club membership.

The classes in which model ships are sailed and judged are as follows:

(a) Exact Scale Class. Models in this class

A fine model of the motor tug *Edengarth* sailing in competition at Doncaster in the 1994 finals.

(Above)
An attractive steam tug negotiating obstacles on the water at the Dome Leisure Centre, Doncaster on finals day 1994.

Sand Heron moving through the channel between buoys and boom at Doncaster in 1994. Model by Roger Thayne (see Chapter 2).

kit and even if enhanced with better-quality fittings to give a better appearance, they must be recognisably the model depicted by the kit illustrations.

(d) Modified Kit Class. The models in this class are generally of ships built from kits but extensively modified to improve either appearance or performance or to indicate a ship of different outline while retaining the kit materials and fittings.

(e) Junior Class. Juniors must have built their model ships substantially by their own hands with only as mall amount of adult help. A junior can enter the other classes but will be judged without regard to age. In the junior class the models are marked on the water but are not judged statically.

To enter the National Finals which are held annually in one of the three areas of the country a competitor must compete in four area qualifying events and reach the necessary marks that permit entry into the National Final.

Competitions

In a competition regatta each entrant is required to sail his or her model twice round a set course, the course being in accordance with the scale sail recommendations. During the first round of sailing the models will be judged on the water earning up to a maximum of 18 points. Between the two sailing rounds, each model in the Stand-off, Kit and Modified Kit classes will be judged on a table usually by two qualified judges viewing the model from a distance of 6ft (2m). Points for this section can be to a maximum of 50. Those models in the Exact Scale class will be judged usually by two or three highly-qualified judges and here the maximum points scored can be 100. When sailing round the set steering course, each model starts with a score of 100 points from which penalty points are deducted when the model fouls a buoy or sails the wrong way round an obstacle.

must be models of full-size ships that have been built. The models must be accurate to scale and must have documentation, drawings etc, to support them. High marks depend upon fidelity of scale and the appearance of the model. The models must be scratch-built and contain only a very few commercial fittings, all of which must be listed in the documentation.

(b) Stand-Off Scale Class. Models in this class are basically scratch-built in the same way as the Exact Scale but may depict a ship that was only a design and never built. Freelance models fall into this class and documentation is not required. Those models which do not fall clearly into the other categories are generally placed in this one.

(c) Standard Kit Class. In this class all models must be built from the boxed

The final scores determine the winners in each class and prizes and trophies are distributed at the end of the day, usually by some person of note.

Details of the scoring for these competitions are as follows:

On the water marks for all models.

Realism of turns of speed	6 points
Controlled stop and getting under way	6 points
Correct waterline and general trim	6 points

Static Judging Marks
Stand-off, kit and modified kit.

(Maximum of 50 points as below).

Degree of difficulty and detail	10 points
Workmanship and finish	20 points
Realism and fidelity to type	20 points

Exact Scale

Realism	15 points
Detail	20 points
Degree of difficulty	20 points
Quality of workmanship	20 points
Finish	15 points
Documentation	5 points
Judge's Bonus	5 points

These categories and their apportioned points are as listed in the MPBA Year Book for 1996 and raise some queries. For instance, what will happen to the points for correct waterline and general trim if a model is depicted as unladen and therefore with the hull well out of the water and the propeller perhaps only partly submerged? In the points system for Exact Scale should there not be more points for 'Documentation' and therefore for research, and finally what is a 'Judge's Bonus'? Of all the MPBA members

questioned, including some qualified judges, no one seems to be able to answer any of these queries. Within only a few days of completing this section of the book the author learned that some of the rules were to be revised.

For entry into competition, a modeller must make sure that all the data accumulated during the research into the ship has been retained. The model must be built with particular attention to accuracy and with the detail work and painting done with great care. There must be nothing on the model to which the judges can point and state with conviction that there is an error. Unfortunately the judges at ship model competitions are only human and they can make mistakes like anyone else but they do have one fact in their favour: they are usually modellers of some experience themselves and do try to be impartial at all times.

Not all events held by the various model boat clubs are competitive and some are purely for the modeller to display a model for the interest of the general public and to raise funds for the benefit of the club. At most clubs there are sailing sessions where a model can be sailed in company with other members' craft, and the builders enjoy friendly conversation and exchange ideas, often solving problems. In

A junior receives help from dad during the finals at Doncaster. There were at least six models sailing at one time.

Diminutive 1:96 scale tug *Thor* sailed by Dave Milton and lying along-side the dock awaiting the start of its run.

press each year. The competition is held during the first days of each year opening just before New Year's Day and lasting about eight days.

The organisers of the exhibition insure all entries and each competitor or exhibitor is required to place a value on his exhibit for this purpose. Gold medals are the top awards in any section going to the entries which gain 500 or more points. If no entries reach the 500 mark then no golds will be awarded, silver medals are awarded for 400 to 499 points and bronze for 300 to 399 points. There is no limit to the number of medals that can be awarded and more than one of each kind can be given in all classes if the marks justify this. Further down the scale the Judges can award certificates of merit in three categories, 'Very Highly Commended, Highly Commended and Commended'.

Judges look for quality of workmanship, finish (painting and detail), complexity, suitability of materials, scale authenticity and originality, and more information on these points is contained in the information booklet supplied to all competitors.

Most of the photographs in this chapter were taken at the MPBA Scale National Finals held in 1994 at the Dome Leisure Centre, Doncaster and run by the Conisbrough and District Modelling Association who normally sail on this lake.

There does not appear to be a central organising body for ship modellers in the USA like the MPBA in the UK. The Scale Ship Modellers' Association of North America lists some twenty-four ship model clubs as members for 1997. Regretfully at the time of preparation no contact address for this association was found. T he magazine *US Boat & Ship Modeler* carries a Boat Club Directory among which were noticed a number of clubs also listed by The Scale Ship Modelers' Association so that it would

this atmosphere one learns most how a model ship will be judged and how to display a model to the best advantage.

One of the largest competitions in the UK is the annual exhibition held under the auspices of Nexus Exhibitions and known as the International Model Show. This exhibition, held in recent years at Olympia in London, covers all types of modelling and the section for model ships is usually wide ranging. There are no restrictions for entering a model, it is not necessary to be a member of a club or other body and the models are not judged by sailing them. They are judged by expert judges purely on the table and the classes are different from those of the national sailing events. Awards come in the form of Gold, Silver and Bronze medals, Highly Commended and Commended Certificates, and within the section devoted to model ships there are a number of trophies which, when won, are held for a year and then returned. A scale model has to be of very high standard to win a medal or certificate at this event. Details of the International Model Show can be obtained from Nexus and information can be found in the model be possible for US readers to locate a local club from these sources.

The hobby is obviously very active in the USA as a number of prestigious regattas are listed among which are the following:

1. The Great Lakes Sailing Regatta (formerly the 'Internats') which is sponsored by Mid-Michigan Scale Model Ship Association. This event is held annually in mid-August. For a contact address see Appendix 2.
2. The Golden Gate Concurs run annually by the San Francisco Model Yacht Club which combines scale sailing with a tugboat regatta. For contact address see Appendix 2.
3. The annual WRAM show held at Westchester County Center, White Plains, New York, usually in February. For contact addresses see local and national press.

There are other shows and regattas in the USA in all parts of the country from East to West coasts and from North to South including some clubs listed for Canada although not so well publicised. The New York Model Ship & Boat Festival run by the South Street Seaport Museum is an annual event not to be missed. The South Orange Seaport Society, New Jersey and the Valley Forge Model Ship Society in Pennsylvania both hold annual regattas and festivals as does the Buffalo Model Powerboat Club and the Maritime Modelers of Los Angeles.

Almost all competitions in the USA use the same formula for models as the UK, *ie* Exact Scale, Kit, Modified Kit and Junior but there is no 'Stand off' class and such models are usually entered in Exact or Modified Kit.

Obviously it is not possible to list individual model boat clubs but prospective members and newcomers to the hobby are advised to seek out their local club by means of the model press, local library and similar information services. It is rare to find that new members and modellers are not welcome and most clubs have a varied and interesting programme each year to entice the members to compete with one another in a friendly fashion. Sharring information and experiences is one of the best ways of enjoying the hobby.

Protecting the model

An important point is the question of protecting the finished model. Dust is the bane of all modellers' lives. It settles on paint that has just been applied and on glazing from which it is difficult to remove.

A delighted competitor receives his trophy from MPBA scale secretary Mike Finnis at the end of the finals hosted by the Conisborough & District Modelling Association at the Dome Leisure Centre, Doncaster in September 1994.

Chrysalis Showcases
display and carry case
for model of
Scott Guardian.
DAVID MILTON

It is certainly sensible to consider making or buying a cover of some description to protect the model from dust etc. It should also be substantial to protect the model from accidental damage. The very best cover or case in which to place a model is one which will, not only protect it and allow it to be seen clearly but also one in which it can be transported to the lakeside.

There will always be spectators who will appear when the model ship is sailed at the lake, since most lakes used by model boat clubs are located in public parks or similar places. If the model can be kept in a case which allows inspection without touching, then it will be safe until it can be placed on the water and away from curious hands. A carry/display case is not too difficult to construct from plywood and clear acrylic sheet together with suitable corner mouldings and a substantial base, but it will take time. The author's models are placed in display or carry/display cases made at very reasonable cost and to required size by Chrysalis Showcases, Grantham (see Appendix 2). Their carry

cases have an acrylic front panel for easy viewing of the model, lightweight plywood back, ends and sides and a baize-covered base of heavy ply incorporating brass catches. Carrying handles are provided usually at both ends and the whole case is very light in weight despite its strength. One of the photographs shows a carry case made for the model of *Scott Guardian*. It is possible to purchase purpose made cases from a number of sources but the majority use glass in preference to acrylic sheet and this results in a very heavy case suitable only for display purposes.

A piece of equipment which is becoming more widely available from a number of sources is a tiny, battery powered, vacuum cleaner complete with nozzles, brush and dust bag. These very small cleaners are ideal for removing dust and swarf from model ships and for reaching into awkward places. Being small and light they can be used safely on delicate fittings and on rigging. The cost is small, probably under £10.00 ($15.00). They will also blow dust away if the tubes are placed on the dust bag outlet.

24
Hints & Tips

Many of the simple tasks carried out from day to day as a matter of course by modellers can prove difficult to a novice model shipbuilder and this chapter is designed to assist those who have little or no experience.

Using the craft knife

When cutting plywood or card, having done the necessary measuring and marked the lines on the material to be cut, place the steel rule on the line and make a gentle first cut with the knife. Do not press too hard and hold the knife blade against the edge of the rule while drawing it along the marked line. Once the first gentle cut has been made the knife can be used more firmly so that after two or three runs the material is separated.

When cutting styrene sheet with the craft knife or scalpel it is only necessary to score the sheet as it will break apart cleanly at the score if it is deep enough. Also with styrene sheet one will notice that the edge where it has been scored and broken will have a raised lip on both pieces, to remove this lip draw the blade of the knife over the edge of the sheet with the blade almost vertical and scrape the lip away. The lip can, of course, be gently sanded away using a medium-grit sandpaper on a block.

If all cuts are made in this way one will soon become accustomed to using the knife and will know when the point and the edge have become blunt and so require a new part of the blade to be brought into use when using a snap-off blade knife. With other types of knife the blade will need to be replaced when it loses its point or edge. Some modellers hone and sharpen their knife blades to gain longer life from them but the small cost involved in replacement blades hardly justifies the time needed to re-sharpen a blade.

Soldering

Soldering is a task which also seems to mystify some modellers and the following notes should prove of assistance. Soldering is the means of joining two metals in a technique similar to welding using a metal bonding material – solder – and heat. Basically there are two types of soldering, soft soldering and hard soldering. Soft soldering covers the making of joints using a soldering alloy of tin and lead and comparatively low temperatures, such as are produced by an electric soldering-iron. Hard soldering is akin to brazing and welding, using an alloy of silver and tin and high temperatures. Almost all solders can be obtained for use within a small range of selected temperatures and one company (Carrs) which regularly advertises can supply a very comprehensive range of solders and fluxes. With each type of solder there is a suitable flux which is used to prevent the cleaned surface of the metals to be joined from oxidising and thereby stopping the solder from flowing freely into the joint. With both hard and soft soldering the watchword is cleanliness. It is not possible to make a good soldered joint if the metals to be joined have not been thoroughly cleaned.

Soft soldering

Soft soldering is the method likely to be used most often by a model shipbuilder, for example for joining pieces of copper to copper, copper to brass etc, for connecting wires to circuit boards, or for sealing the thin core wires of a cable together for secure fastening into a jointing block (chocolate block) having screw-down connections. This method can also be used for joining together brass tubes one inside another to make tapered masts or derrick booms and, where a brass tubular mast is used, soft soldering will safely secure fittings to it. Such joints are good conductors of electricity provided they are well made and soft soldering is used extensively when attaching electronic components to circuit boards.

To prepare two pieces of metal for soft soldering the area to be joined must first be cleaned very thoroughly with fine emery or wet-and-dry abrasive paper and coated with flux, which will prevent the cleaned surfaces from oxidising. With a suitable soldering-iron, the pieces of metal are heated separately and a small quantity of solder is applied while holding the hot iron on the metal. The solder will be seen to melt and run over the cleaned surface which should be quickly wiped over with a soft cloth while the solder is still fluid. This operation is known as 'tinning the metal'. When both pieces of metal have been tinned, a small amount of flux should be applied to one surface and the two brought together. Holding the two together, heat should be applied again with the hot soldering-iron until a thin bright silver line of solder can be observed round the two parts. If necessary, a small additional quantity of solder can be applied to the edges of the joint. Once the hot iron has been removed leave the pieces for a minute or two to cool slightly and the joint will be found to be secure. The final stage is to cool the joint and to wash it well in warm water and detergent to remove any remaining flux which would prevent successful future painting.

Note that the soft soldering method described above is suitable for joining copper, brass, bronze, tinplate and mild steel and the type of solder and flux is that which is easily obtained from the local ironmongery or DIY store. Soft soldering can be used for joining aluminium and for joining cast white metal parts but in both cases a special flux and special solder is needed. Aluminium has a tendency to oxidise almost as soon as it has been cleaned and the operation of soft-soldering aluminium parts to each other is one which requires practice. In the same way, practice is needed when soldering white metal castings. A special solder and flux is required and the temperature needs to be watched carefully. White metal parts melt at very much lower temperatures than those of other metals such as copper etc. Solders and fluxes for aluminium and white metal can be obtained from specialist outlets found in the advertising pages of model magazines.

There is a movement today for using cyanoacrylate adhesives where soldering would have been used in earlier days and, while such adhesives are perfectly adequate for most lightly-loaded applications, they cannot replace the soft-soldered joint completely. A joint made with Superglue does not conduct electricity. Therefore, adhesives cannot be used on circuit boards or to interconnect electrical and electronic components. For this soft soldering is necessary and it is wise to use a cored solder wire designed for electrical circuit duty where the flux within the cores of the solder wire is of a non-corrosive kind. A non-corrosive paste flux should be used to aid making a sound joint. Some joints made on circuit boards can look sound yet subsequently be found to be poor. These are known as 'dry joints', where penetration of the solder to the wire and circuit of the board has not been correctly completed. This generally happens because the person making the joint either hurries or applies too little heat with the iron to gain a good joint.

When two pieces of copper or brass are to be joined, it is possible to use a gas blowlamp in place of an electric soldering-iron and, in some cases, a blowlamp is to be preferred where two large pieces of material have to be joined, or the joint is a long one. When using an electric iron on a fairly large section of metal, it will be found that the metal absorbs the heat very quickly so that the area where the joint is to be made does not heat up sufficiently. In this case, the use of a blowlamp with a good pencil flame can provide the heat needed to obtain a good flow of solder. In all cases the metal surfaces need to be clean and fluxed before heat is applied. Coils of flux-cored solder will be a most useful purchase for a modeller and practice with electric irons and blowlamp will bring good results in time.

Hard soldering

More complex is the technique of silver soldering or hard soldering. As mentioned above this method uses solder which contains a percentage of silver and which requires much higher heat to effect a satisfactory joint. To make joints using silver solder needs a fairly powerful blowlamp, a base to work upon which is heat-resistant and heat-retaining such as a firebrick or a number of firebricks, and a supply of suitable flux and silver solder. As with soft solder, silver solder can be bought in a range of temperatures. Using the higher temperature solders first in a series of joints will allow the lower temperature solders to be used later without the first joints melting in the heat and falling apart. Where a model steam plant is to be installed, then it is almost certain that some joints which are

heat-resistant at temperatures higher than those that would melt soft solder will need to be made.

As with any other form of soldering the pieces of metal to be joined must be cleaned thoroughly. Silver solder flux usually comes as a white powder (Borax) which has to be mixed with water into a stiff paste and applied to the cleaned metal. The cleaned parts must then be brought together and held together while heat is applied. The blowlamp is used to heat the metal pieces until they reach a dull red colour when a small amount of silver solder can be applied. If the heat is correct the piece of silver solder will melt, run into the joint between the two pieces of metal and show a thin, bright line against the dull red. The blowlamp can then be removed and the metal parts allowed to cool or be doused in a waterbath. In most cases the joint will be found to be stronger than the metal surrounding it. The parts can safely be placed in boiling water and scrubbed to remove any remaining traces of flux.

Using a suitable jig to hold the pieces together, the author has successfully repaired bandsaw blades with silver solder, thus extending the life of the blade and, of course, saving the cost of a new one. When watching the heat build up for silver soldering, the first sign of reaching the correct temperature will be the flux melting and glistening in the flame. The solder can be applied with the solder stick held to the work or a small piece of solder can be cut and placed on the work pieces and pressed into the flux before the heat is applied. Either method of placing the solder to the joint is acceptable. Parts of a steam boiler such as the flue pipe cannot be extended or altered to suit a model unless they are silver-soldered. Soft soldering would not stand up to the heat.

When attempting to solder using either soft solder or silver solder it is always sensible to try out the technique on a scrap or two of material, which can be discarded afterwards, to ensure that the attempts will not spoil a finished part of a model. Always wait until the heat from the iron or blowlamp has built up sufficiently to melt the selected solder properly. Solder applied to the tip of a soldering-iron, for instance, should immediately run and become bright silver in colour if the iron is at the correct temperature. If the solder is reluctant to run then the heat is insufficient and the joint will be poor. Practice makes perfect, and successful soldering is very nearly an art form

Veneers

Not previously mentioned but of value to the modelmaker is the use of veneers. Many of the earlier merchant ships had open bridges, often finished in vertical match boarding and made of varnished timbers. Making vertical matchboarding is very much like making deck planking, but the finished bridge really needs to have the work done in the correct timber and

this is where the timber veneer comes in useful. They can be bought from good timber importers and from some of the better shops that cater for the marquetry maker. Veneers are very thin layers of timber cut to exhibit the fine grain patterns of the material and used mostly in furniture-making to cover blockboards and to simulate quality timbers. The thin sheets tend to be very brittle and break apart very easily. When attempting to cut veneer with a sharp knife the blade usually tries to follow the grain, with disastrous results. Cutting veneers into narrow strips is very difficult unless a few simple shortcuts are used.

Select first a piece of veneer of the type of timber to be used, for example,

(Right)
View of bridge of *Arran Mail* from port side and before navigation lamps were installed. Single stanchions on top of front rail would carry canvas dodger in poor weather.

(Below)
Bridge on model of *Arran Mail* showing gypsy, binnacle and telegraph. Note use of mahogany veneer for match boarding and mahogany strip for top rails.

mahogany. Coat one side with PVA adhesive which has been thinned 50/50 with clean water and place a layer of thin tissue paper on to the coating of glue. Roll the tissue well into the glue. Lay the veneer to one side and place some weights on it to hold it flat until the adhesive is thoroughly dry (at least twenty-four hours). The veneer can now be handled much more safely and it will have less tendency to break. The veneers most likely to suffer damage are those which are very open-grain, such as teak. Teak also is an oily type of timber

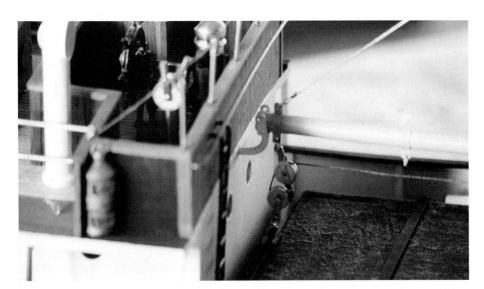

Starboard corner of *Arran Mail* bridge showing both oil and electric navigation lamps.

which is very reluctant to accept varnishes and paint.

Once the veneer has been stabilised with tissue paper it is easy to cut off narrow strips which can have the edges sanded and coloured with a black felt tipped pen to show clearly when used to simulate vertical match boarding. The bridge shown in the photographs of *Arran Mail* was made using strips of mahogany veneer. Veneers can also be used to cover deckhouses and to simulate timber panelling on certain types of vessel. Many of the magnificent paddle-steamers of the Mississippi and other American rivers carried wonderful panelling and decoration and veneers can be used for showing such beautiful work. Possibly the best adhesive to use when attaching veneer to a plywood or similar timber surface is a contact adhesive such as Evostik, but the extremely fast grab time allows only one chance to lay the two pre-pared parts together accurately. Once joined they cannot be parted without damage.

Paint masking for small areas

In addition to standard masking tape, which is readily available in various widths, there are a number of liquid masking products on the market and available from model shops. These come in small bottles and the liquid is applied with a brush. Being latex-based liquids they dry very rapidly leaving a skin on the surface of the work piece which can be peeled away after the part has been painted. This material is ideal for use in covering glazing or port-lights when spray painting a deckhouse or similar structure. The removal of the skin leaves no residue on the model. Obviously, it is necessary to make sure that the liquid masking is dry before applying any paint. At some artists' supply outlets very fine masking film can be bought and applied to sections of a model where masking tape cannot be used or, perhaps, where a small design needs to be covered, such as the logo on a ship's funnel. This film is trans-parent, permitting the surface underneath to be seen clearly. It can be cut with a sharp scalpel or knife to the required shape. Once the area has been painted it will remove cleanly leaving no sticky residue. Such film is a little on the expensive side but the cost is justified in some cases where only a small quantity is needed.

Cyanoacrylate adhesive

When using cyanoacrylate glue (Superglue) from a small plastic bottle with a long neck and fine nozzle, small amounts of the glue will collect round the nozzle making it difficult to remove the cap after repeated use. If the nozzle is coated with grease or petroleum jelly, the glue will not stick to the spout and the cap can be removed easily. The drops of glue which collect round the nozzle will harden and can be rubbed away and then the grease can be replaced.

General hints

Small detail parts for a model can be attached to pieces of scrap ply using double-sided adhesive tape to hold them firmly for painting. After each part has been painted, use a small box or carton to store such finished parts until they are required. Very small parts can become lost or damaged if left lying in the clutter on the workbench, with attendant frustration.

If space permits, hanging a sheet of insulation board on one wall of the workshop will permit drawings to be pinned up during the time the model is being constructed. It is easy to take measurements from a drawing so mounted and the picture of the model is always in view. Frequent opening-up and folding a drawing purely to measure a small section, will result in the drawing becoming creased and damaged.

Proportional dividers are quite expensive but extremely useful where the only drawings available for a model are in an unsuitable scale. The proportional dividers can be set to convert one dimension to another with consistent accuracy. They have fine needle points at both ends and an adjustment slide and scale in the centre. Setting the slide to a given point on the scale allows the points at one end of the instrument to measure from a drawing and the points at the other end give the required measurement in a different set scale. For example, if the drawing in use is at a scale of 1:50 and the model is 1:25, then setting the proportional dividers to this difference means that each time they take a measurement from the drawing using the points at one end, those at the

other end equate to 1:25 and give the measurement needed for the model. The range over which they work is quite large and, of course, they are equally useful for reducing the scale. For addresses of suppliers of this very useful instrument, see Appendix 2.

When making parts from brass or similar sheet metal it is often difficult to see pencil lines where cuts are to be made. In fact, making marks that are easily visible on most metals can be difficult. The best way, and one which does not require the purchase of engineer's blue marking, is the spray-can of primer – almost any colour will do. Spray the surface of the metal lightly with the paint and allow it to dry. Make the required lines using a fine needle point. The bright metal will shine through the paint and when the cutting has been done the paint can be cleaned away using cellulose thinners or acetone on a soft cloth.

Much data and a number of drawings will be accumulated before and during the construction of a scale ship model. Such material should be carefully preserved for reference and a manilla pocket or similar file is suitable for storing records. It is pleasant to be able to look back on the work through such records which can include photographs illustrating the various stages of building the model. Taking photographs to show stages of construction and to highlight some of the methods of making fittings is always useful. Most model magazine editors welcome articles describing the building of ship models but need good photographs as well. Photography for ship modellers is a subject outside this publication but there are often articles in the model press to assist and the local library will probably be able to recommend books to those interested. Some of the data and information obtained may also be useful to other modellers wishing to build similar vessels and this information can be passed on to assist them. Many modellers find that they can avoid repeating mistakes by reading through their records of previous building.

Appendix 1
Useful Conversion Factors

Length

Inches	x	25.4	=	Millimetres	x	0.0394	= Inches
Feet	x	0.305	=	Metres	x	3.281	= Feet
Miles	x	1.609	=	Kilometres	x	0.621	= Miles

Volume

Cubic Inches	x	16.387	=	Cubic cm	x	0.061	= Cubic Ins
Imperial Pints	x	0.568	=	Litres	x	1.76	= Pints
Imperial Galls	x	4.456	=	Litres	x	0.22	= Gallons

Weight

Ounces	x	28.35	=	Grams	x	0.035	= Ounces
Pounds	x	0.454	=	Kilograms	x	2.205	= Pounds

Velocity (Speed)

Miles per Hr	x	1.609	=	Kilometres/hr	x	0.621	= mph

Temperature

Degress F = Deg C x 1.8) +32   Degrees Celcius = (Deg F – 32) x 0.56

Additional Data

One knot = 0.5 Metres per second
One knot is one nautical mile per hour or 6080 feet per hour.

Appendix 2
Suppliers

Specialist model ship shops (kits, timber, styrene sheet, fittings, radio controls etc)

UK

Westbourne Model Centre, 41 Seamoor Road, Westbourne, Bournemouth, Dorset BH14 9AF. Tel: 01202 763480
Sambrook Maritime Models, 214 Roxley Lane, West Ewell, Surrey KT19 9EZ. Tel: 020 8391 5144
The Model Dockyard, 17, Tremorvah Barton, Tregolls Road, Truro, Cornwall TR1 1NN Tel:01872 222120. Mail Order Only.
Midway Models, 157 St Leonards Road, Leicester LE2 3BZ. Tel:0116 270 1609
Derby Marine Models, 16 George Street, Derby DE1 1EH. Tel:01332 202706
E Radestock, 2 Government Road, Hoylake, Wirral, Merseyside L47 2DB Tel: 0151 632 1566
Marcle Models, Turnagain, Finch Lane, Amersham, Bucks HP7 9NE Tel: 01494 765910
   Card models such as the SD14 cargo vessel.

USA

Model Expo Inc., PO Box 1000, Mt.Pocono Industrial Park, Tobyhanna, Pa. 18466-1000.

The Dromedary, 6324 Belton Drive, El Paso, Texas 79912
Valley Plaza Hobbies, 3633, Research Way, Carson City, Nevada 89706-7900
Bluejacket Shipcrafters, PO Box 425, Stockton Springs, Maine 04981

Glass fibre suppliers

Trylon Ltd, Wollaston, Northants. NN29 7QJ. Tel:01933 664275
Scott-Bader Ltd (Strand Glass) Various centres in UK: see Yellow Pages.

Specialist suppliers of steam outfits

Cheddar Models Ltd, Sharpham Road, Cheddar, Somerset BS27 3DR Tel: 01934 744634
John Hemmens Steam Engineer The Steam Gallery, Thorganby, York, North Yorkshire YO4 6DA Tel: 01904 448 331
Marten, Howes & Bayliss, 216 Bredhurst Road, Wigmore, Gillingham, Kent ME8 0RD Tel: 01634 233146
R M Marine, 20 Greenfield Road, Colwyn Bay, Clwyd LL29 8EL (Stour Valley Steam Engines) Tel:01492 530363
Saito Steam Outfits (Japanese). Available in the UK from Westbourne Model Centre, Bournemouth. Usually to order only.
Unit Steam Engines (USE), The Coach House, Rose Cottage, London Rd., Mickleham, Surrey RH5 6EH Tel: 01372 378075

Manufacturers of model ship fittings

James Lane (Display Models), 30 The Broadway, Blyth, Northumberland NE24 2PP. Tel: 01670 352051
   Etched brass & nickel silver ladders, stanchions etc, in fine scales.
Precision Controls, 3 Chantry Avenue, Bideford, Devon EX39 2QW. Tel: 01237 476820
   Fine scale ship fittings in brass and resin to high standard.
Quay Craft, Harbour Cottage, 2 Quayfield Road, Ilfracombe, North Devon, EX34 9EN Tel: 01271 866837
   Scale model ship's lifeboats etc, in resin, various scales, high quality.
E Radestock (see above) Specialist maker of propellers of high standard and propeller shafts, Kort nozzles etc.
The Prop Shop, Unit 5, Alscot Park Stables, Preston-on-Stour, Warwickshire CV 37 8BL Tel: 01789 450905
   Scale propellers made to order, standard sizes from stock – large range available.
Hand Made Flags, 64 Copse Avenue, West Wickham, Kent BR4 9NR Tel: 0181 777 1942
   Silk flags, ensigns and pennants in sizes from 10 to 160 mm long and in wide range of designs. All countries covered.

Display cases and carry cases

Chrysalis Showcases, 21 Gorse Road, Grantham, Lincs. NG31 9LH Tel: 01476 565202

Cases in clear Acrylic and timber and carry cases with clear front panel in sizes to order.
Timbercraft Cabinets, Abercorn House, Unit M, Watling street, Towcester NN12 8EU.
Cases in glass and delivered UK only.

Tools and gears suppliers

Proops Brothers Ltd, Technology House, 33 Saddington Road, Fleckney, Leicester LE8 0AW Tel: 0116 240 3400
Mail Order and at some exhibitions
Squires Model & Craft Tools, The Old Corn Store, Chessels Farm, Hoe Lanes, Bognor Regis, West Sussex PO22 8NW Tel: 01243 587009
Mail Order and at some exhibitions

Suppliers of specialist materials

Electronise Design, 2, Hillside Road, Four Oaks, Sutton Coldfield B74 4DQ
Tel: 0121 308 5877
Electronic Speed Controllers etc.
Hunter Systems, 24, Aspen Road, Eastbourne, East Sussex BN22 0TG
Tel: 01323 503336
Suppliers of electronic units.
Action, 140 Holme Court Avenue, Biggleswade, Beds, SG 18 9PB.
Suppliers of Electronic kits for Radio Control Boats.
Alec Tiranti Ltd., 70, High Street, Theale, Reading RG7 5AR Tel: 0118 930 2775
Suppliers of Silicon Rubber, White metals Etc.

Model boating organisations

UK
Model Power Boat Association, General Secretary; Mrs A Finnis, 7 The Ridgeways, Linthwaite, Huddersfield, HD7 5NP.
SAE with enquiries please.

USA
Mid-Michigan Scale Model Ship Association, Chairperson Kevin Garth, 716 Maple Street, Grand Ledge, MI 48837. Tel: 517 627 1091
San Francisco Model Yacht Club, 450 Taraval Street, Suite 235, San Francisco, CA 94116

Appendix 3
Publications and Plans Services

Magazines

Model Boats (Monthly) Nexus Special Interests, Nexus House, Boundary Way, Hemel Hempstead, Herts HP2 7ST

Marine Modelling (Monthly) Traplet Publications Ltd., Traplet House, Severn Drive, Upton-upon-Severn, Worcs. WR8 0JL
Model Shipwright (Quarterly) Conway Maritime Press, 33 John Street, London WC1N 2AT
US Boat & Ship Modeler (Quarterly) Gallant Models Inc. 34249 Camino Capistrano, Capistrano Beach, CA 92624 USA
Seaways Ships In Scale (Bi-monthly) Seaways Publishing Inc, 2271 Constitution Drive, San Jose, Cal. 95124 USA

Plans services

Model Boats Plans Service - Address as above
Marine Modelling Plans Service - Address as above
Model Shipwright plans from Sambrook Maritime Models. Address above

David MacGregor Plans, 12 Upper Oldfield Park, Bath BA2 3JZ
Jecobin, 31 Romans Way, Pyrford, Woking, Surrey GU22 8TR.
Taubman Plans Service International,

11 College Drive, Jersey City, New Jersey 07305, USA

Reference sources

Bowen, John, *A Ship Modelmakers Manual* (Arco Publishing 1982). Out of print. Possibly available from libraries.
Conway's History of the Ship. Two volumes relevant: Greenway, Ambrose (ed), *The Golden Age of Shipping: The Classic Merchant Ship 1900-1960* (Conway Maritime Press 1994); Couper, Prof. Alastair, *The Shipping Revolution: The Modern Merchant Ship* (Conway Maritime Press 1993).
Freestone, Ewart, *Model Open Boats* (Conway Maritime Press 1975). Now out of print.
Frost, Ted, *From Tree to Sea* (Terence Dalton 1985) Available from most model shops and bookshops.
Thomas, P N, *British Steam Tugs* (Waine Publications 1983). The definitive work on steam tugs, available from model shops and booksellers.
Waine, C V, and Fenton, R S, *Steam Coasters and Short Sea Traders* (Waine Publications 1976). Available from booksellers.

Appendix 4
Radio Control Frequencies

27 Megahertz.
(26.960 to 27.280)

40 Megahertz (Green Flag with 3 numbers)
(40.665 to 40.995)

Frequency	Flag Colour	Frequency	Flag Number
26.975	Black	40.665	665
26.995	Brown	40.675	675
27.025	Brown/Red	40.685	685
27.045	Red	40.695	695
27.075	Red/Orange	40.705	705
27.095	Orange	40.715	715
27.125	Orange/Yellow	40.725	725
27.145	Yellow	40.735	735
27.175	Yellow/Green	40.745	745
27.195	Green	40.755	755
27.225	Green/Blue	40.765	765
27.255	Blue	40.775	775
27.275	Purple	40.785	785
		40.795	795
		40.805	805
		40.815	815
		40.825	825
		40.835	835
		40.845	845
		40.855	855
		40.865	865
		40.875	875
		40.885	885
		40.895	895
		40.905	905
		40.915	915
		40.925	925
		40.935	935
		40.945	945
		40.955	955

Note Some of the above frequencies also apply in Europe where they are given freqency numbers and some bands are peculiar to the UK only. It will be seen that there are many more available channels on the 40-Meg frequencies than on the older and less tolerant 27-Meg band.

NB Some of the frequencies in the 27-Meg channel are used by Cb (Citizen's Band) radios and there can be interference as a result. It is wise for ship modellers to select new equipment that operates on the 40-Meg system. The model press and most model clubs will have up-to-date information on the use of the 27-Meg band and they should be consulted before selecting such radio gear.

Index

Page numbers in *italic* refer to illustrations.
Ship names in *italic*

abrasives and files   *30*, 32-3
adhesives
    Cascamite   35
    contact adhesives   36
    Cyanoacrylate (superglue)
      35-6, 179-180
    Epoxy   35
    liquid polystyrene cement
      35
    Polyvinl acetate   35
    Spraymount   36
Akron (US tug)   *10*
anchors   122-5, *122, 123*,
    152
    winch   *153*
Arran Mail (coaster)   *12, 90, 96, 117, 136*,
    178-9

Badger (Customs cutter)
    12, 95, 146
Bailey Gatzert (US stern-wheeler)
    64
ballasting   165-6
balsa wood, *see under* timber
basin trials   166-7
batteries, *see under* electric motors
blocks   133-4, *134*
boilers, *see under* steam
bollards   118-19, *118*
bread-and-butter construction, *see under* hulls
bridges   98-9
    elevating   *104*, 105
Britannia (pilot cutter) *105, 121, 139, 143*,
    150, 151

camber curves   88-9, *88*
capstans   140-41, *140, 141*
cardboard and pasteboard
    26
cargo ships   13, *13, 14, 95*
carry/display cases   173-4, *174*
casting in white metal and resin
    126-8, *126-8*
chain cable   123-4, *123-4*
Chimaera (pilot cutter) *68, 79, 101, 112*,
    116, 140, 148
coastal vessels   11, *12*, 39, 98, *90*,
    95, 96, 99, 100,
    102-4, 105, 106, *109*,
    117, 118, *122*, 129,
    136, 139, 140, 155,
    162, 178-9
competitions   169-73, *169-73*
    classes   169-70
cranes   153-4, *154*

Customs vessels   11-13, *12*, 95, *146*

davits   *129*, 131-4, *131, 132,*
    133
decks   87-96
    beams   89-91, *87, 89-90*
    caulking of   93-5
    laying of   92-3
    materials   27, 91-2
    planking   27, *92*, 93
Denebula (fishing vessel)
    101, 109
depth marking   *162, 163*
derricks   *107*, 110-12, *111, 112*
dredgers   15, *15*, 153, *170*
Duchess of Fife (paddle steamer)
    6, *7, 64, 75, 131, 150*,
    151

Edengarth (tug)   *169*
electric motors   68-75, *68, 69*
    batteries   70
    calculations   68-9
    control equipment   70-2, *71-4*
    paddle-wheels driven by
      75, 75

fairleads   119, *119*
fire monitors   *152*
fishing vessels   10, *10, 11, 21, 22*,
    83, 90, 100, 101,
    109, 112, 115, *116*,
    121, 129, 139, 147,
    158
Formidable (fishing vessel)
    11, 112, 115
fuel, *see under* steam
funnels   105-7, *105-7*

General Arrangement plans, *see under* plans
glass-reinforced plastic (GRP) 28, 54-5
    adhesives for use with
      35-6
    moulding, *see under* hulls
Glenrose I (trawler)   *100, 101, 109, 116*,
    139

hatches   95-7, *95, 96*, 122
    access   *94*, 122
    adjacent fittings   97
    coaling   122
    coamings   *91*, 95-7
    flush pattern   97
    making watertight 97
    types   95-7
Heron (pusher tug)   *104*, 105
hulls
    bread-and-butter construction

      37-40, *38*
    Kirby method   39-40
    GRP moulding   *55-6, 57-8*
    hull plug   53, 55, *55, 56*
    painting   160-3
    plank-on-frame construction
      40-50, *41-47, 49, 50*
    plating   51-2, *51, 52*
    rivets   52-3, *53*
    timbers   26-7

Idlewild (US stern wheeler)
    14

Jelutong, *see under* timbers
Jonrix (coaster)   *95, 100*, 106, *117,*
    118, 122, 139

Keila (fishing vessel)   *21, 22, 90, 147*, 158
Kingston Peridot (trawler)
    10, 83, 121, 129
Kort nozzles   156

ladders and companions 117-18, *117, 118*
lifeboats   129-31, *129, 131*,
    132
    fittings   133-4, *133*
lights   149-150, *150*
    navigation   125-6
    wiring   *110*
lines plan, *see under* plans
Lizrix (coaster)   *162*
Lloyd's Register of Ships
    22-3, *23*

masts   *108-10*, 109-10
metals
    adhesives for use with
      35-6
    tin plate   6, 26
    white metal (casting) 126-7
model clubs and societies
    25, App. 2
moulding of hulls, *see under* hulls

Norland (passenger ferry)
    14, 132
Norsea (passenger ferry) *135*

oil rig support vessels   15, *24, 41-3, 99, 120*,
    139, 140, 141, 145,
    154, 156-7, 158, 159

paddle vessels   6, *7, 14, 14, 64, 75*,
    131, 150, 151
paddle-wheels   63-5, *64, 65, 75*, 75
painting
    hull   160-3, *161*

masking   162-3, 179
paints   160
superstructure   163-4
passenger vessels   13-14, *14, 132, 135,*
                                  153
pasteboard and cardboard
                                  26
    adhesives for use with 35-6
pilot cutters   11, *68, 79, 101, 105,*
                                  112, 116, 121, 139,
                                  140, 143, 148, 150,
                                  151
pipework   141, *141*
planking   27, 93
plank-on-frame construction, *see under* hulls
plans
    General Arrangement plans
                                  18, 19, 19-20
    lines plan   16-19, *17*
    shipbuilders' plans 23
plating, *see under* hulls
Plimsoll Line   162-3, *162*
plywood, *see under* timbers
portholes   100-2
propellers and shafts   59-63, *59-62*

radar scanners   151-2, *151*
radio control
    equipment   142-6, *143, 144,*
                                  146-8
    testing   147-8
    wiring   *145,* 146-7
rails   *111,* 115-17, *115-16*
resin, *see under* casting
rigging   112-14, *113*

rivets, *see under* hulls
Rovuma (coaster)   39, 98, *99, 102-4,*
                                 105
rudders   65-7, *65-7*

sailing the model   167-8
Sand Heron (dredger)   *15, 170*
Savannah (US nuclear-powered cargo ship)
                                 159
scales   20
scale speed   72-5
Schottel drive   158, *159*
Scott Guardian (oil rig support vessel)
                                 24, 41-3, 99, 120,
                                 139, 140, 141, 145,
                                 154, 156-7, 158, *159*
Shell Technician (tanker) 13
shipbuilders' plans, *see under* plans
Smit Duitsland (tug)   167
smoke units   150-1, *150, 155*
soldering   175-8
    hard soldering   177-8
    soft soldering   176-7
sound systems   154-5
steam
    boilers   80-3, *80-3*
    engines   76-80, *76-9, 85*
    fuel   83-6
    operation of models   86
styrene sheet   27-8
    adhesives for use with
                                 35
superstructure
    construction of   99-100, *99-104*
    materials   98

tankers   13, *13*
thrusters, bow and stern 156-58, *156, 157*
Thor (tug)   *166,* 172
timbers
    adhesives for use with 35-6
    balsa wood   26-7
    Jelutong   27
    plywood   26
    see also under decks, hulls *and* veneers
Timrix (coaster)   *109, 129, 140*
tin plate, *see under* metals
tools
    hand tools   29-32, *30, 31*
    power tools   33-4
    use of   29, 175
towing hooks   138, *138*
tugs   9, *9,* 10, *104,* 105,
                                 166, 167, 169, 172

vehicle ramps   152-3, *152*
veneers   178-9, *178-9*
    adhesives for use with 36
    timber   27
ventilators   119-22, *119-22*
Voith Schneider drive   158-9

water discharges   *153,* 154, *154*
white metal, *see under* metals *and* casting
winches   135-8, *135, 136, 137*
windlasses   *135,* 138-40, *139*
windows   100-2, *101*
wiring, *see under* radio control *and* lights

Yvonne VI (tug)   9